*Adolf Hitler, thirty-six, posing with his books
in his first Munich apartment.*

Hitler's Private Library

The Books That Shaped His Life

WITHDRAWN FROM STOCK

WITHDRAWN FROM STOCK

Hitler's Private Library

The Books That Shaped His Life

TIMOTHY W. RYBACK

THE BODLEY HEAD
LONDON

Published by The Bodley Head 2009

2 4 6 8 10 9 7 5 3 1

Copyright © Timothy W. Ryback 2009

Timothy W. Ryback has asserted his right under the Copyright, Designs
and Patents Act 1988 to be identified as the author of this work

Grateful acknowledgment is made to Mary Sharp for permission
to reprint previously published material from *This Is the Enemy* by
Frederick C. Oechsner (Boston: Little, Brown, 1942).

First published in Great Britain in 2009 by
The Bodley Head
Random House, 20 Vauxhall Bridge Road,
London SW1V 2SA

www.rbooks.co.uk

Addresses for companies within The Random House Group Limited can be found at:
www.randomhouse.co.uk/offices.htm

The Random House Group Limited Reg. No. 954009

A CIP catalogue record for this book
is available from the British Library

ISBN 9781847920720

The Random House Group Limited supports The Forest Stewardship
Council (FSC), the leading international forest certification organisation. All our titles that
are printed on Greenpeace approved FSC certified paper carry the FSC logo. Our paper
procurement policy can be found at www.rbooks.co.uk/environment

Mixed Sources
Product group from well-managed
forests and other controlled sources
www.fsc.org Cert no. TT-COC-2139
© 1996 Forest Stewardship Council
FSC

Printed and bound in Great Britain by Clays Ltd, St Ives PLC

To my mother,
who taught me the love of books,
and in memory of my father.

A little learning is a dangerous thing;
Drink deep, or taste not the Pierian spring:
There shallow draughts intoxicate the brain,
And drinking largely sobers us again.

ALEXANDER POPE, "A Little Learning"

I know people who "read" enormously, book for book, letter
for letter, yet whom I would not describe as "well-read."
True, they possess a mass of "knowledge," but their brain is
unable to organize and register the material they have taken
in. They lack the art of sifting what is valuable for them in a
book from that which is without value, of retaining the one
forever, and, if possible, not even seeing the rest.

ADOLF HITLER, Mein Kampf

CONTENTS

The Man Who Burned Books

HE WAS, OF COURSE, a man known better for burning books than collecting them and yet by the time he died at age fifty-six he owned an
estimated sixteen thousand volumes. It was by any measure an impres-
sive collection: first editions of the works of philosophers, historians,
poets, playwrights and novelists. For him the library represented a Pierian spring, that metaphorical source of knowledge and inspiration. He
drew deeply there, quelling his intellectual insecurities and nourishing
his fanatic ambitions. He read voraciously, at least one book per night,
sometimes more, so he claimed. "When one gives one also has to take,"
he once said, "and I take what I need from books."

He ranked *Don Quixote,* along with *Robinson Crusoe, Uncle Tom's Cabin,*
and *Gulliver's Travels,* among the great works of world literature. "Each
of them is a grandiose idea unto itself," he said. In *Robinson Crusoe* he
perceived "the development of the entire history of mankind." *Don
Quixote* captured "ingeniously" the end of an era. He owned illustrated
editions of both books and was especially impressed by Gustave Doré's
romantic depictions of Cervantes's delusion-plagued hero.

He also owned the collected works of William Shakespeare, published in German translation in 1925 by Georg Müller as part of a series
intended to make great literature available to the general public. Volume six includes *As You Like It, Twelfth Night, Hamlet,* and *Troilus and
Cressida.* The entire set is bound in hand-tooled Moroccan leather with a
gold-embossed eagle flanked by his initials on the spine.

He considered Shakespeare superior to Goethe and Schiller in every respect. While Shakespeare had fueled his imagination on the protean forces of the emerging British empire, these two Teutonic playwright-poets squandered their talent on stories of midlife crises and sibling rivalries. Why was it, he once wondered, that the German Enlightenment produced *Nathan the Wise,* the story of the rabbi who reconciles Christians, Muslims, and Jews, while it had been left to Shakespeare to give

Hitler was given this anthology of Goethe's poetry
shortly after his release from prison in December 1924,
for his "serious and lonely hours."

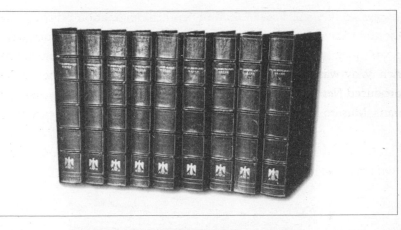

*Hitler kept this hand-tooled leather edition of
Shakespeare's collected works at his alpine retreat
near Berchtesgaden. Note his initials on the spine.*

the world *The Merchant of Venice* and Shylock?

He appears to have imbibed his *Hamlet*. "To be or not to be" was a favorite phrase, as was "It is Hecuba to me." He was especially fond of *Julius Caesar*. In a 1926 sketchbook he drew a detailed stage set for the first act of the Shakespeare tragedy with sinister façades enclosing the forum where Caesar is cut down. "We will meet again at Philippi," he threatened an opponent on more than one occasion, plagiarizing the spectral warning to Brutus after Caesar's murder. He was said to have reserved the Ides of March for momentous decisions.

He kept his Shakespeare volumes in the second-floor study of his alpine retreat in southern Germany, along with a leather edition of another favorite author, the adventure novelist Karl May. "The first Karl May that I read was *The Ride Across the Desert*," he once recalled. "I was overwhelmed! I threw myself into him immediately which resulted in a noticeable decline in my grades." Later in life, he was said to have sought solace in Karl May the way others did in the Bible.

He was versed in the Holy Scriptures, and owned a particularly hand-some tome with *Worte Christi,* or *Words of Christ,* embossed in gold on a cream-colored calfskin cover that even today remains as smooth as silk. He also owned a German translation of Henry Ford's anti-Semitic tract, *The International Jew: The World's Foremost Problem,* and a 1931 handbook on poison gas with a chapter detailing the qualities and effects of prussic acid, the homicidal asphyxiant marketed commercially as Zyklon B. On his bedstand, he kept a well-thumbed copy of Wilhelm Busch's mischie-vous cartoon duo Max and Moritz.

WALTER BENJAMIN ONCE SAID that you could tell a lot about a man by the books he keeps—his tastes, his interests, his habits. The books we retain and those we discard, those we read as well as those we decide not to, all say something about who we are. As a German-Jewish culture critic born of an era when it was possible to be "German" and "Jewish," Benjamin believed in the transcendent power of *Kultur.* He believed that creative expression not only enriches and illuminates the world we inhabit, but also provides the cultural adhesive that binds one generation to the next, a Judeo-Germanic rendering of the ancient wisdom *ars longa, vita brevis.*

Benjamin held the written word—printed and bound—in especially high regard. He loved books. He was fascinated by their physicality, by their durability, by their provenance. An astute collector, he argued, could "read" a book the way a physiognomist deciphered the essence of a person's character through his physical features. "Dates, place names, formats, previous owners, bindings, and all the like," Benjamin observed, "all these details must tell him something—not as dry isolated facts, but as a harmonious whole." In short, you *could* judge a book by its cover, and in turn the collector by his collection. Quoting Hegel, Benjamin noted, "Only when it is dark does the owl of Minerva begin its flight," and concluded, "Only in extinction is the collector comprehended."

When Benjamin invoked a nineteenth-century German philosopher, a Roman goddess, and an owl, he was of course alluding to Georg Wilhelm Friedrich Hegel's famous maxim: "The owl of Minerva spreads its wings only with the falling of dusk," by which Hegel meant that philosophizing can begin only after events have run their course.

Benjamin felt the same was true about private libraries. Only after the collector had shelved his last book and died, when his library was allowed to speak for itself, without the proprietor to distract or obfuscate, could the individual volumes reveal the "preserved" knowledge of their owner: how he asserted his claim over them, with a name scribbled on the inside cover or an ex libris bookplate pasted across an entire page; whether he left them dog-eared and stained, or the pages uncut and unread.

Benjamin proposed that a private library serves as a permanent and credible witness to the character of its collector, leading him to the following philosophic conceit: we collect books in the belief that we are preserving them when in fact it is the books that preserve their collector. "Not that they come alive in him," Benjamin posited. "It is he who lives in them."

FOR THE LAST HALF CENTURY the remnants of Adolf Hitler's library have occupied shelf space in climatized obscurity in the Rare Book Division of the Library of Congress. The twelve hundred surviving volumes that once graced Hitler's bookcases in his three elegantly appointed libraries—wood paneling, thick carpets, brass lamps, overstuffed armchairs—at private residences in Munich, Berlin, and the Obersalzberg near Berchtesgaden, now stand in densely packed rows on steel shelves in an unadorned, dimly lit storage area of the Thomas Jefferson Building in downtown Washington, a stone's throw from the Washington Mall and just across the street from the United States Supreme Court.

The sinews of emotional logic that once ran through this collection—
Hitler shuffled his books ceaselessly and insisted on reshelving them
himself—have been severed. Hitler's personal copy of his family genealogy is sandwiched between a bound collection of newspaper articles
titled *Sunday Meditations* and a folio of political cartoons from the 1920s.
A handsomely bound facsimile edition of letters by Frederick the Great,
specially designed for Hitler's fiftieth birthday, lies on a shelf for over-
sized books beneath a similarly massive presentation volume on the city
of Hamburg and an illustrated history of the German navy in the First
World War. Hitler's copy of the writings of the legendary Prussian general Carl von Clausewitz, who famously declared that war was politics
by other means, shares shelf space beside a French vegetarian cookbook
inscribed to *"Monsieur Hitler végétarien."*

When I first surveyed Hitler's surviving books, in the spring of 2001, I
discovered that fewer than half the volumes had been catalogued, and
only two hundred of those were searchable in the Library of Congress's
online catalogue. Most were listed on aging index cards and still bore the
idiosyncratic numbering system assigned them in the 1950s.

At Brown University, in Providence, Rhode Island, I found another
eighty Hitler books in a similar state of benign neglect. Taken from his
Berlin bunker in the spring of 1945 by Albert Aronson, one of the first
Americans to enter Berlin after the German defeat, they were donated
to Brown by Aronson's nephew in the late 1970s. Today they are stored
in a walk-in basement vault, along with Walt Whitman's personal copy
of *Leaves of Grass* and the original folios to John James Audubon's *Birds of
America*.

Among the books at Brown, I found a copy of *Mein Kampf* with
Hitler's ex libris bookplate, an analysis of Wagner's *Parsifal* published in
1913, a history of the swastika from 1921, and a half dozen or so spiritual
and occult volumes Hitler acquired in Munich in the early 1920s, including an account of supernatural occurrences, *The Dead Are Alive!,* and a
monograph on the prophecies of Nostradamus. I discovered additional

Hitler books scattered in public and private archives across the United States and Europe.

Several dozen of these surviving Hitler books contain marginalia. Here I encountered a man who famously seemed never to listen to anyone, for whom conversation was a relentless tirade, a ceaseless monologue, pausing to engage with the text, to underline words and sentences, to mark entire paragraphs, to place an exclamation point beside one passage, a question mark beside another, and quite frequently an emphatic series of parallel lines in the margin alongside a particular passage. Like footprints in the sand, these markings allow us to trace the course of the journey but not necessarily the intent, where attention caught and lingered, where it rushed forward and where it ultimately ended.

In a 1934 reprint of Paul Lagarde's *German Letters,* a series of late-nineteenth-century essays that advocated the systematic removal of Europe's Jewish population, I found more than one hundred pages of penciled intrusions, beginning on page 41, where Lagarde calls for the "transplanting" of German and Austrian Jews to Palestine, and extending to more ominous passages in which he speaks of Jews as "pestilence." "This water pestilence must be eradicated from our streams and lakes," Lagarde writes on page 276, with a pencil marking bold affirmation in the margin. "The political system without which it cannot exist must be eliminated."

British historian Ian Kershaw has described Hitler as one of the most impenetrable personalities of modern history. "The combination of Hitler's innate secretiveness," Kershaw writes, "the emptiness of his personal relations, his unbureaucratic style, the extremes of adulation and hatred which he stirred up, and the apologetics as well as distortions built upon post-war memoirs and gossipy anecdotes of those in his entourage, mean that, for all the surviving mountains of paper spewed out by the governmental apparatus of the Third Reich, the sources for reconstructing the life of the German Dictator are in many respects

Books were frequently the gift of choice for Adolf Hitler.
The Nazi leader receiving presents on his fiftieth birthday.

extraordinarily limited—far more so than in the case, say, of his main adversaries, Churchill and even Stalin."

Hitler's library certainly contains its share of "spewed" material; easily two-thirds of the collection consists of books he never saw, let alone read, but there are also scores of more personal volumes that Hitler studied and marked. It also contains small but telling details. While perusing the unprocessed volumes in the rare book collection at the Library of Congress, I came across a book whose original contents had been gutted. The front and back boards were firmly secured to the spine by a heavy linen cover with the title, *North, Central and East Asia: Hand-*

book of Geographic Science, embossed in gold on a blue background. The original pages had been replaced by a sheaf of cluttered documents: a dozen or so photonegatives, an undated handwritten manuscript titled "The Solution to the German Question," and a brief note typed on a presentation card that read:

> My Führer
>   On the 14th anniversary of the day you first set foot in the Stern-ecker, Mrs. Gahr is presenting to you the list of your first fellow fighters. It is our conviction that this hour is the hour of birth of our wonderful movement and of our new Reich. With loyalty until death.
>   Sieg Heil!
>
>   The Old Comrades

The card bore no date and the list of early Nazi Party members was missing, but the mention of "Mrs. Gahr," presumably the wife of Otto Gahr, the goldsmith, whom Hitler charged with casting the first metal swastikas for the Nazi Party, as well as the reference to the fourteenth anniversary of Hitler's first appearance in the Sternecker Beer Hall, pre-serves in briefest outline the trajectory of Hitler from political upstart in 1919 to chancellor of the German Reich in 1933.

For this book, I have selected those surviving volumes that possessed either emotional or intellectual significance for Hitler, those which occu-pied his thoughts in his private hours and helped shape his public words and actions. One of the earliest is a guidebook he acquired for four marks on a dreary Monday in late November 1915 while serving as a twenty-six-year-old corporal on the western front. The last is a biogra-phy he was reading thirty years later in the weeks leading up to his sui-cide in the spring of 1945. I have attempted to be judicious in my choice of Hitler volumes, selecting only those books for which there is com-pelling evidence that Hitler had them in his possession. I have exercised similar caution when it comes to the marginalia since the "authorship" of penciled intrusions cannot necessarily be determined definitively. Once again, I have relied on corroborating evidence, and I discuss individual cases in the text, drawing when available on the determinations of previous scholarship. To make titles accessible to the non-German reader, I generally use English translations of the original titles except in such obvious cases as Hitler's *Mein Kampf,* or My Struggle.

In closing his essay on book collecting, Walter Benjamin considers the emotional as well as financial investment he has made in individual volumes. He recalls vividly the day in 1915 when he purchased a special edition of Honoré de Balzac's *The Magic Skin* (Peau de chagrin) with its magnificent steel plate engravings, and details the exact circumstances under which he acquired a rare 1810 treatise on "occultism and natural philosophy," *Posthumous Fragments of a Young Physicist*, by the German writer Johann Wilhelm Ritter.

The books flood Benjamin with memories: "memories of the rooms where these books had been housed, of my student's den in Munich, of my room in Bern, of the solitude of Iseltwald on the Lake of Brienz, and finally of my boyhood room, the former location of only four or five of these several thousand volumes."

Hitler left no equivalent narrative of his own collection, no account of how one or the other volume came into his possession or its particular emotional significance, but the various inscriptions, marginalia and other details provide insight into their personal and intellectual significance for his life. What follows are the stories they tell.

Hitler's Private Library

BOOK ONE

Frontline Reading, 1915

What the world of the twentieth century finds most fascinating about the capital of the German Reich are things other than the beauty of its historical monuments or its rich cultural heritage.

MAX OSBORN, *Berlin*, volume 41 in the series *Famous Cultural Sites*, published in Leipzig, 1909

O N A DREARY MONDAY in late November 1915, Adolf Hitler, then a corporal in the Sixteenth Bavarian Reserve Infantry Regiment, left his billet in a two-story farmhouse on the edge of Fournes, two miles behind the front in northern France, and with his trench coat pulled tight against the autumnal chill and his hobnailed boots clacking on the dank cobblestones, walked into town to buy a book.

For the twenty-six-year-old frontline soldier, it promised to be a quiet week, not unlike the previous one whose tranquillity had been broken only occasionally by enemy gunfire and the threat of gas attacks. On the previous Tuesday, when the dense fog had briefly lifted, three British biplanes had circled the sector for several hours. Their appearance was followed by clanging gas alarms that sent frontline soldiers fumbling for their rubber masks and goggles. In November 1915, poison gas was relatively new to the front.

Only a few weeks earlier, several "black soldiers," subjects from India pressed into British service, had defected to the German lines, warning of an imminent attack. Fearful of this silent new weapon, the men built fires and stood in the billowing wood smoke to test these awkward contraptions. That evening, they watched as an eerie yellow cloud drifted into no-man's-land, lingered menacingly, and then, as the breeze shifted, returned with equal leisure to the British lines. Several gas alarms had followed since, but without incident. For Tuesday, November 16, 1915, the regimental log records: "false alarm."

The following Monday, when Hitler bought his book, the day dawned gray and cold with a dense ground fog that continued to dampen all but the most sporadic gunfire. As the mist lifted in late morning, British artillery peppered the regiment's two-mile sector with scattered barrages, targeting the command posts and littering Sector H with shrapnel shells. From his "rest quarters" in Fournes, Hitler would have heard the bombardments as muffled thunder along the horizon.

As a *Meldegänger,* or "message runner," assigned to regimental headquarters, Hitler generally worked a rotating shift: three days at the front and three days resting in Fournes. From Fournes, Hitler would walk along a country road to the neighboring village of Fromelles, where the frontline command post and dressing station were located amid the ruined buildings, and from there through a series of communications trenches into a nightmare landscape of cratered fields and ruined villages. To facilitate troop movements and help orient the message runners, the French villages had been assigned German names.

The place-names echoed the devastation: *Knallhüte* (Blasted Hut), *Backofen* (The Oven), and at a bend where the British and German trenches nearly touched, *Totes Schwein* (Dead Swine). One village was named Petzstadt after Friedrich Petz, the regimental commander. On the left flank, where the RIR 16 abutted on the RIR 17, a razed farm had been dubbed "Dachau," after the picturesque artists' colony just north of Munich, which had earned two stars in the Michelin guides of the era, but would acquire very different resonances in the decades to come.

While *Meldegänger* assignments were frequently mundane, the work could be perilous in the extreme. When shelling disrupted telephone lines, runners were forced to dart amid flying shrapnel while most sol-

* Kriegsfreiwilliger A d o l f H i t l e r,
Gefechtsordonnanz des List-Regiments, Mai 1915

*Image from Hitler's copy of a war memoir by fellow
veteran Adolf Meyer. The German caption reads:
Volunteer Adolf Hitler, orderly with the List Regiment, May 1915.*

diers huddled in underground bunkers. The messages were supposed to
be coded for priority—X for normal delivery, XX for heightened importance, XXX for urgent—but men frequently found themselves placed at
gratuitous risk. "I was repeatedly exposed to heavy artillery fire even
though it was nothing but a postcard that needed to be delivered," Hitler
later recalled. During the first day of fighting at the battle of Wytschaete
in the fall of 1914, the eight-man unit was cut in half, with three men
killed outright and one critically wounded. By the autumn of 1915, Hitler
was the only original member left in the unit.

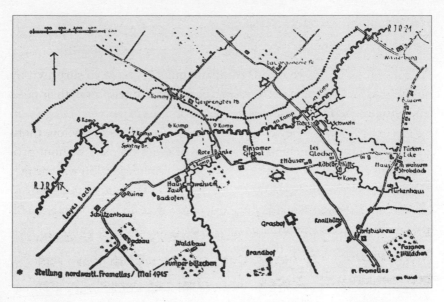

RIR 16 sector map, from Adolf Meyer's memoir. Note "Dachau" on lower left.

In early October 1915, during a battle to dislodge British troops from a salient known as the Hohenzollernwerk, the message runners were given an even more precarious assignment when they were pressed into service shuttling armloads of grenades to the front, as the frontline soldiers literally blasted the British from their trenches yard by yard, using fifteen hundred hand grenades to clear one three-hundred yard stretch of trench and another two thousand to clear five hundred more yards. "The battle for the Hohenzollernwerk demonstrated again that the hand grenade is the most horrific and effective weapon for close combat," Petz reported after the battle.

In October, rain brought the autumn offensives to a standstill as soldiers on both sides of no-man's-land turned to battling mud rather than one another. Among Hitler's remnant books, I found his unit's five-hundred-page regimental history, *Four Years on the Western Front: History of the List Regiment, RIR 16; Memoirs from a German Regiment,* exquisitely bound in brown leather, in which the misery and desperation of those weeks is vividly preserved. When the incessant rain pushes a river over its banks, the water floods into the RIR 16 trenches with near apocalyptic consequences. "Two of our company units . . . were so surprised by the deluge that the men in the trench barely had time to grab their guns and equipment and to rescue themselves on the rampart," the regimental history records. "They clung there and cowered, a mire before them and a raging stream behind them, many of them exposed without protection to the open view of the enemy." Their only salvation was the fact that the British were equally occupied with rescuing themselves from the flood. The regimental history calculates that for each frontline soldier poised to fight the British, ten men were battling the mud.

The daily log, now at the Bavarian War Archive in Munich, not only confirms the frontline soldier's uneven battle against the elements but also his equally uneven struggle with technology at the frontline pumping stations. For November 22, 1915, the regimental commander records a typical day:

Electric pumps in Sector A 6–11 in the evening power shortage
11–11.30 evening, Damaged hose
7.45 morning–12.30 afternoon power shortage
In sector c 8–12 morning power shortage

In these rain-idled weeks, Hitler was quartered in Fournes with only occasional assignments. On October 21, Petz dispatched him and another message runner, Hans Lippert, to the city of Valenciennes, to requisition a new mattress. According to the requisition slip, Hitler and Lippert were permitted to remain there overnight. On the return trip, Hitler carried the mattress most of the way since Lippert held a superior rank.

A month and a day later, still idled by the elements, Hitler walked into Fournes and purchased an architectural history of Berlin by the celebrated art critic Max Osborn. Despite its three hundred pages, Osborn's

Berlin is a notably slender volume, as easily slipped into the pocket of a trench coat as into the handbag of a cultural tourist, with a water-resistant, olive drab cover with BERLIN embossed in bold crimson and complemented by a profile of the Brandenburg Gate, whose six Doric columns stand in parallel ranks with the rigidly spaced letters of the book's title.

At some point that day, Hitler returned to the relative comfort of his two-story farmhouse billet, opened this hardbound volume, and laid claim to its content in a notably timid hand, scribbling his name and the place and date in the upper-right-hand corner of the inside cover in a space no larger than that of a small postage stamp.

Eighty years later, Osborn's book attests to its frontline service.

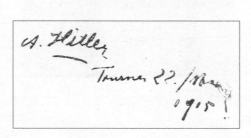

Blunted and brown, the corners curl inward like dried lemon rind. The spine dangles precariously from fraying linen tendons, exposing the thread-laced signatures like so many rows of rope-bound bones. A mud stain blots out the final letters in "November." When I opened this fragile volume in the Rare Book Reading Room of the Library of Congress, with the muffled sounds of late-morning traffic wafting through the hushed silence, a fine grit drizzled from its pages.

AT ROUGHLY THE SAME TIME that Hitler acquired his copy of *Berlin*, Max Osborn passed within a few miles of Fournes, on the road from Lille to Auber. He had arrived at the front the previous January, a few

*Hitler acquired this architectural guide to
Berlin in late November 1915, while serving
on the western front.*

months after Hitler, on assignment for the *Vossische Zeitung,* the presti-
gious Berlin newspaper for which he had been writing for nearly two
decades.

Born into the same privileged Berlin milieu that had shaped Walter
Benjamin's intellectual tastes and interests, Osborn had established himself as one of the leading art critics of the day, gaining a wide readership
with his irreverent commentaries on aesthetics and culture. In a cultural
history of Satan, Osborn declared angels "the most boring of God's crea-
tures" and devoted three hundred pages to chronicling diverse satanic

follies in art, music, and literature. He befriended the painter Max
Liebermann and coined the phrase "expressionist rococo."

In 1908, when the publisher Seemann Verlag asked Osborn to author
a guide to Berlin, he agreed but with the understanding that he was an
art critic not a tour guide. Thus, he welcomed the reader to his *Berlin*
with this impious caveat: Why would his publisher consider this city
among the "cultural capitals" of Europe when "what the world of the
twentieth century finds most fascinating about the capital of the German Reich are things other than the beauty of its historical monuments
or its rich cultural heritage"?

Osborn arrived on the western front with this same sporting diffi-
dence. As he traversed the battlefields of northern France, visiting the
devastation along the Somme, at the Marne, and near Verdun, Osborn
found little that was new or shocking. The human slaughter there appeared to be little more than flesh-and-blood re-creations of the sprawling canvases he had studied in the National Gallery in Berlin. Osborn
had seen it all before.

The German soldiers in their spiked headgear and with their bayo-
nets appeared as latter-day incarnations of the pike-bearing warriors
from sixteenth-century murals. The flamethrowers with their plumes of
smoke and fire spewing across the broken earth had been vividly woven
into these early tapestries. "And that favored horrific instrument of close
combat today, the hand grenade," Osborn wrote for his readers in Germany, "already played a role in the seventeenth century, as well as in the
armies of the grand dukes." When the battlefront critic glimpsed a message runner on a horse galloping across an open field, both man and
beast fitted with gas masks, he likened it to a scene from a canvas by
Hieronymus Bosch.

In late May 1915, Osborn and Hitler nearly crossed paths on the battlefield at Ypres, where the Germans had repulsed the second major British
offensive along this front, with both sides suffering massive casualties.
The RIR 16 lost more than half its men: sixteen hundred soldiers and all
but one officer. Osborn arrived shortly after the slaughter and surveyed

the battlefield from the unscathed spire of the Ypres cathedral, which towered miraculously above the ruined town. Amid the ravage, Osborn found himself witness to the "second act" of the war's greatest battle.

"Crushed trench defenses and bunker emplacements rise from the ground," he observed. "Crumbling walls of earth, crushed sandbags, scattered debris, stretches of barbed wire twisted and broken: Filthy remnants litter the ground, shreds of uniforms, bloody rags, socks, canteens, fragments of French newspapers, torn pages from English magazines, ration cans, empty cartridges, unspent ammunition." The bodies had already been removed, but the smell of death lingered, tainting the air with an aroma of antiseptic and decaying flesh.

That autumn, Osborn toured the battlefields west of Lille, visiting the frontline towns of Richebourg and Neuve-Chapelle and passing along the front near Fournes. "When you arrive at the villages, they are pathetic and ruined, houses gutted by bombs, farms burned, walls riddled with bullet holes," he wrote. "A hopeless landscape!"

By then, Osborn's poetic enthusiasms had tempered. "There lie the rotting corpses the attackers have left behind," he observed. "Hordes of rats feed on them, growing large and fat, almost like disgusting little dogs, nauseating to look at, and when they mistakenly run into the trenches, the soldiers, filled with disgust, kill them." He found it "terrifying, simply incomprehensible" that "all the images of grace have transformed into images of horror."

As the war entered its second full year, with no end in sight to the butchery, Osborn sensed a shift not only in himself but also among the soldiers. On both sides of no-man's-land, men were growing increasingly antagonistic and embittered. "The fierce days of fighting toward the end of September have brought a new emotion into the war that has moved from trench to trench," Osborn wrote on October 22, 1915. "The fighting has grown grimmer, more bitter, more vicious. The bitterness with which the great offensive was launched and beaten back can still be felt." Times had changed.

On Christmas Eve 1914, soldiers on both sides had gathered in no-man's-land to celebrate the holiday, and in the months that followed tossed friendly notes to one another, shared jam and cigarettes, and even held their fire so the enemy could retrieve or bury his dead.

They now exchanged insults and "hateful and nasty" missives. The French composed rhymed couplets insulting the Kaiser and the crown prince. One message tossed across no-man's-land read "The Boches are swine and should be guillotined not shot." Years later, Hitler would recall a similar hardening of the human spirit. "By the winter of 1915–16, this inner struggle had for me been decided," he wrote in *Mein Kampf.* "At last my will was undisputed master. If in the first days I went over the top with rejoicing and laughter, I was now calm and determined." Hitler noted that his nerves and reason had been hardened by constant battle. "The young volunteer had become an old soldier," he wrote. "And this transformation had occurred in the whole army."

BY NOVEMBER 1915, after more than a year at the front, Hitler's "transformation" was already in evidence, an emotional shift that is preserved in remnant artifacts in the Hitler library. In a leather-bound photostat copy of Hitler's military record, which includes his enlistment papers, he gives his permanent domicile as Munich, and does not list any immediate blood relatives, not his older half-siblings Alois and Angela, nor his younger sister Paula. By 1914, all regular contact with his immediate family appears to have been broken. Paula later said she assumed he was dead.

Another bound folio containing photostat copies of postcards and letters Hitler sent to Ernst Hepp, a Munich acquaintance, also suggests a severed relationship. In extended and rambling sentences, punctuated with emotional pleas that anticipate his rhetorical style in decades to come, Hitler fills page after page with vivid accounts of frontline fighting and his longing to return home. "I think so often about Munich, and each of us has only the one wish that we will have finally settled accounts with this gang, regardless of the outcome," Hitler writes Hepp.

"To get it over with, cost what it will, and that those of us who have the good fortune to see their homeland again, will find it cleaner and cleansed further of the foreign elements, that through the sacrifice and suffering that so many hundreds of thousands of us daily bring, that through the stream of blood flows here day after day against an international world of enemies." The last missive to Hepp is dated February 5, 1915.

By the time the RIR 16 took up position in Fournes in March 1915, where it was to remain for the next eighteen months, Hitler appears to have made the front his home. His closest companion was an English terrier he snatched that spring when it strayed into the German lines while chasing a rat across no-man's-land. He named it Foxl and taught it tricks, such as walking on its hind legs and climbing a ladder, much to the bemusement of his comrades. Foxl accompanied him on his assignments to the front until that October, when the British introduced poison gas.

We have several photographs of Hitler and Foxl in Fournes. In one, Hitler leans on a sawhorse, a gangly, awkward man with sallow cheeks, a bushy moustache, and large, protruding ears. He squints against the sunlight into the camera while Foxl, who stretches across the laps of two seated soldiers, cranes his neck back toward Hitler.

Max Amann, the company sergeant, remembered Hitler as a decidedly odd but notably selfless man. Amann recalls that when he discovered a surplus in the company budget and offered it to Hitler because the Austrian appeared to have so little money, Hitler thanked Amann and suggested he give it to someone more needy. Similarly, when Amann recommended him for a promotion, Corporal Hitler declined. He said he commanded more respect without an officer's stripes. He appeared to be selfless in the extreme. "Even if I came in at three in the morning, there were always a few men on duty," Amann recalled. "When I said, 'Messenger,' no one moved, only Hitler jumped up. When I said, 'You again!' he said, 'Let the others sleep. It doesn't matter to me.' "

While Amann's anecdotes are to be viewed with caution given that he was to become a close Hitler associate, and most notably the publisher of *Mein Kampf,* once again, the Hitler library provides corroborating evidence. In a tattered war memoir, *With Adolf Hitler in the Bavarian Reserve Infantry Regiment 16 "List,"* written by fellow RIR 16 veteran Adolf Meyer and presented to Hitler in 1934, we watch the twenty-something corporal cutting a zigzag pattern across an open field—overgrown with unharvested crops from the previous summer—while fellow soldiers huddle in a trench. As the man leaps into the safety of their company, he reports crisply, "Messenger, Regimental Headquarters 16, Hitler."

Hitler's dedication to duty is also preserved in his personal copy of the RIR 16's five-hundred-page regimental history, which bears a handwritten inscription to Hitler from Maximilian Baligrand, the RIR 16's last commander: "To his brave message runner, the highly decorated former corporal Mr. Adolf Hitler in memory of serious but great times, with thanks." Dated "Christmas 1931," a full year before Hitler's seizure of power, the handwritten inscription was made well before there was an obvious reason to pander to the former corporal.

Most consequential, of course, is the large folio with Hitler's complete military service record. Compiled in July 1937 for the Nazi Party Archives, this series of eighteen photostat documents from the Central Office for War Injuries and Graves was made in duplicate for Hitler. Along with a record of Hitler's two war injuries, his two citations for bravery—an Iron Cross Second Class in 1914 and an Iron Cross First Class in 1918, the highest military award for a noncommissioned officer—and his discharge papers from the army in March 1920, the folio also contains an assessment of his four years of service. Document 16 records: "Comportment: Very Good, Penalties: 0."

IN NOVEMBER 1915, for a frontline corporal to pay four marks for a book on cultural treasures of Berlin, when cigarettes, schnapps, and

Mit Adolf Hitler

im Bayer. Ref.-Inf.-Reg. 16 Lift

Von Adolf Meyer

Hitler's battered copy of Adolf Meyer's memoir,
With Adolf Hitler in the Sixteenth
Bavarian Reserve Infantry Regiment List

women were readily available for more immediate and palpable distraction, can be seen as an act of aesthetic transcendence, a vicarious escape from the ruined world of refinement and beauty that Osborn watched dissolving in the mud of the Somme, or in Hitler's case, possible evidence of the enduring aspiration for an artist's career, as suggested by the gritty fingerprints I found beside a reproduction of Rubens's *Diana and Her Nymphs Assaulted by Satyrs* on page 282, and further smudges along the margin on page 292, beside a Botticelli illustration for Dante's *Divine Comedy,* in which a despairing figure clings to an angel as he is lifted from the Inferno.

With a rush of busy lines running through the angel's robes and the man's anguished face, Botticelli conveys both urgency and desperation, which he contrasts with a flawless half circle that emanates from the angel's raised hand, enclosing the scene in a hemisphere of serenity and safety. With remarkable economy of line, Botticelli creates a powerfully emotive moment of salvation as well as a technical lesson in contrast and drama for students of the penciled line. As Hitler studied this sketch, his fingers left a series of gritty prints along the right-hand margin that showed the course of his attention.

This attention to artistic detail suggests the resilience of an obstinate artistic spirit that had survived his father's hard-knuckled objections ("A painter? Never!"), the devastating rejection from the Royal Academy of Arts in Vienna ("It struck me as a bolt from the blue"), and the subsequent realization that even his true calling in life, architecture, was beyond his reach. "One could not attend the Academy's architectural school without having attended the building school at the *Technik,* and the latter required a high-school degree," Hitler later lamented. "I had none of all this." Five subsequent hardscrabble years as a freelance painter in Vienna and Munich could not dampen his artistic ambitions. Yet, when Hitler enlisted in the army in early autumn 1914, he registered his profession as "artist."

Hitler was not the only soldier to march to the front with artistic intent.* The RIR 16 ranks were filled with professional painters who spent much of the war recording the daily life and horror at the front and whose works are preserved in the regimental history. There was Wilhelm Kuh, who penned a series of ink drawings of the ruins of Fromelles, including a farmhouse that had taken a direct hit that left a splintered roof with a gaping hole in its center; Alexander Weiss, who sketched the graves of dead soldiers along the trenches near Fromelles;

---

* At Brown University, I found a cache of thirty-three etchings made between 1914 and 1916 by the artist Fritz Gärtner, depicting Bavarian frontline soldiers; the signed etchings were found among Hitler's remnant papers in the Berlin bunker after his suicide.

Botticelli drawing, Osborn's Berlin.

and Max Martens, whose watercolor of his frontline quarters with its reinforced roof and sand-bagged entrance bears a painted sign on a high post that blends bitter irony with sweet nostalgia by using the name of the legendary beer hall of his native Munich, "Löwenbräu."

None of Hitler's wartime efforts are included in the regimental history. His own library preserves six of his watercolors in a folio published by his photographer Heinrich Hoffmann in 1935. The oversize hardcover, embossed with the words *Hitlers Aquarellen*, contains a one-page introduction, and presents reproductions of a half dozen watercolors, each with an additional onionskin overlay, that Hitler painted between autumn 1914 and summer 1917. The earliest is *Sunken Road near Wytschaete* from November 1914, where Hitler earned his first Iron Cross and where the RIR 16 message-running unit was decimated. "In Wytschaete alone, on the day of the first assault, three men of our eight men were shot dead, and another critically wounded," Hitler wrote afterward to Ernst Hepp. "We four survivors and the wounded man received medals." His watercolor from Wytschaete shows a vacant trench running through a war-ravaged forest with butchered trees standing in for butchered men.

In another painting, he depicts a ravaged, ruined monastery at Messines, where the following month the RIR 16 was again mauled in battle. Hitler also includes a scene from Fromelles, the *Dressing Station*, which shows the frontline first-aid station in a shrapnel-pocked farmhouse. Most notably, Hitler includes a painting of his farmhouse billet in Fournes where he was quartered with his fellow message runners, which they facetiously dubbed "Dark-Haired Maria's Place," after the strong-willed farmer's wife who attended to them. In this painting, Hitler shows us a sturdy, two-story farmhouse with an attached barn and scattered debris in the courtyard. Propped against the wall is a bicycle. For a time, Hitler served as the regimental bicyclist.

One recent observer pointed out that the reproduction of the farmhouse billet included in *Hitler's Watercolors* shows significant alterations from a copy of an original that survives in the Nazi Party Archives, suggesting that Heinrich Hoffmann had the Hitler originals doctored for public consumption. Indeed, the copy reveals a much less practiced hand. The bicycle is rendered only in a vague outline, and the details of the house are crudely drawn. Nevertheless, the deception embedded in the folio and included among Hitler's remnant books expresses an authentic emotion: Hitler's aspiration to be a better artist than he actually was.

BERLIN ALSO PRESERVES some of the earliest traces of Hitler's lifelong obsession with the German capital and the militant Prussian chauvinism

Hitler's sketch of his farmhouse billet near Fournes. From Hitler's personal copy
of his wartime artwork compiled by his photographer Heinrich Hoffmann

he shared with Max Osborn. Just as Hitler writes of his desire to see Germany "cleansed" of "foreign elements," Osborn rails against the influences of derivative nineteenth-century architectural styles that plagued this "Sparta on the Spree" with "orgies of an unspeakable debasement in taste." Osborn laments the "wilding" of taste (*Geschmacksverwilderung*) that has despoiled the Prussian purity of Berlin and burdened it with a "cornucopia of artistic curses."

   Osborn has particular disdain for those architects whose slavish imitation of foreign influences, especially "dogmatic Hellenism," have ruined the aesthetic texture of countless German cities. At the same time, he praises those architects who had retained a distinctively Teutonic vision, lauding the massive domed German Reichstag as "an artistic reflection of the multifaceted organism of the German Reich," admiring Karl Friedrich Schinkel for the "Prussian martialness" of the New Guard House, built in honor of the Germans who died in the Napoleonic Wars, and Karl Gotthard Langhans, who graced Berlin with its signature monument, the Brandenburg Gate. Though Langhans placed six Doric columns atop Ionic bases in a nod to Mediterranean classicism, he wisely avoided, Osborn notes, the temptation of employing a "Hellenic pediment." Instead, Langhans crowned his structure with the dramatic copper mise-en-scène, the quadriga with the four horses transporting a chariot with the sword-bearing goddess of victory.

To Osborn, the Brandenburg Gate represents "the ultimate essence of Prussianness," a balance between the perfected beauty of the ancients and the distinctly martial style of the north German plain—"Ancient Greece on Prussian soil!"—the German Grecomania run through a Prussian boot camp, brought to order and taught to stand crisp and smart at attention. "Its columns have something singularly orderly and erect, perhaps one could say, almost like a grenadier," Osborn writes.

Osborn's paeans to Prussian grace and grandeur evidently spoke to the young Austrian corporal as indicated by the volume's dog-eared pages and broken spine. The book bears evidence of careful scrutiny— smudges, bent pages, a drip of residual red paraffin still viscous after eighty years—in a thirty-page chapter on Frederick the Great, the legendary eighteenth-century warrior-king who established Prussia's preeminence as a military power. Frederick came to serve Hitler as a late-life role model of leadership and personal comportment, though rendered with catastrophic imperfection, in his own final years as a military commander.

Osborn casts Hitler's future idol as a meddling, cheapskate monarch who scrimped on quality and excelled at cut-rate imitation and shabby pomposity. "The king, entirely a child of the artistic mediocrity of his age when it came to taste, saw solutions only in the frivolous arbitrariness of this powder-wig era," Osborn complains. "More than his predecessors Frederick meddled in the plans of all his artists through personal intrusions and changes. More than his father he impatiently insisted that work be performed quickly and was satisfied with outward appearances for which inferior materials like plaster and stucco seemed adequate." Worse still, Frederick avoided "artists and geniuses in preference to dutiful and less opinionated second- and third-rate craftsmen." The resulting architectural missteps damaged not only the city's appearance but also the regent's health and reputation.

When planning his private residence, Sanssouci, in Potsdam, Frederick initially engaged the respected Berlin architect Georg Wenzeslaus von Knobelsdorff, but meddled incessantly with the design. According to Osborn, Frederick forced Knobelsdorff to forgo the construction of subterranean spaces, a decision, Osborn notes, that resulted in a chronic moisture problem that plagued the king's rheumatism to his dying day. Knobelsdorff was eventually released from the project and replaced with a more pliant architect.

Osborn takes particular pleasure in recounting the collapse of the redbrick church on the Gendarmenmarkt in 1746. Frederick rushed the builders to complete the church in half the allotted time and with a significantly reduced budget. As roof construction was nearing completion, the church walls collapsed, transforming the site into a heap of rubble and killing forty laborers. Osborn reproduces a period etching of the ruined structure with its tumbled stone, smashed beams, and broken scaffolding, along with clusters of gawking bystanders. "The Berliners were naturally unsparing in their mockery," Osborn writes. "In a brochure with the wry title 'Sorry About That,' the ironic theory was advanced that the structure had been built with gingerbread rather than stone."

On the night of October 22, 1941, a quarter century after Hitler acquired Osborn's *Berlin*, he recounted his early fascination with the Prussian capital, echoing Osborn's assessment.

"I always liked Berlin and even if it did bother me that a lot of it was not very beautiful it still meant a lot to me," he recalled. "Twice during the war I had ten days of vacation. Both times I went to Berlin, and from that time I know Berlin's museums and collections." Hitler, faithful to Osborn's assessment, called Berlin the "sandbox of the old Reich," which had accumulated a grab bag of architectural styles determined by rulers with little sense of aesthetic judgment—"Wilhelm II did have taste, it just happened to be extremely bad"—and recalled his own architectural vision of "Germanic-northern Ur-forms" that derived from "a Greek source," an echo of Osborn's own architectural incantation, "Ancient Greece on Prussian soil!"

Unlike Osborn, however, who could do little more than laud, lament, or lampoon, Hitler in 1941 possessed mettle and the means to undo the past. "We want to eliminate whatever is ugly in Berlin, and whatever Berlin gets now it should represent the epitome of what we are capable of achieving with modern means," he said. "Whoever enters the Reich Chancellery should have the feeling that he is standing before the masters of the world, and even the route along the way, through the triumphal arch on the wide streets past the Hall of the Soldier to the Square of the People should take his breath away." He foresaw the day when Berlin would emerge as "the capital of the world."

Hitler evidently bought Osborn's book with touristic intent, as is suggested by a companion volume from the Seemann series, a guide to Brussels I found among his remnant books. Like *Berlin, Brussels* is bound in an olive-drab cover with the title embossed in crimson, and as with the Osborn volume, Hitler's name is scrawled in the upper right corner on the inside cover.

Though Hitler includes neither the location nor date of purchase, we can assume the book was in his possession by the first week of July 1916, when, just after the battle for the Argonne Forest, he used a one-week furlough to visit Brussels, an event preserved not only in his military service record but also in a postcard sent to an RIR 16 comrade. "This trip is the most wonderful I have ever taken, despite the eternal rain which has been falling constantly," Hitler wrote from Brussels on July 6. Three months later, Hitler found an unanticipated opportunity to visit Berlin.

IN LATE SEPTEMBER 1916, after eighteen months near Fournes, the RIR 16 was ordered to bolster the defenses at the Somme. The three thousand men marched to Haubourdin and boarded a train to Iwuy. Here they exchanged their spiked *Pickelhauben* for steel helmets and marched to Cambrai, then on to Fremicourt and, eventually, in the first days of October, were thrown into battle between the towns of Bapaume and Le Barque. The regimental log notes 250 dead, 855 wounded, and 90 missing. Virtually the entire message-running unit was either killed or wounded, as recounted by one surviving soldier.

"The message runners were in an underground passage that was so narrow and low that two people could not pass each other," he recalled. "You could hardly sit. We kept tripping over each other's legs. The air was so thick and heavy you could barely breathe. A small stairway led outside. I had just sat down next to Hitler when the passage took a direct hit. The roof was demolished and torn into a thousand pieces. Shrapnel flew everywhere." Only two men emerged unscathed.

Hitler was taken to a nearby field hospital at Hermies with a piece of shrapnel in his leg. He was treated early the following morning in the company of Ernst Schmidt, who had also been wounded and transported by train to a Red Cross military hospital in Beelitz, a small town near Potsdam, forty miles southwest of Berlin. He was to spend the next two months there. "What a change! From the mud of the Battle of the Somme, into the white beds of this miraculous building!" Hitler later recalled. A photograph dated October 26, 1916, shows Hitler in a white hospital jacket with twelve other patients. He stands in the back row, his arms crossed, the only one without a hat, his hair unkempt, his moustache overgrown and bushy, his eyes dark and intense, his expression somber. He looks older, more serious than in the photographs taken in Fournes the previous year.

While recovering at Beelitz, Hitler had a chance to see Berlin, briefly visiting its museums and touring the city's most prominent sites, including Unter den Linden, the elegant tree-lined boulevard anchored at one end by the Brandenburg Gate and, at the other, by an imposing monu-

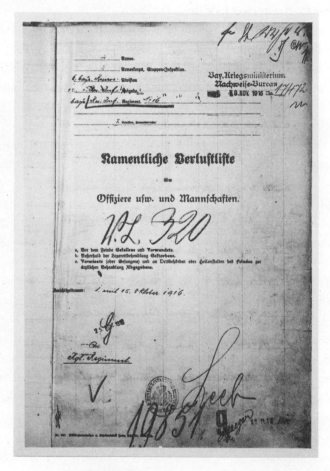

*Casualty report for Hitler dated October 15, 1916, from
Hitler's personal photostat copy of his military record*

ment to Frederick the Great. With this massive bronze equestrian of the Prussian king—in his cape and his signature headpiece—set atop a three-tiered stone pedestal carved with scenes of the warrior-king leading his troops, Osborn claims that the sculptor Christian Daniel Rauch struck the perfect balance between "classicism" and "Prussianism." "Rauch understood how to suppress all his classical impulses," Osborn rhapsodizes, "and to create in the Old Fritz with his three-cornered hat and wig and cane a masterwork of Berlin realism."

In December, Hitler was released from Beelitz and traveled to Munich, where he spent Christmas before rejoining the RIR 16 at the front. He returned to Berlin in October 1917, where he spent a ten-day furlough with the parents of an RIR 16 comrade, Richard Arendt. "The city is tremendous," Hitler wrote Ernst Schmidt on October 6, 1917. "A real metropolis. The traffic is also overwhelming. Am under way almost the entire day. Have finally found time to study the museums better. In short: I have everything I need." Including, we can assume, Osborn's *Berlin*.

Hitler evidently relied on Osborn as a guide to Berlin's museological holdings, which the author held in especially high regard and claimed "compensated" for the city's architectural shortcomings. Osborn faults a museum for showcasing the works of the Bavarian painter Peter Cornelius at the expense of the Prussian artist Adolph Menzel and the Austrian Moritz von Schwind. "The entire floor plan of the National Gallery has suffered so much from the demand of having the two large Cornelius galleries," Osborn says, "that the consequences of this step will never be completely remedied." In his sketch for an imagined reordering of the collection, Hitler rectifies this curatorial shortcoming by relegating the works of Cornelius to a single modest room, accommodating the von Schwind collection in three successive galleries, and devoting an entire wing to the works of Menzel. Hitler made a second ten-day visit to Berlin in early autumn 1918 and passed his time again exploring the museums and architectural sites.

He returned to the front in the last days of September, just as the final

British offensive of the war was under way. Here he was blinded in a gas attack. "On a hill south of Wervick, we came on the evening of October 13 into several hours of drumfire with gas shells which continued all night more or less violently," Hitler remembered. "As early as midnight, a number of us passed out, a few of our comrades forever." Hitler was taken from the front and transported to a lazarette near Pasewalk, in East Prussia, where he gradually regained his eyesight. That November, when he learned of the German capitulation, he was briefly stricken with a second attack of blindness.

A few years later, Hitler made much of his Pasewalk blindness, claiming that along with the combined trauma of the German capitulation, it precipitated his epiphany to enter politics, as he writes in *Mein Kampf*.

Although there is an approximate alignment between the end of Hitler's frontline service and the beginning of his political activity, there is no indication that he returned from the war in December 1918 with any intent to act on his political views.

Hitler arrived in Munich with his eyesight and a slightly battered copy of Osborn's guide to Berlin—as well as the companion volume to Brussels—that he was to keep with him for the rest of his life. In the early 1920s, *Berlin* joined a growing number of books in a wooden book-case, first in his apartment at 41 Thiersch Street, and, after August 1929, accommodated in his more elegant third-floor residence on Munich's Prince Regent's Square. In the protective safety of Hitler's collection, this volume survived the book burnings of May 1933—as a Jew, Osborn was on the list of banned authors and eventually immigrated to America— and the subsequent Allied bombings of the 1940s.

At some point in the spring of 1945, *Berlin* was packed into a crate with three thousand of Hitler's other books and transferred to a salt mine near Berchtesgaden, where they were discovered by a unit of the American 101st Airborne Division, taken to a "collecting point" in Munich, and eventually shipped, via Frankfurt, to a warehouse in Alexandria, Virginia. After several years, the book became part of the rare book collection of the Library of Congress, where it was assigned the call number N6885.07.

In the spring of 2001, when I first opened Osborn's *Berlin* in the subdued atmosphere of the Rare Book Reading Room, with the muffled sounds of midday traffic, I discovered, tucked in the crease between pages 160 and 161, a wiry inch-long black hair that appears to be from a moustache. An extension of the Benjaminian conceit—the collector preserved within his books, literally.

BOOK TWO

The Mentor's Trade

His idea of becoming the king of the world should not be taken literally as the "Will to Power." Hidden behind this is a spiritual belief that he will be ultimately pardoned for all his sins.

From DIETRICH ECKART's introduction to his stage adaptation of HENRIK IBSEN's *Peer Gynt*

ITLER'S COPY OF *Peer Gynt* is a corpse of a book. It is a second edition, published by Hoheneichen Verlag in 1917. The cover boards are warped, bowed at the center, and turned inward. The cheap, wide-weft linen cover has faded unevenly. A patch of dirty green at the center drains into lifeless brown along the edges, like a scorched lawn in late summer. A tasteless strip of lime-green paper has been pasted along the spine, bearing traces of the original gold-stenciled title: the upper portions of a *G* and a *T*. The jagged letters of the Fraktur script jangle the eyes.

The volume flops open effortlessly, revealing a personal dedication from Dietrich Eckart to Adolf Hitler, scrawled in a bombastic cursive script that spirals across the page, to "his dear friend"—*seinem lieben Freund*—which is rendered in the shorthand initials: S. L. Freund.

Few people could consider Hitler a "friend," let alone a "dear" one, and yet Eckart was more than that. He was patron, mentor, and father figure, the man who bought Hitler his first trench coat, and took him on his first airplane ride and to his first theater production in Berlin. Eckart

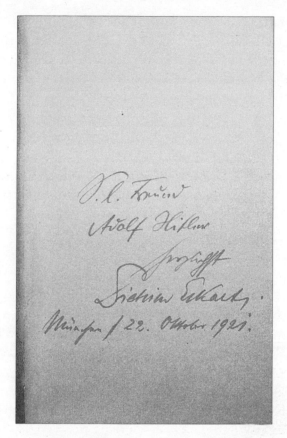

"Intended for his dear friend Adolf Hitler"
—*Dietrich Eckart's inscription in* Peer Gynt

taught Hitler how to write and he published his first essays. He circulated Hitler among his well-heeled friends with the icebreaker "This
man is the future of Germany. One day the entire world will be talking
about him."

Most significant, Eckart shaped the soft clay of Hitler's emotional and
intellectual world. When they first met, Hitler was thirty-one and just

finding his way onto the Munich political scene. Eckart was a generation older and a commanding figure in not only Munich but also much of Germany. His adaptation of *Peer Gynt* was one of the most successful theater productions of the age, allegedly with more than six hundred performances in Berlin alone.

He was a man of strong appetites—for women, alcohol, and morphine—and even stronger opinions, especially when it came to Jews. He published the hate-mongering weekly *Auf gut deutsch* (In Plain German) and cofinanced, also in Munich, Hoheneichen Verlag, a publishing house that specialized in anti-Semitic literature. One Munich newspaper claimed that Eckart's hatred of the Jews was so fierce that he could "consume a half dozen Jews along with his sauerkraut for lunch." Eckart gave focus, form, and fire to Hitler's own anti-Semitism.

"Eckart was the man who, according to Hitler's own repeated statements, had the greatest significance for his personal development," a close Hitler associate observed. "He was Hitler's best friend and one can also consider him his intellectual father. This is true especially of the beginning; his fanatic racial patriotism and his radical anti-Semitism made Eckart the greatest influence on his political development." On his deathbed, Eckart is reported to have said, "Follow Hitler! He will dance, but it is I who called the tune!" Hitler hailed Eckart as the "polar star" of the Nazi movement.

In late 1918, Hitler returned from war to find Germany in chaos. In Berlin, the socialists had toppled the kaiser and proclaimed a socialist republic. In Munich, a socialist radical named Kurt Eisner declared Bavaria an independent country, only to be assassinated by a right-wing count. In the ensuing turmoil, the government was taken over by Bolsheviks—including an anarchist, a playwright, and a psychiatric patient who, in his brief stint as foreign minister, declared war on Switzerland—who established a shortlived Soviet state of Bavaria. Eventually, a force of nine thousand regular troops supported by a *Freikorps* of thirty thousand decommissioned soldiers toppled the Bolsheviks and, after executing their leaders, reestablished relative order.

Amid the turmoil Hitler found refuge in the Oberwiesenthal barracks on the outskirts of Munich. For a few weeks, he stood guard at a prison in the nearby town of Traunstein, along with former fellow RIR 16 message runner Ernst Schmidt, then for a month or so with the watch detail at Munich's main train station. At the barracks, he began circulating among military units agitating against Bolshevik insurgency, and was briefly assigned to a decommissioning interrogation panel that determined soldiers' political loyalties before approving their release from the army.

In these weeks, Hitler came to the attention of Captain Karl Mayr, who was impressed by his strong anti-Bolshevik sentiments and compelling manner of speaking. That spring, Mayr suggested Hitler attend a one-week course in political ideology at the University of Munich, and in August, he sent him on a two-week training course in propaganda and public speaking at a military training facility near Augsburg. When Hitler returned, Mayr dispatched him on intelligence-gathering forays among the upstart extremist parties proliferating in the uncertain political atmosphere.

On Friday, September 19, 1919, Hitler attended a meeting of the Deutsche Arbeiterpartel (German Workers Party), a new movement founded that January by a sports journalist, Karl Harrer, and a local railroad mechanic, Anton Drexler, at which Dietrich Eckart was scheduled to speak. When Eckart fell ill, Gottfried Feder, whose book on "interest slavery" Hitler had read earlier that year, stood in. "My impression was neither good nor bad, a new organization like so many others," Hitler later said of the meeting. "This was a time in which anyone who was not satisfied with developments and no longer had confidence in existing parties felt called upon to found a new party. Everywhere these organizations sprang out of the ground, only to vanish silently after a time."

During the discussion that followed Feder's lecture, an argument erupted over Austria—a professor called for the creation of an Austrian-Bavarian state—and Hitler launched into a tirade against the professor, who eventually fled the room hat in hand. Impressed by Hitler's oratorical skills, Drexler handed him a political pamphlet he had written about his personal conversion to radical rationalism.

That same evening at the Oberwiesenthal barracks, Hitler read the Drexler treatise, *My Political Awakening: From the Diary of a German Social-ist Worker*. In this forty-page political coming-of-age story, Hitler read about Drexler's transformation from an apathetic and near destitute teenage laborer in Berlin—"As a result of unemployment I survived by playing zither in a night club"—to a fervent German nationalist and equally virulent anti-Semite. "By anti-Semite one means all those who recognize the destructive Jewish influence on the life of our people, who fight against it and who protect themselves from the economic strangu-lation by the Jews!" Drexler traces his conversion to anti-Semitism to a night in November 1917 when he encountered a Jewish businessman in Antwerp and engaged in an argument on German nationalism that ended with Drexler unconscious in a local prison. "I cannot say whether this apostle of the Talmud poured something in the wine," Drexler wrote, "but later the more I thought about it, it led me to a clue that I only now recognize." Drexler's epiphany, of course, was the alleged per-vasiveness of Jewish influence and control.

Drexler claims to have traced Jewish influences into the press, includ-ing the *Vossische Zeitung;* into finance, where he asserts that 80 percent of Germany's assets are "in Jewish hands"; into the trade unions; political parties; the Bolshevik movement; and ultimately into the collapse of the German war effort. Drexler speaks ominously of the "corrosive Jewish influence on the life of our people" and underscores the alleged eco-nomic threat, peppering his treatise with excerpts from the Talmud, his own speeches, a poem by Dietrich Eckart, and with eerily portentous concepts like "eradication" (*Ausrottung*) and "extermination" (*Vernich-tung*). "From the moment that I recognized the true enemy of all work-ers, there was no stopping me," Drexler wrote. "With the great love that I felt for my fatherland I set myself the task to use every means at my dis-posal to help to open the eyes of those poor misled souls to the true enemy."

When Hitler read Anton Drexler's My Political
Awakening, *he saw "my own development
come to life before my eyes."*

As Hitler read Drexler's treatise, he found familiar resonances with his own experiences. "Once I had begun, I read the little book through with interest; for it reflected a similar process to the one which I myself had gone through twelve years before," Hitler remembered. "Involuntarily, I saw my own development come to life before my eyes." A few days later Hitler received a postcard saying he had been "accepted" into the German Workers Party. He deliberated on membership and decided to join. "Now we have an Austrian. Man, he really knows how to talk," Drexler later quipped. "We can certainly use him."

When Hitler attended a second meeting in a back room at the Stern-ecker Beer Hall, he found himself with thirty or forty others listening to an extended and tedious speech by Karl Harrer. Harrer had gone on for some time when suddenly he was interrupted by the "rasping deep voice" of an elderly man: "Will you finally stop driveling. No one gives a damn about what you are saying!" Hitler turned and saw staring at him an imposing figure with a fiercely bald head, intense blue eyes, and a paintbrush moustache. "I could have thrown my arms around him," Hitler later recalled.

Harrer sputtered to a conclusion, and as the meeting dispersed, Anton Drexler led Hitler to the older man and introduced him as Dietrich Eckart. Hitler sensed an instant affinity. Eckart asked Hitler if he had seen either *Peer Gynt* or *Lorenzaccio,* a play Eckart had written—Hitler had not—then invited him to his house. It was a landmark moment. The next week, Drexler accompanied Hitler to Eckart's handsome villa, where they were escorted to Eckart's upstairs library.

As the men entered, Eckart rose majestically from his desk, turned toward them, peered over the top of his reading glasses, raised his imperious head—Hitler vividly recalled every detail—and, removing his spectacles, stepped forward to welcome his guests with a handshake. "A powerful forehead, blue eyes, his entire visage like that of a bull, not to mention, a voice with a wonderfully forthright tone," Hitler remembered.

Hitler had never met anyone quite like Eckart. His own father, Alois Hitler, had been a midlevel civil servant whose lack of formal education idled his career early on, despite his acknowledged intellectual capacities, leaving him to occupy a series of modest posts in customs offices along the Inn River, on the border between Austria and Germany. Late in life, he purchased a large country home that so taxed his resources and energies that he eventually abandoned it and moved to a more modest residence near Linz, where he was to spend the rest of his days. By the end, his only ambition in life was to see his two daughters married and his two sons gainfully employed. His obituary in the local paper noted his achievements in beekeeping, his irascible nature, and his resonant voice.

As the son of a middling government official, Hitler was awed by Eckart's stature, both physical and material, and flattered by his attentions. Eckart appears to have been similarly impressed with Hitler. Unlike Karl Harrer, whom Eckart found tedious, or even Drexler, who had spent the war years engaged in home-front politics, Hitler possessed the passion and frontline credentials Eckart had long been seeking.

"We need someone to lead us who is used to the sound of a machine gun. Someone who can scare the shit out of people," Eckart allegedly proclaimed three years earlier over drinks in Munich's Café Nettle. "I don't need an officer. The common people have lost all respect for them. The best would be a worker who knows how to talk. He doesn't need to know much. Politics is the stupidest profession on earth." Eckart claimed that "any farmer's wife" in Munich knew as much as any political leader. "Give me a vain monkey who can give the Reds their due and won't run away as soon as someone swings a chair leg at him," he said. "I would take him any day over a dozen educated professors who wet their pants and sit there trembling with their facts. He has to be a bachelor, then we'll get the women."

The description is so evidently tailor-made for Hitler that it would strain credibility, but there is nonetheless independent evidence of Eckart's pre-Hitler search for a future leader. In *Lorenzaccio*, a play that premiered in the autumn of 1916, Eckart recounts the travails of a Florentine prince in search of a leader—Eckart uses the word *Führer*—who can instill pride and reestablish order in his faltering city-state. Eckart has the Florentine prince despair that there is "no one" (*keiner*) to be found: *"Keiner, keiner, keiner, keiner!"* he cries, echoing King Lear's grief-wracked lament "Never, never, never, never, never."

When *Lorenzaccio* opened on the stage of the Royal Court Theater in Berlin, the play spoke powerfully to the growing disillusionment with the German leadership, and a war that appeared stalemated in a seemingly permanent and senseless bloodletting.

With the substantial income he received from his theatrical successes, Eckart helped fund right-wing societies such as the Fichte Club in Berlin, and the Thule Society in Munich, which promoted virulent strains of nationalism and anti-Semitism in the guise of Aryan mysticism; Thule was the purported capital of an ancient Aryan empire situated in Scandinavia. In 1917, he financed, with Gottfried Grandel, a wealthy Augsburg businessman, the acquisition of Hoheneichen Verlag and, the next year, he cofinanced *Auf gut deutsch.*

At the same time, Eckart prowled Munich's political fringes in search of writing talent. In December 1918, he engaged Alfred Rosenberg, a handsome twenty-one-year-old Baltic German who shared his twin hatreds of Jews and Bolsheviks as well as membership in the Thule Society. The following spring, Eckart hired Hermann Esser, a poison-pen boulevard journalist with an instinct for the scandalous and salacious.

Most notably, Eckart began courting Wolfgang Kapp, a Prussian aristocrat whose bellicose condemnations of the Versailles Treaty and Weimar democracy had made him a leading spokesman of the radical right across Germany. In the same weeks when Eckart and Hitler first met, Eckart traveled to Berlin for a tête-à-tête with Kapp. "I had been admiring your person only from a distance, and suddenly you have become so close to me," Eckart wrote to Kapp afterward. In March 1920, when Kapp staged a military coup with disaffected units of the German army, Eckart borrowed a plane and pilot from Grandel and flew to Berlin. He invited Hitler to join him.

When the two men arrived at the Hotel Adlon, which was serving as Kapp's headquarters, Eckart saw Ignatius Timothy Trebitsch-Lincoln, a Hungarian journalist whom Kapp had appointed as press spokesman. Immediately, Eckart knew Kapp was not his man. Trebitsch-Lincoln was a Jew. Eckart took Hitler by the arm. "Let's go, Adolf," he allegedly said. "We don't want anything to do with this sort of thing." Hitler echoed

Eckart's sentiments in an intelligence report he filed upon his return to Munich. "When I saw and spoke with the press spokesman for the Kapp government," Hitler wrote, "I knew that this could not be a national revolution and that it would have to fail since the press spokesman was a Jew."

In the days that followed, Eckart and Hitler watched the Kapp putsch disassemble into chaos and ultimate calamity. Bolshevik strikes paralyzed the city. The rebellious Reichswehr units waffled. The German Reichstag escaped Berlin and reconvened first in Weimar, then in Stuttgart, and continued to run the country. Within a week, the putsch was over. Kapp fled, and the Weimar government returned. Eckart and Hitler remained in Berlin, visiting Eckart's wealthy friends and, quite likely, attending a performance of *Peer Gynt* at the National Theater.

Neither Hitler nor Eckart provided details of their time together in Berlin, but subsequent words and actions suggest they established a strong personal bond. "I felt myself drawn to his person, and I soon saw that he was the right man for the entire movement," Eckart later observed, "and my relationship to him grew more personal during the time of the Kapp putsch." Though we do not have an equivalent testimonial from Hitler, his actions are as revealing as Eckart's words. Immediately upon his return to Munich, he resigned his commission in the army, left his quarters at the barracks, and, with a handful of possessions carefully itemized in army records, moved into a second-floor apartment at 41 Thiersch Street, in a quiet area near the Isar River and just down the street from Eckart's office.

With Hitler only a few doors away, it was convenient for Eckart to assume a proprietary claim over the younger man's career. He circulated Hitler among his friends, added his own right-wing gravitas to Hitler's early beer hall appearances, and stage-managed Hitler's public persona. With an instinct for the theatrical, Eckart withheld Hitler's image from the press as a means of heightening the Hitler mystique. Storm troopers were instructed to assault photographers attempting to photograph him; generally, film was merely removed by force, though on occasion, cameras were smashed. When William Randolph Hearst requested a photograph of Hitler to accompany a news story, he was allegedly told it would cost him thirty thousand dollars. If you wanted to see Hitler, you had to go hear him. A more prosaic explanation holds that Hitler's image was suppressed to avoid his easy identification by the police.

In any event, even as late as 1923, while Hitler was filling the largest venues in Munich and had become a staple in the German press, his physical appearance remained elusive. When the Munich-based political cartoonist Thomas Theodor Heine visited Berlin, he was asked about Hitler's appearance so frequently that he responded with a full page of Hitler caricatures, rendered in grotesquely overstated dimensions, each focused on a distinctive feature—his mesmerizing gaze, his legendary voice, his fanatic gestures. "But what did Hitler really look like?" Heine mused. "The question must remain unanswered. Hitler does not exist as an individual. He is a condition."

Most significantly, of course, Eckart scripted Hitler's role as history's most infamous anti-Semite. By Hitler's own admission, he had only passing exposure to anti-Semitic thought or rhetoric before he met Eckart. He claimed that his father would have considered it a sign of "cultural backwardness" to have used the term *Jew* in the Hitler household. Hitler recalls being "horrified" by the occasional anti-Semitic remark he heard at school. "Not until my fourteenth or fifteenth year did I begin to come across the word 'Jew' with any frequency, partly in connection with political discussions," Hitler said. "This filled me with a mild distaste, and I could not rid myself of an unpleasant feeling that always came over me whenever religious quarrels occurred in my presence."

In Vienna, where Hitler was first confronted with the "Jewish question," he found himself torn between the inbred "tolerance" of his home life and the anti-Semitic rhetoric of the city's political right, as well as his own firsthand encounters with Jews in the streets of the city. "As always in such cases, I now began to try to relieve my doubts by books," Hitler observed. "For a few hellers I bought the first anti-Semitic pamphlets of my life." He dismissed them as "unscientific."

Now Hitler's anti-Semitism took form and fire under Eckart's tutelage. "Dietrich Eckart himself dealt with the literary and intellectual aspects," Hitler said, "but mastered the entire subject matter like few others." In particular, Hitler credits Eckart with forging the link between Jews and Bolshevists.

While there is no way to gauge the specific influences that Eckart had on Hitler's nascent anti-Semitism, or what Hitler may have imbibed from other associates and his own reading, we are able to gain some sense of the tone and spirit of the Eckart tutelage in a "Conversation" Eckart was writing at the time of his death. In this fragmentary, perverse sort of Socratic dialogue between mentor and protégé, Eckart and Hitler engage in a sparring match of anti-Semitic one-upmanship, each attempting to outdo the other in terms of viciousness. Hitler blames the Jews for the collective excesses and missteps of the Catholic Church: the selling of indulgences is a blatantly "Jewish practice"; the Crusades that allegedly bled Germany of "six million men" and sent "tens of thousands of children" to their deaths were the brainchild of the Jews. "Some religion!" Hitler rages. "This wallowing in filth, this hate, this malice, this arrogance, this hypocrisy, this pettifogging, this incitement to deceit and murder—is that a religion? Then there has never been anyone more religious than the devil himself. It is the Jewish essence, the Jewish character, period!"

"Luther expressed his opinion of it plainly enough," Eckart responds. "He urges us to burn the synagogues and Jewish schools and to heap earth on the remains so that no man would ever again see one stone or cinder of them."

Hitler adds with conviction, "Burning their synagogues, I am afraid, would have been of damn little avail. The fact of the matter is: even if there had never been a synagogue, never a Jewish school, never an Old

Testament, and never a Talmud, the Jewish spirit would still have been there and had its effect."

Eckart's "Conversation" runs eighty pages, then ends abruptly. The fragment was published by Hoheneichen Verlag in March 1923, three months after Eckart's death, while Hitler was on trial following his failed attempt to topple the Bavarian government. Hitler's biographers have generally disregarded this bizarre document, since it is clearly an invented dialogue, with no evidence that Hitler had a hand in its creation. While there is good reason to dismiss the "Conversation" as a document of record, it not only captures the tone and spirit, if not the verbatim content, of Eckart's exchanges with Hitler, but also preserves a more significant personal fact: in these eighty handwritten pages, Eckart allows Hitler to match him point for point in terms of fact and vitriol in a rite of passage in which the student shows himself to be every bit the equal of his master.

WHEN ECKART INSCRIBED *Peer Gynt* to his "dear friend Adolf Hitler" in the autumn of 1921, he had more than two dozen works—plays, poetry anthologies, novels, collections of essays—from which to choose, several of them more appropriate at first glance than the Ibsen epic. He could have presented Hitler a copy of *Tannhäuser on Vacation*, his 1895 homage to Richard Wagner. And then, of course, there was *Lorenzaccio*, with its prescient "Führer" references, a copy of which Eckart inscribed to Hitler's younger sister, Paula, a gift that flattered equally both the giver and the recipient.* In selecting *Peer Gynt* for Hitler, however,

---

* I found the book among a cache of Hitler family memorabilia taken from Paula Hitler's Vienna apartment at the end of the war by a neighbor who later donated them to a Linz archive. Along with diverse family items dating back to Hitler's youth, including an account book of daily household expenses, postcards, and embroidery with the initials of Hitler's mother, there is also a picture book of Munich that Hitler inscribed to his sister when she visited him for two weeks in February 1922.

Eckart intended to be less self-congratulatory than intensely personal. His stage adaptation of *Peer Gynt* was not only his most successful work, but also the one with which he most closely identified.

When Eckart first read Ibsen's epic poem in the spring of 1911, he was a forty-four-year-old failed writer who had squandered his artistic promise and his financial resources, and was reduced to sleeping on park benches in Berlin. Only the death of his father and a resulting inheritance delivered him from destitution. The story of Ibsen's "Nordic Faust" spoke to him. The namesake protagonist sets off into the world brimming with youthful hubris from an isolated Norwegian village intent on becoming "king of the world." He journeys across Europe and North Africa, through the magical world of trolls and into the courts of kings, leaving ruined lives and betrayed promises in his wake, only to return home at the end of his life in ruin and shame. There he finds his abandoned but faithful lover, Solveig—her name means "path of the soul"—waiting for him and offering him salvation. Eckart was so moved by Peer Gynt's fate that he wrote to Ibsen's son in Norway requesting permission to adapt the poem for the German stage.

"I *experienced* Peer Gynt, not just because of his inner life, but remarkably, to a large degree, by the things that happened to him," Eckart explained. "Likewise, Solveig's song plays a melancholy role in my existence, but because that happens to every sensitive soul, there's nothing unusual about that. It's only striking in more remote events, for instance with the finger that is cut off—as a dumb boy I once stuck my hand in a lathe so I wouldn't have to go to school—but most strikingly with the insane asylum. More than twenty years ago I ended up there because of a serious morphine addiction." Eckart noted a further parallel. In the summer of 1867, while Ibsen was first envisioning his epic hero, Eckart's parents conceived their son. "Let anyone who wants to laugh about the resulting mysticism," Eckart wrote. "For me this fact holds a transcendent epiphany, an unshakeable comfort that will endure until the end of my earthly journey." Eckart went on for fourteen pages like this, noting, in addition, that the authorized German translation by Christian Morgenstern was a travesty of the original. In Eckart's opinion, Morgenstern, who was Jewish, was little more than a "gravedigger" of language whose lyrics were barely fit for a beer hall newspaper. To underscore his intensely personal identification with the Ibsen character, Eckart had "Peer Gynt" embossed on his stationery. When Eckart gave *Peer Gynt* to his "dear friend" Adolf Hitler, it was an exceedingly personal gesture.

Hitler, unfamiliar with *Peer Gynt* when he first met Eckart in the autumn of 1919, would have sensed similar resonances to those that moved Eckart. In his youth, like Gynt, Hitler had been possessed by a wanderlust, fueled in good part by adventure stories such as James Fenimore Cooper's Leatherstocking tales, Daniel Defoe's *Robinson Crusoe,* Karl May's *Ride Across the Desert,* and the real-life adventures of the Swedish explorer Sven Hedin, who in the first decades of the twentieth century traversed some of the earth's last uncharted regions and returned with riveting accounts of unknown peoples and untold dangers. "As a boy, he often mentioned the name Sven Hedin around the house," Paula Hitler once recalled.

> He followed his explorations through Inner Asia as closely as everything else that seemed of importance for the future of the world. And then—he had barely outgrown his children's shoes when he was taken with an irrepressible longing for distant places, one after the other, he wanted to go to sea and then into the desert, to throw off the chains that kept his restless wandering spirit contained within a ten-kilometer radius. Initially he remained within these ten kilometers which was a great relief to Mother to whom he was so attached.

Hitler recalled that he first saw *Peer Gynt* in Berlin, in the company of Eckart, noting with distaste Munich's preference for the Morgenstern adaptations. Though Hitler mentions nothing more specific about the performance, neither the year nor circumstances, Hitler's library preserves resonances of that memorable event in the gramophone registry,

"I want to achieve greatness," Peer Gynt declares. The opening scene to Dietrich Eckart's stage adaptation of the Ibsen classic. One of nine etchings included in the edition Eckart inscribed to Hitler.

which lists four separate recordings of Grieg's incidental music to *Peer Gynt,* and in the inscribed copy of Eckart's stage adaptation with its nine woodcut illustrations to individual scenes. Collectively, these artifacts convey the spirit and tone of that evening as Hitler sat with Eckart and listened to the haunting notes of the woodwinds as the curtain rose to reveal a modest hut in the foreground and craggy peaks beyond.

"I want to achieve greatness," Peer proclaims to his mother in the opening scene. "I want fame and honor for you and me." Despite the maternal warning that such ambition must come to no good, Peer sets forth—*allegro con brio*—into the world to realize his dreams, traversing Europe, voyaging by sea, encountering real men and mythical beasts, and eventually crossing the deserts of North Africa, where he settles in Morocco amid wealth and splendor. Along the way, Peer Gynt forges a path of human destruction in his single-minded bid to become "king of the world." Gynt betrays friendships, commits murder, and seduces and then abandons Solveig, a village maiden who patiently awaits his promised return. When Peer Gynt finally returns, ruined in body and soul and on the verge of death, he seeks absolution.

"Denounce my crimes!" he demands, as he stands before her. "Denounce my crimes!"

Unaware of the dimensions of his crimes and transgressions, Solveig responds, "I don't know what you are talking about! You kept your promise, my loved one, you returned." The rest, she says, must be left to God. As Solveig takes Peer into her arms, he drifts into a delusional state thick with Freudian innuendo. "Lover and mother, so you will protect me from doom?" he gasps. "Take me, protect me within your womb." Accepting her role as a mother-lover, Solveig absolves Peer of his sins and, in the closing scene, sings a lullaby as a beam of light bathes the couple in a luminous circle.

Eckart generally remains true to the Ibsen original, but in the final scene he adds a theatrical touch that significantly shifts the story's moral dramaturgy. "Only when he lies dying in Solveig's lap, illuminated by the rising sun, should he turn his face to the audience," Eckart instructs. "It's no longer the tortured, fear-stricken face of the old Peer, but rather the fresh, young, clear countenance of the young Peer." In that instant, a lifetime of sin has been washed clean. Peer is absolved, restored to the purity and innocence of youth. It proved to be a singularly emotive theatrical turn, as suggested by the reviews of the premiere performance. "When the curtains closed for the last time on the final scene, the audience was so moved that it took some time before they began to applaud," one critic wrote, noting that the applause then rose to a deafening roar. "It went right to the heart," noted another critic. "It shook and moved all of one's emotion." Two decades later, Hitler was still talking about

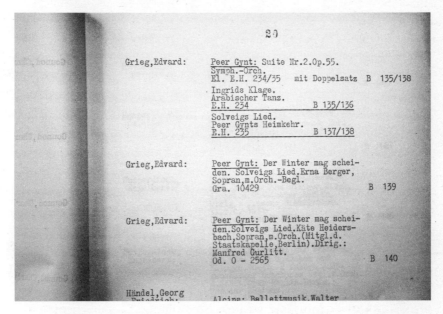

20

Grieg,Edvard: Peer Gynt: Suite Nr.2.Op.55.
                  Symph.-Orch.
                  El. E.H. 234/35   mit Doppelsatz B 135/138
                  Ingrids Klage.
                  Arabischer Tanz.
                  E.H. 234   B 135/136
                  Solveigs Lied.
                  Peer Gynts Heimkehr.
                  E.H. 235   B 137/138

Grieg,Edvard: Peer Gynt: Der Winter mag schei-
                  den. Solveigs Lied.Erna Berger,
                  Sopran,m.Orch.-Begl.
                  Gra. 10429   B 139

Grieg,Edvard: Peer Gynt: Der Winter mag schei-
                  den.Solveigs Lied.Käte Heiders-
                  bach,Sopran,m.Orch.(Mitgl.d.
                  Staatskapelle,Berlin).Dirig.:
                  Manfred Gurlitt.
                  Od. O - 2565   B 140

Händel,Georg
Friedrich: Alcina: Ballettmusik.Walter

*Excerpt from Hitler's gramophone registry listing three of
his four recordings of Edvard Grieg's incidental music to* Peer Gynt

the performance and in a bizarre reprise, ended his life in a Gyntian
mise-en-scène, broken in spirit and body with his companion Eva Braun
on a sofa and a portrait of his mother on the wall but without a hint of
remorse.

AT FIRST GLANCE, there seems to be no readily evident reason why
Eckart waited until October 1921 to inscribe a copy of his *Peer Gynt* to
Hitler. By then, the men had known each other for two years. The explanation, as I was to discover among Eckart's papers, was as much political
as it was personal, with *Peer Gynt* providing a bookend, both literally and
figuratively, to the first major crisis of Hitler's political career in which
Eckart appears to have played the role of kingmaker, as suggested from

the several dozen Eckart letters, essays, receipts, and other documents from Eckart's private papers that I was shown in Berchtesgaden.* "It's barely a year-and-a-half since I first spoke at the party meeting," Eckart observes with proprietary ease in an undated letter from mid-1921. "There were about fifteen people present, eight of whom I brought with me, and today every meeting draws thousands upon thousands." Eckart goes on to detail his central role in the acquisition of the *Völkischer Beobachter* (People's Observer) the previous December, noting that he had personally vouched for a 60,000-mark loan from one donor and committed another 50,000 marks of his own money. A number of remnant IOUs from the Nazi Party to Eckart attest to his ongoing patronage of the movement almost until his death in late autumn 1923.

In particular, a letter from fellow patron Gottfried Grandel suggests the central role that Eckart played in influencing both Hitler and the movement Hitler came to lead. Under Eckart's tutelage, Hitler was able to assert himself almost immediately after joining the movement.

In January 1920, just two months after Eckart had silenced Karl Harrer with a "gravel voiced" intervention, Hitler forced the party co-founder out of the chairmanship of the party, marginalized Anton Drexler, renamed the party the National Socialist German Workers Party, and framed a twenty-five-point program that would serve as the Nazi Party manifesto for the next quarter century. Hitler's own sense of authority was cemented by Eckart's mentoring but also by his ability to draw crowds. Though Hitler held no official decision-making capacity, he was regularly consulted on party decisions, as confirmed by surviving internal documents that bear scribbled comments such as "To be forwarded to Herr Hitler" and "Will be handled personally by Herr Hitler." In February 1921, Hitler forced the party leadership to cede him significant authority.

---

*The papers were part of the estate of Anni Obster, Eckart's companion at the time of his death. I was able to study the original documents in Berchtesgaden before they were transferred to a private collection outside Germany.

When Drexler entered into negotiations to merge the Nazi Party with other nationalist movements, Hitler quashed the plan by threatening to resign from the party. A few weeks later, Hitler again took action when he discovered that Drexler was engaged in another negotiation, this time with Otto Dickel, a professor of philosophy at Augsburg University and a protégé of Gottfried Grandel.

At the time, Hitler was with Eckart in Berlin lobbying members of the conservative National Club for additional financing for the party newspaper, the *Völkischer Beobachter*, which they had acquired the previous December with the financial assistance of Grandel and others. In Hitler's absence, Drexler invited Dickel to Munich to talk about his book *Resurgence of the West,* a four-hundred-page paean to resurgent nationalism that had been published a few months earlier and was receiving good press in conservative circles. In *Resurgence,* Dickel provided a positive, nationalist antidote to the pessimism of Oswald Spengler's best-selling treatise *The Decline of the West.* Challenging Spengler's claim that the Occident was a spent civilization, Dickel argued that a more assertive nationalism, coupled with economic socialism and officially sanctioned anti-Semitism, could revive European culture. The "tyranny" of the Jews, Dickel claimed, was the greatest threat not only to Germany but to the entire continent. "The Jewish question is not just an internal German matter that is more important to one person and less important to the other," he asserted. "It is at present the most important issue for the Western world." Dickel claimed that the Jews controlled the press, the arts, and education, and had thereby become the masters and shapers of the *Volksseele,* the collective soul of the people. Dickel's solution: purge these mechanisms of control of Jewish influence. Only Aryans should be informing, entertaining, and educating other Aryans. There was not much new here, except that it had been written by a university professor with full academic credentials. The *Völkischer Beobachter* quickly declared Dickel's *Resurgence* "required reading" for all good German nationalists.

On Friday, May 12, 1921, Dickel appeared in the main hall of Munich's

Hofbräuhaus before a packed crowd. Dickel proved to be, in Drexler's view, not only an insightful intellectual but also an inspiring, even mesmerizing speaker. For two hours, he held the audience captive with his vision for a German future. Afterward, Drexler noted that Dickel, like Hitler, had "a popular touch." He immediately booked Dickel for several more speaking engagements, and accepted an invitation to bring the Nazi Party leadership to Augsburg to discuss potential cooperation. The journalist Hermann Esser called Hitler in Berlin and informed him of Dickel's Munich appearance and Drexler's merger plans. Hitler was furious. He had read *Resurgence* earlier that year, and had told Drexler it was "rubbish." Drexler had gone ahead and invited Dickel to speak anyway, and in no less a place than the Hofbräuhaus, the site of Hitler's own beer hall triumphs. More vexing still, Hitler had not been consulted or even informed about the merger talks. Enraged, he left Berlin for Augsburg.

Hitler arrived to find Dickel holding forth before the assembled Nazi Party leadership. With academic precision, Dickel methodically dissected Hitler's twenty-five-point party program, underscoring its weaknesses and internal contradictions point by point. He found the party name cumbersome, unwieldly, and, worst of all, misleading. Hitler repeatedly interrupted Dickel with protests and emotional outbursts, and eventually stormed out in a fury. "When, after three tedious hours, I attempted to bring a quick close to these proceedings by exiting the room, the official representatives of the Party who were present not only did not support me, but quite the opposite continued the negotiations," Hitler complained later. Even Eckart stayed.

WHEN HITLER ROSE to his feet and fled the meeting room in Augsburg, his instincts almost certainly told him he had no other viable option. His brief political career had been built on bullying, cajoling, and subterfuge. He was a master of the dismissive quip or cutting remark that silenced criticism or diverted attention. When that failed, he drowned dissent in a deluge of rage and rant, or relied on the fisticuffs and boot tips of his brown-shirted storm troopers.

The technique worked well in the overheated clamor of beer halls but was less effective in the more staged setting of a meeting room, especially against rational, measured arguments delivered by an articulate opponent with a demonstrated rhetorical ability. Unlike the professor whom Hitler had chased from the room with his first public tirade back in September 1919, Dickel could match Hitler in word and wit and Hitler knew it. Hitler had shared a podium with him in Augsburg the previous January, and was as aware of Dickel's strengths as he was of his own limitations, especially when it came to formal education.

Against Dickel's distinguished academic pedigree, Hitler's only formal education since dropping out of high school seventeen years earlier had been the crash course in political ideology, recommended by Karl Mayr, at the University of Munich in the spring of 1919. For a full week, commencing Thursday, June fifth, Hitler had sat in the main university lecture hall listening to morning lectures on subjects ranging from "German history since the Reformation" to the "political history" of the Great War to the "economic terms" of the Treaty of Versailles. Afternoons and evenings were devoted to workshops on debating techniques that trained the students in "unified concepts" of German identity and the "sober selection" of facts in framing arguments. "The main part of the course however consists of oral exercises, debating and discussion of catch phrases, and the sequencing of ideas in individual presentations," the instructions read.

Despite his deficiencies in formal education, Hitler was possessed by a voracious appetite for reading. Some of Hitler's earliest recollections in *Mein Kampf* relate to "rummaging" through his father's library and his own obsession with particular authors. We have similar attestations by Hitler's acquaintances from his years in Linz, Vienna, and Munich. Hermann Esser recalls that the first piece of furniture for Hitler's Thiersch

Street apartment was a wooden bookcase, which he quickly filled with books from friends and antiquarian bookshops near the Isar River. When this first bookcase was filled, he bought a second, and quickly filled that as well.

Ernst "Putzi" Hanfstaengl, Hitler's Harvard-educated associate, remembers surveying Hitler's bookcases in those years and finding the shelves cluttered with dime-store detective novels, Spamer's illustrated encyclopedia, a memoir by Sven Hedin, an account of the First World War by Gen. Erich Ludendorff, a copy of Karl von Clausewitz's classic *On War*, biographies of Frederick the Great and Richard Wagner, and historical treatises that ranged from a standard world history by Maximilian Yorck von Wartenburg to a treatise by the late-nineteenth-century historian Heinrich von Treitschke, who coined the phrase "Jews are our misfortune," and a copy of *German History*, by Heinrich Class, a radical nationalist who wrote under the pseudonym Einhardt.

Friedrich Krohn, who founded a lending library of right-wing literature at the National Socialist Institute in Munich, compiled an inventory of titles Hitler borrowed between 1919 and 1921 that suggests a similar eclecticism. The four-page list contains more than a hundred entries on subjects ranging from early church history—*Papal Fables of the Middle Ages*—to the writings of the acclaimed historian Leopold von Ranke, to firsthand accounts of the Russian Revolution, and numerous works on Austrian territorial sovereignty. There are also works by Montesquieu and Rousseau, Kant's treatise *Metaphysical Elements of Ethics*, and Spengler's *The Decline of the West*.

Not surprisingly, Hitler devoured the institute's extensive anti-Semitic holdings, including the classics on the subject: Houston Stewart Chamberlain's *Foundations of the Nineteenth Century*, the German translation of Henry Ford's *The International Jew: The World's Foremost Problem*, condensations of titles such as *Luther and the Jews*, *Goethe and the Jews*, *Schopenhauer and the Jews*, and *Wagner and the Jew*, and anthologies of anti-Semitic remarks ranging from Martin Luther to Émile Zola. Krohn's inventory also includes Anton Drexler's *My Political Awakening,* Gottfried Feder's *Manifesto for Overcoming the Interest Slavery of Capital,* back issues of Dietrich Eckart's *Auf gut deutsch* (In Plain German), and a study published by Krohn himself, *Is the Swastika Appropriate as the Symbol of the National Socialist Party?* "At the time, I became aware of Hitler because of his rather superficial and haphazard choice of readings," Krohn later observed, "so that I had the impression he could not possibly have 'digested' everything that he read."

Although Krohn's recollections of Hitler, like those of Kubizek, Esser, and Hanfstaengl, contain questionable assertions, we possess empirical evidence that corroborates their accounts of Hitler's bibliophilic interests. A rare interior photograph of his Thiersch Street apartment by Heinrich Hoffmann shows Hitler posed in a dark suit before one of his two bookcases—with books piled on top—his arms crossed in an assertively proprietary gesture.

Most significant, of course, we have the books themselves. Of the thirteen hundred or so remnant Hitler volumes in Washington, Providence, and elsewhere, I found at least forty that date from the early 1920s and that provide a snapshot of the intellectual world that lay behind Hitler's shoulder in the Thiersch Street portrait: biographies of Julius Caesar, Frederick the Great, and Immanuel Kant; a 1919 edition of Heinrich Class's *German History,* probably the volume Hanfstaengl noted on Hitler's shelf; a 483-page treatise on "the future state as a socialist monarchy"; an exposé on British culpability for starting the First World War; a study on the role of destiny in Wagner's *Parsifal;* a handful of books on the occult and the mystical, including an interpretation of the prophecies of Nostradamus; a 1918 translation of *Nationalism,* by Rabindranath Tagore, the Bengali poet who won the Nobel Prize for literature in 1915, with an inscription from an early Nazi Party member indicating the book had been given to Hitler for his thirty-second birthday. And, of course, Hitler's frontline copies of Osborn and Hymans.

These are the remnant pieces from Hitler's intellectual world at

41 Thiersch Street, the quiet corner in Munich to which he withdrew after his clamorous beer hall triumphs and street battles. These were the books that fueled his racist tirades, satiated his gnawing intellectual hunger, and bolstered him for his confrontations with the likes of Otto Dickel. In 1921, it was still an unequal fight. Against Hitler's one-week class at the University of Munich and his two-year crash course in right-wing literature cobbled from the National Socialist Institute's collection and his own two-bookcase home library, was Dickel, the professor. Against Hitler's handful of articles for the *Völkischer Beobachter*, Dickel hoisted a dense three-hundred-page treatise packed with sentences that flaunted his philosophic breadth. "For his part, Schelling, driven by the same dissatisfaction he harbored toward Kant, felt compelled to transcend even Fichte," Dickel wrote with intellectual sovereignty. At this point, Hitler was still misspelling *Schopenhauer* with two *p*s, as indicated in surviving notes to his handwritten speeches.

Hitler's limitations were not lost on the party members gathered in Augsburg, not even on Dietrich Eckart—in a handwritten note to Eckart the previous December, Hitler had written, "Liber Herr Eckart," an error equivalent to "Deer Mr. Eckart"—who, for all his loyalty to his "friend," demonstrably harbored an even greater loyalty to the National Socialist and anti-Semitic causes, as proven by his abandonment of Alfred Kapp a year earlier.

After Hitler's abrupt departure, Dickel continued with his presentation, outlining his vision for the future of a National Socialist movement that could reach beyond Bavaria and lay claim to all of Germany. The party leaders returned to Munich that evening convinced of two things: that Dickel indeed had the capacity to provide both the vision and leadership the Nazi Party needed at the time and, more significant, that Hitler, "as a simple man, despite his diligence," was not up to the task of leading the movement.

"Hitler was certainly the agitator who knew how to bring in the masses, but not the architect who envisions a plan and form for a new

Hitler, with a book at his desk in Nazi Party headquarters,
was well aware of his academic deficiencies.

building and undertakes the actual work of placing one stone on top of the next with calm resoluteness," said Max Maurenbrecher, a pastor and conservative political leader. "He required someone larger behind him whose orders he could carry out."

HITLER NOW REREAD Dickel's *Resurgence* with a vengeance, scrutinizing every page for inconsistencies and contradictions, noting specific passages and keeping a running list of Dickel's ideological, racial, and political transgressions, which he then transcribed verbatim into a blistering refutation. Dickel, he noted, described Karl Marx as an "idealist" and praised Walther Rathenau, Germany's Jewish foreign minister, for his patriotic inclinations. He observed that Dickel defended the Weimar Republic and denounced the "folly and baseness" of those who sought to undermine its democratic structures.

Hitler found his most damning evidence in a passage on page 81, in which Dickel calls for a moderated form of anti-Semitism, proposing that the German economy be left in Jewish hands. Hitler quoted Dickel: "As businessmen, their sons fertilize the sluggish domestic commerce. They are therefore of inestimable significance for the health of our economy." Dickel praised Lloyd George for his cooperation with Jewish business interests in London. How, Hitler wondered, could the party leadership "dare to trust" a man who could write such things? "I accuse the Party of not taking the trouble to read through, let alone study, the works of a man to whom you are considering giving such significant influence on the movement," Hitler raged, and shortly thereafter resigned from the party. "I can and will not be any longer a member of such a movement," he said.

As intended, Hitler's resignation precipitated a crisis. The leadership found itself torn between Hitler, with his proven ability to move the masses, and Dickel, with his promise of visionary leadership. They also faced the certainty that Hitler would splinter the party and form his own movement, a potentially fatal blow that might well add the Nazi Party to the long list of other failed political initiatives of those years. The choice was as stark as it was simple: Hitler or Dickel.

On Wednesday, July 13, 1921, Drexler dispatched Eckart to discuss Hitler's return to the party. The exact details of the discussion between mentor and protégé are not known, but the next day Hitler agreed to rejoin the party, but only on the following terms: "The immediate summoning of a membership meeting within eight days, as of today, with the following agenda: the current leadership of the party will resign and with the new elections I will demand the position of the chairman for myself with dictatorial powers to immediately create an action committee that is to ruthlessly purge the party of the foreign elements that have penetrated it."

When Gottfried Grandel learned of the Hitler coup, he was dismayed. "I like and value Hitler, but his striving for total power concerns me," Grandel wrote Eckart in protest. "It's going to come to a bad end if he doesn't change his ways and allow others to share power. We have to keep in mind that violence and cronyism scare away the best comrades and cripple the best forces, and in so doing empowers the less desirable elements." Grandel argued that Dickel was absolutely vital to the Nazi movement if it ever hoped to extend itself beyond the confines of Bavaria and become a national force. He also expressed concern that the Nazi Party would "degenerate into screaming and destruction," and that Hitler's single-minded and fanatical anti-Semitism would bleed attention from more urgent issues. "Anti-Semitism is necessary, but the preparation for the forthcoming German Reich is also important," Grandel wrote. He urged Eckart to exercise his "sizable and decisive influence" in Munich to bring Hitler into line and the party back into balance.

Eckart was not to be moved. In a front-page editorial in the *Völkischer Beobachter,* he threw his full ideological weight behind Hitler. "No human being can be more selfless, more willing to sacrifice himself, more devoted, more devout, more upright than Hitler in serving our cause," Eckart wrote. He praised Hitler for his vehement objections to changing the party name, to altering the party program, to shifting the locus of the Nazi movement away from Munich. "Do we need any further proof as to who deserves our trust, and to what degree he has earned it?" Eckart concluded. "I think not."

That August, during a membership meeting, Hitler was accorded dictatorial powers. At a meeting of the party leadership on September 10, Hitler exercised his new mandate. He replaced Drexler as party chairman, put Max Amann in charge of party finances, and ejected Otto Dickel from the party. The meeting record preserves this last action in explicit detail: "Mr. Otto Dickel from Augsburg, the author of the book *Resurgence of the West,* is expelled, by a unanimous vote of the board, from the National Socialist German Workers Party."

Five weeks later, on October 22, 1921, Hitler exercised full authority over the movement by issuing a broad-ranging memorandum that provided for an overhaul of the nascent movement. The Nazi Party was to be moved from its makeshift headquarters in a back room at the Sternecker Beer Hall to its first independent office, at 12 Cornelius Street. A party archive was to be created that would preserve the history of the Nazi movement.* It provided for the establishment of a "secret service," the forerunner to the Gestapo, intended to provide Hitler with intelligence on potential threats both within and outside his movement. With the issuance of Memorandum 10, the thirty-two-year-old political upstart came into his own, exercising his full authority to shape the Nazi Party at will, and institutionalizing a state of paranoia that was to become a signature feature of his movement. That same Saturday, his sixty-year-old mentor inscribed a hardcover second edition of *Peer Gynt* to his "dear friend."

Even though Hitler effectively sidelined Dickel as a political threat, he also recognized the need to address what we might call the Nazi Party's "Dickel deficit," the absence of a philosophical or ideological canon. On party membership cards, along with relevant personal data—date of birth, date of membership, party number, and photograph—a list of recommended readings was now included. The titles appear to be cobbled together from Hitler's intellectual rummaging at the National Socialist Institute and writings snatched from his immediate circle of associates: three books by Gottfried Feder on "interest slavery" and tax reform; six works by Alfred Rosenberg, including *Traces of Jews in the Course of Time, Amorality in the Talmud,* and *Zionism as an Enemy of the State;* a detailed, point-by-point annotation of the Nazi Party's twenty-five points, *Essence, Principles, and Goals of the National Socialist Workers Party;* and a collection of poems by Dietrich Eckart. It also included Henry Ford's *The Interna-*

---

*The Third Reich Collection at the Library of Congress contains copies of more than two hundred primary source documents prepared for an exhibition of the early Nazi Party history. The materials include internal Nazi Party correspondence, posters of beer hall rallies, an excerpt from an accounting book, and diverse materials recording early Nazi Party confrontations with the police, among them Dietrich Eckart's fingerprints from his police file.

tional Jew. A boldface headline at the head of the list reads, "Books that every National Socialist should read." Beneath it is the address for the German Nationalist Bookstore, 15 Thiersch Street, just down the street from Eckart's office, and for a bookshop adjacent to the Hofbräuhaus in central Munich.

Hitler's personal trauma over the Dickel affair continued to echo in his speeches for months and years to come. In handwritten notes for a

*Hitler's list of recommended readings printed on
Nazi Party membership cards included works by
Dietrich Eckart, Alfred Rosenberg, Gottfried Feder,
and Henry Ford.*

speech in August 1921, he wrote "Dr. Dickel" in bold letters, underlined it twice, then scrawled "bad tendency." That December, Hitler
denounced *Resurgence* as an "Egyptian dream book" and its author as a
"professor whose detachment from the real world soars to the clouds."
The following month, Hitler threatened that "any Dickel" who "claims
to be a National Socialist, whether in mind or spirit, is our enemy and
must be vanquished." Four years later, Hitler was still fulminating over
Dickel. During a speech on loyalty to a gathering of Nazi Party leaders
in June 1925, he recounted his personal challenge to Dickel. "Where was
the promised obedience?" Hitler asked. Nothing short of blind obedience would be tolerated, he insisted, even in the face of folly. "A leader
can make mistakes, no question about that," Hitler said. "But following
a bad decision will achieve the final goal better than personal freedom."
It was, of course, a dictum to which an entire nation ultimately adhered,
with catastrophic consequences.

Dickel also haunts the pages of *Mein Kampf,* an invisible presence
never mentioned by name but shadowing the author as he rails against
the "intellectual" who "believes himself in all seriousness to be 'educated,' to understand something of life" while in fact "growing more and
more removed from the world." Such people, Hitler says, belong either
in "a sanatorium or in parliament." Dickel also seems to be on Hitler's
mind when he makes his case for his singular ability to hold a crowd by
tallying the shortcomings of others: Gottfried Feder is a "theoretician
not a politician"; Karl Harrer is "certainly widely educated" but "no
speaker for the masses"; and Anton Drexler is "likewise not very significant as a speaker."

Like a beer hall Banquo, Dickel haunts a closing scene of *Mein Kampf*
as Hitler trumpets the coherency and comprehensibility of the Nazi
Party program. "And when I finally submitted the twenty-five theses,
point for point, to the masses and asked them personally to pronounce
judgment on them, one after another was accepted with steadily mounting joy, unanimously and again unanimously," Hitler writes. "And when

the last thesis had found its way to the heart of the masses, there stood before me a hall full of people united by a new conviction, a new faith, a new will."

Amid this beer hall triumphalism, one cannot help but sense a belated response to Dickel's challenge in Augsburg, and in the shrill insistence, the insecurity of a man who, Hanfstaengl recalled, once responded to counsel given by a distinguished Munich professor, *"Ach Herr Professor, that is all very good but you must never forget how terribly difficult it is for someone without a name or position or academic qualification to work himself up to the position where his name is identified with a political program. You underrate all the bitter hard work involved."*

BOOK THREE

The Hitler Trilogy

*The problem for me is that after my release on October 1, I don't expect
significant income from my book until mid-December . . .*
ADOLF HITLER, in a letter from Landsberg Prison,
September 13, 1924

A MONG THE TWELVE HUNDRED surviving Hitler books at the
Library of Congress are a dozen or so copies of Hitler's legendary
twin-volume best seller, *Mein Kampf.* The earliest of these is a special second edition of both volumes, individually bound in cream-colored calf's
leather with gold embossing, and dated 1926. Each book bears the
printed notation: "There were 500 copies of this work produced as a
deluxe edition in the following design and personally signed by the
author. This copy bears the number 155." The space for Hitler's signature
remains blank.

There is also a special numbered edition of volume two from 1927,
bound in red leather and bearing the number 178, and a specially bound set
of volumes one and two printed on parchment in a handsome leather slip-
case, but without a publication date. In addition, there are three unbound
copies of volume two numbered 70, 110, and 122; two bundles of unsorted
signatures from 1940; a twenty-seven-page typewritten manuscript for a
name and subject index; and several six-volume sets of *Mein Kampf* in a special Braille edition. These latter books are the size of small tombstones—
they must be lifted with two hands—with large swastikas blind-stamped

into the thick cardboard covers. The eclectic nature of these books and the absence of the Hitler ex libris suggest that they were probably taken from the plundered storage of the Nazi Party's Central Publishing House, Dietrich Eckart's old office, at 11 Thiersch Street, in the summer of 1945, and were mistakenly included among Hitler's remnant books.

Only two editions of *Mein Kampf* are known with certainty to have been in Hitler's personal collection. One is a leather-bound edition from 1930, taken from the basement of the Berghof by Edgar Breitenbach, a member of the Library of Congress "mission" in May 1945, which was donated to the rare book collection by his widow in 1991.* When I looked at the volume, I found extensive marginalia, clearly not in Hitler's hand, with numerous question marks and, in one place, the scribbled notation, *"im Gegenteil,"* or "quite the opposite." I found a second copy among the eighty books taken from the *Führerbunker* by Albert Aronson shortly after Hitler's suicide in the spring of 1945, and now at Brown University. This second copy, almost certainly acquired for Hitler's collection in the Reich Chancellery, is a 1938 "people's edition," with both volumes bound together in a dark blue linen cover; the Hitler ex libris is pasted on the inside cover.

Of all the possible means of book collecting, Walter Benjamin has observed, "writing them oneself is regarded as the most praiseworthy method," and recalls Schoolmaster Wutz, the endearing protagonist of a popular eighteenth-century novel, who is so poorly paid and of such limited financial means that he cannot afford to buy books and resorts to visiting book dealers, where he notes especially intriguing titles, then returns home to author his own books using the plagiarized titles.

In this manner, the frugal schoolteacher amasses a sizable personal library. However, most real authors, Benjamin notes, feel compelled to

---

* The book was returned on October 4, 1991, by Breitenbach's widow along with a second Hitler book taken by her husband, a 1933 edition of *Reflections on World History* by the nineteenth-century Swiss historian Jacob Burkhardt. This latter volume bears an inscription from Elsa Bruckmann to "my friend and Führer" with the date December 24, 1934.

write books out of existential rather than material poverty. "Writers are really people who write books not because they are poor but because they are dissatisfied with the books which they could buy but do not like," he says with a waggishness that belies the profundity of this passing remark: Most writers feel compelled to put words into the world to express ideas or stories that have not yet been articulated, or that they feel have not been adequately expressed or, at the very least, seem to require or deserve repeating in their particular idiom. In Adolf Hitler's case, the initial motivation was vengeance.

ON THE EVENING OF THURSDAY, November 8, 1923, around eight-thirty, Hitler stormed into the Bürgerbräu Beer Hall in Munich with a squadron of armed storm troopers, silenced the room with a single pistol shot into the ceiling, extracted at gunpoint a loyalty oath from Munich's assembled political leadership—Gustav von Kahr, Hans Ritter von Seisser, and Otto von Lussow—and declared a "national revolution." The following morning, Hitler assembled two thousand right-wing radicals in central Munich, intending to replicate Mussolini's March on Rome that had established a fascist government in Italy the previous autumn. Hitler planned to seize power in Bavaria then proceed to Berlin where he intended to topple the democratic government with a popular uprising. On this gray Friday morning, Hitler, accompanied by the war hero Erich Ludendorff, marched his men through the streets of Munich to the Odeon Square, where they were met with salvos of gunfire from a military cordon. In the ensuing chaos, sixteen putschists died. Hitler dove to the pavement when the men on either side of him were killed. He was then rushed to a waiting vehicle and taken to safety, only to be arrested three days later at the lakeside villa of Ernst Hanfstaengl, where he was nursing a shoulder wrenched in the fall.

Almost immediately, Kahr, Seisser, and Lussow distanced themselves from the failed enterprise. They claimed to have counseled Hitler against the attempted coup, which they had, and that Hitler had coerced their cooperation at gunpoint, which he had. Hitler was alternately distraught and enraged by their "betrayal." He first contemplated suicide, then staged a brief hunger strike, and finally decided to "settle accounts." He borrowed a typewriter from the prison administration and pounded out a sixty-page "accounting"—*Abrechnung*—of the two-day debacle, much of which served as a basis for his defense in his monthlong trial for treason, which concluded with Hitler declaring, "Even if you declare us 'guilty' a thousand times, the eternal goddess of the last judgment"—by which he meant history—"will smile and shred the prosecution's indictment, and will smile at the court's verdict, because *she* will acquit us." Despite the belligerence, Hitler's prison sentence was scandalously light: five years with the possibility of early parole and credit for time served. By Hitler's calculation, he could be free by October.

Hitler's incarceration was a fitting complement to his light sentence. The detention center in Landsberg am Lech, just west of Munich, resembled a faux medieval castle complete with twin turrets and an inner courtyard for daily constitutionals and soccer matches. The prison included meeting rooms and a lending library. Until Hitler's arrival, the most renowned inmate was Anton von Arco-Valley, a Bavarian count who was condemned to death for the murder of a socialist political leader; that sentence was commuted to *Ehrenhaft* in Landsberg, from which the count was released after less than four years.

As a right-wing political radical, Hitler held a privileged status in Landsberg. He was assigned to a second-floor suite of rooms—*Stube 6*—that consisted of a central sitting area and adjacent private bedrooms, which were assigned to convicted fellow putschists. From his bedroom, he looked out across the rolling hills and fields of central Bavaria. He was permitted to retain his dog, and visitor privileges were expanded to accommodate the incessant pilgrimage of associates, patrons, and well-wishers. The Landsberg registry records scores of them.

Hitler in Landsberg Prison, 1924, from
Hans Kallenbach's memoir, With Adolf Hitler
in Landsberg Prison. *The author's*
inscription to Hitler reads:
"May God protect our Führer!"

Hans Kallenbach recalled that the electricity curfew—*Stromsperre*—
was lifted to permit Hitler to pursue his habitual nocturnal reading.
"Only a single light burned, usually late into the night, and that was the
lamp in the room of the Führer," Kallenbach wrote in his memoir. "In
these lonely night hours Adolf Hitler sat bent over his books and papers
and worked on Germany's resurrection." Prison guards were said to
greet him with "Sieg Heil!" In this atmosphere of commodious and
courteous confinement, the celebrity inmate prepared himself to write
a book.

On Monday, May 5, 1924, Hitler sent a letter to Richard Wagner's son
Siegfried, in Bayreuth, describing his intention to write "a thorough

settling of accounts with those gentlemen who on November 9th enthu-
siastically shouted 'Hurrah' " and afterward attempted to show the
"impulsiveness of the insane undertaking." As the month progressed,
Hitler's authorial ambitions grew. What began as a mere "settling of
accounts" assumed greater proportions as he expanded the book into
the story of his political career in Munich, which he initially titled *A Four
and a Half Year Battle Against Lies, Stupidity and Cowardice.*

While vengeance was certainly the initial driving force behind Hitler's
decision to write a book, financial considerations also played a role.
Hitler's legal counsel, Lorenz Roder, from Linz, had worked closely with
him to prepare his defense, even securing testimony from Hitler's high-
school history teacher, but his efforts came at a high price. In one letter,
Hitler wrote that Roder's legal fees "make my hair stand on end."
Hitler's financial concerns seem to have been common knowledge, as
suggested by a prison memorandum: "He is expecting a large printing,
and hopes to be able to meet his financial obligations," Otto Leybold,
the prison director, noted.

Hitler assumed that the drama of the failed putsch, coupled with the
subsequent publicity generated by his trial, positioned him to negotiate
a favorable arrangement with a publisher. He was wrong. Ernst Hanfstaengl, who visited Hitler five times that April, was unable to convince
his brother to consider Hitler's book for the family publishing house.
Another prominent publisher, Ernst Boepple, reportedly offered Hitler a
"pathetic" royalty arrangement. Walter Stang, head of Ring Publishers
in Munich, visited Hitler in Landsberg on April 25 and returned three
weeks later with two additional Ring representatives. Stang was to pay
two subsequent visits in the weeks ahead. At the same time, Max
Amann began assessing the potential of Hitler's book for Franz Eher
Verlag, the Nazi Party press. In early May, Amann commissioned a study
of the market potential for a special edition of a Hitler book. The assessment, completed at the end of the month, determined "that if a collector's edition of Hitler's work in a special binding with a printing of only

500 books, numbered and signed by Herr Adolf Hitler, were to appear it should be worth at least 500 marks."

Apparently, this was enough to convince Amann. In early June, Eher issued a publicity brochure announcing the July publication of *A Four and a Half Year Battle Against Lies, Stupidity and Cowardice: An Accounting.* It was accompanied by a photograph of the author, not as the demonic beer hall orator, or even as the storm trooper who arrived on the morning of the putsch in a steel trench helmet and bundled in a thick military jacket, but instead dressed in a suit and tie with his hair slicked back and his signature moustache carefully manicured. A swastika pin was discreetly positioned on his left lapel. But as was so often the case with Hitler, ambition outstripped his capacity to deliver on his promises. July came and went without a book.

Hitler missed his July deadline in good part because of his preoccupation with visitors and his attempt to stage-manage the banned Nazi movement, issuing underground decrees under the code name "Rolf Eidhalt," a scrambling of letters from his own name Eidhalt translates to mean "Keep the Oath." As political infighting increased and the movement began to fracture, Hitler withdrew from politics and turned his full attention to his book.

"Herr Hitler has announced from Landsberg that he has given up leadership of the National Socialist movement and will avoid any form of political activity for the length of his imprisonment," the *Völkischer Kurier* (People's Courier) reported in early July. "The reason for this decision lies in the impossibility at present of assuming any practical responsibility, as well as the general overload of work." The *Kurier* noted in particular that Hitler was occupied with a "lengthy book" and wanted to make certain he had "adequate time" to devote to its completion.

Hitler reduced outside visitors to all but his closest associates—Anton Drexler, Gottfried Feder, Max Amann—and a few friends and family members, among them Helene Bechstein and Elsa Bruckmann and his niece and nephew Geli and Leo Raubal. He abandoned his evening readings of his manuscript, a fact reported by Rudolf Hess in a letter to his wife. Leybold, the prison administrator, confirmed Hitler's change of habits, observing that he had "withdrawn from political discussion" and now spent most of his time working on his book.

As Hitler's work habits changed, so did his vision for his book. What had begun as a "settling of accounts" in December 1923, and expanded into a "four and a half year battle against lies, stupidity and cowardice" in the spring of 1924, now bloomed in the summer heat into a Dickensian epic in which "the connection to the preceding chapters was broken," Hitler told Hess. Hitler now emerged as the hero of his own life.

Once again, Leybold was there to record the moment. He noted that Hitler's book "consists of his autobiography together with his thoughts about the bourgeoisie, Jewry, Marxism, the German revolution and Bolshevism, and the National Socialist movement with the events leading up to November 8, 1923." In expanding his original "accounting" and reframing it as an autobiography, Hitler not only expanded his own authorial ambitions but also brought hermetic closure to the Benjaminian conceit: the author preserving himself in a book that is in turn preserved within his collection.

ADOLF HITLER FAMOUSLY DESCRIBED his time at Landsberg Prison as his "higher education at state expense," and welcomed his incarceration as an opportunity to catch up on backlogged reading. "Personally I have somewhat more time and leisure after the conclusion of the trial," Hitler wrote in his letter to Siegfried Wagner. "I can finally get back to reading and learning. I hardly had time even to familiarize myself with the new nationalist books appearing on the market."

Ernst Hanfstaengl ascribed to the idled Nazi leader a more ambitious intellectual fare that allegedly included the philosophers Arthur Schopenhauer, Karl Marx, and Friedrich Nietzsche, the right-wing historian Heinrich von Treitschke, and the political leader Otto von Bismarck.

Though none of these individuals are represented among the surviving books from Hitler's prison years, I did find an unread biography of the eighteenth-century thinker Immanuel Kant by Houston Stewart Chamberlain as well as a Gandhi biography by the French pacifist and Nobel laureate Romain Rolland, with the inscription, "Fortunate is the man who is a nation—his nation, that lay in its grave and will rise again."

Hitler almost certainly bristled at the association with the Hindu leader. "The admiration of Gandhi is in my eyes a racial perversity," Hitler once observed. The inherently martial nature of Germans was, he noted, incompatible with Gandhi's peaceful civil disobedience. "The so-called 'fight for freedom' of the Indian people holds as little interest for me as the battles of the German people fifteen years ago was of interest to the Indians," Hitler sniped. The book shows no sign of having been read, nor does a six-hundred-page anthology of Gandhi's prison writings given to Hitler in those same months.

The one book I found with extensive marginalia is a collection of short essays by the German surgeon turned best-selling author of self-help counsel, Carl Ludwig Schleich. This thin volume, published in 1924, with "For happiness"—"*Zur Freude*"—scribbled on the inside cover opposite Hitler's ex libris bookplate, contains an eclectic selection of essays on happiness, beauty, creativity, genius, and immortality.

While there is no definitive evidence that the marginalia are from Hitler's hand, the penciled lines repeatedly underscore passages related to politics and the general relationship between the public and the individual, as on page 26, where the following passage has been highlighted with two bold strikes in the margin:

> It is questionable whether there can be geniuses in politics. The political leader belongs to the nation. He has to have character. The genius belongs to all mankind. He is an exemplary personality. There are politicians with genius but no political geniuses.

In one place there is a pencil mark beside the the passage "Geniuses are only recognized after their deaths, especially in Germany."

There has been much speculation on Hitler's sources for *Mein Kampf*, but few specifics. Otto Strasser, an early Hitler associate, attributed key concepts to conversation rather than reading. "In this book you come across Houston Stewart Chamberlain and [Paul] Lagarde, two authors whose ideas were conveyed to Hitler by Dietrich Eckart," Strasser observed, also identifying Gottfried Feder, Alfred Rosenberg, and Julius Streicher as sources.

The one book among Hitler's extant prison readings that left a noticeable intellectual footprint in *Mein Kampf* is a well-thumbed copy of *Racial Typology of the German People* by Hans F. K. Günther, known as "Racial Günther" for his fanatical views on racial purity. Hitler included Günther in his list of recommended reading for National Socialists. Published in 1923, this third edition of Günther's five-hundred-page treatise is inscribed by the book's publisher, Julius Friedrich Lehmann, to Hitler, whom he hails as the "advanced guard in German racial thinking."

Along with Günther's *Racial Typology of the German People*, another consequential influence on the intellectual content of *Mein Kampf* was a German translation of *The International Jew* by Henry Ford. Although we no longer have Hitler's personal copy of the two-volume translation of the infamous racist treatise, we know that Hitler owned one, as well as a portrait of its author, at least a year before he began work on *Mein Kampf*. "The wall beside his desk in Hitler's private office is decorated with a large picture of Henry Ford," the *New York Times* reported in December 1922. "In the antechamber there is a large table covered with books, nearly all of which are a translation of a book written and published by Henry Ford."

Ford's book had been published earlier that year in German under the title *Der Internationale Jude: Ein Weltproblem*, and was an immediate sensation. "I read it and became anti-Semitic," recalled Baldur von Schirach, the future Hitler Youth leader, who was a teenager when Ford's book appeared. "In those days this book made such a deep impression on my friends and myself because we saw in Henry Ford the representative of success, also the exponent of a progressive social policy."

Hitler appears to have been no less affected; this is suggested not only by the portrait on his wall but also by his repeated invocation of Ford's name. In one speech, Hitler praised Ford's creative genius as an industrialist, calling him the "greatest" and noting that Ford was racially pure, "an absolute Northern type." In an attack on the prominent German statesman Gustav Stresemann, Hitler offered Ford as a counterexample. "They say that Mr. Stresemann is working on a system just as Ford worked for a long time on his system," Hitler observed. "Again I must say: Don't compare Mr. Stresemann with Ford. Regardless of what one can say about the automobile from Ford, at least it ran while the politics of Mr. Stresemann are constantly stuck and never go anywhere."

Most notably, Hitler saw in Ford a bulwark against the alleged Jewish-Bolshevik threat in America where, Hitler claimed, Jews were the "regents." "Every year sees them emerging as the rulers of the workforce of a population of 120 million people," Hitler observed. "A single great man, Ford, still stands there today independent, much to their anger."

For Hitler, Ford represented the ideal of the self-made man for his enlightened view of the common laborer. Famously, Ford doubled the wages of his workers as his profits increased. Of equal renown was Ford's vicious and public anti-Semitism, to which he gave vent in a series of ninety-two articles published in the *Dearborn Independent* between 1920 and 1922. Written by two Ford associates but published in bound volumes under Ford's name, the articles detail an alleged Jewish conspiracy that is revealed in the *Protocols of the Elders of Zion*, a forgery of Russian origin that outlines Jewish plans for world domination.

Hitler was taken by Ford's observation that Germany, next to the United States, was most threatened by this global plot. "Germany is today, with perhaps the possible exception of the United States, the most Jew-controlled country in the world—controlled within and from without—and a much stronger set of facts could be presented now than was presented in the original article," Ford asserts. It notes that even though efforts had been made to reduce the Jewish presence in the government of Germany, Jews remain embedded in key aspects of German life and economy. "For their entrenchments stretched further and deeper than mere display of official power," Ford wrote. "Their hold on the basic industries, the finances, the future of Germany has not been loosened in the least. It is there, unmovable."

When Ford was confronted with incontrovertible evidence that the *Protocols* was a forgery, he dismissed the fact, noting that it lost none of its credibility because it nevertheless described realities as they were, a blinkered logic mimicked by Hitler in *Mein Kampf:* "It is completely indifferent from what Jewish brain these disclosures originate," Hitler writes of the *Protocols.* "The important thing is that with positively terrifying certainty they reveal the nature and activity of the Jewish people and expose their inner contexts as well as their ultimate final aims."

Clearly there were many influences in Hitler's writing of *Mein Kampf,* and we will never know the exact admixture of the various things he read or heard, but there is no question that Ford's book entered his career at an early and formative stage and impressed itself on both his thoughts and his writing, as Hitler himself stated in no uncertain terms. When a reporter asked him about the portrait prominently displayed on the wall in his office, Hitler replied in clear and simple terms, "I regard Ford as my inspiration."

WHEN HITLER BOASTED of his education at state expense, he not only flaunted his disdain for the Bavarian penal system but also exposed his meager understanding of serious education, a fact that is revealed in *Mein Kampf* both in terms of its vacuous intellectual content and its painfully flawed grammar. In the surviving bits of unpublished Hitler text I found in archives across Europe and America, the collector-cum-author emerges as a half-educated man who has mastered neither basic spelling nor common grammar. His raw texts are riddled with lexical and syntactical errors. His punctuation, like his capitalization, is as faulty as it is inconsistent.

At age thirty-five Hitler had not even mastered basic spelling. He writes *"es gibt"*—"there is"—phonetically rather than grammatically as *"es giebt,"* and the German word for prison, *Gefängnis,* with a double *s,* the equivalent of writing "prisonn." But the remnant pieces I studied, including Hitler's original draft for the first chapter of *Mein Kampf,* as well as an eighteen-page outline to five subsequent chapters, demonstrate he took his writing seriously.

It has long been assumed that Hitler dictated *Mein Kampf* to his fellow prisoners, in particular his personal secretary, Rudolf Hess, and his chauffeur, Emil Maurice. In fact, Hitler had begun work on his manuscript before either one of them arrived in Landsberg. This first draft, typed in Pica with a faded blue ribbon, shows a fitful start to the four-hundred-page book that was to follow. A single line is typed across the top of the untitled page, "It is not by chance that my cradle," then breaks off, drops two carriage returns, and begins anew. "It must be seen in my opinion as a positive omen that my cradle stood in Braunau since this small town lies directly on the border of two German states whose reunification we young people see as a higher goal in life," Hitler writes with an evidently measured cadence, though he misspells *higher*—*hohre* rather than *höhere*—before pulling two more carriage returns and plunging into an emphatic claim that this reunification is driven not by economic considerations—*"Nein! Nein!"* he hammers—but by the common bond of blood. *"Gemeinsames Blut gehört in ein gemeinsames Reich!"* he writes. "Common blood belongs in a common empire."

At some point in these opening paragraphs, Hitler paused, took a blue pencil, and went back to make amendments, striking out his first failed sentence, making one grammatical correction, but overlooking several others. Like any author, he was clearly conscious that the opening lines of his book were among the most crucial, setting the tone and style for all that was to follow. And he evidently returned to those opening lines for further deliberation and amendment, as indicated by the version that ultimately made it into print, reflecting Hitler's continued

Als eine glückliche Vorbedeutung ... ich es heute, daß meine Wiege ... in Braunau stand; ... doch dieses Städtchen gerade an der Grenze (gelegen) ... deutscher Staaten, deren Wiedervereinigung uns Jüngeren als eine wahrhaft hohe Lebensaufgabe erscheint.

Deutschösterreich muß wieder zurück zum großen deutschen Mutterlande; und zwar nicht etwa aus ... Gründen wirtschaftlicher Erwägungen heraus. Nein nein. Auch wenn diese Vereinigung wirtschaftlich gedacht gleichgültig, ja sogar wenn sie schädlich wäre, sie müßte dennoch stattfinden.

Gemeinsames Blut gehört in ein gemeinsames Reich.

Das deutsche Volk besitzt solange kein moralisches Recht zu kolonialpolitischer Betätigung, solange es nicht einmal seine eigenen Söhne in einem einzigen Staat zu fassen vermag. Erst dann, wenn des Reiches Grenze auch den letzten Deutschen umschließt, ohne die Sicherheit seiner Ernährung bieten zu können, wird die Not des eigenen Volkes zum moralischen Recht auf neuen Grund und Boden.

So scheint mir dieses kleine Grenzstädtchen als ein Symbol einer großen Aufgabe.

Allein auch noch in einer anderen Hinsicht ... wohl in den Kreis und Rahmen unseres heutigen Gefühls und Sinnens. Vor mehr als ... Jahren hatte dieses kleine Städtchen, als Schauplatz eines erschütternden Unglücks, das Glück, in den Annalen zumindest der deutschen Geschichte ...

Hitler's working draft for the opening of Mein Kampf, *written in Landsberg Prison in April 1924. Note the false start to his opening sentence, which was amended again before publication.*

attempt to infuse his opening with a more expansive air of import and portent:

> It has turned out fortunate for me today that destiny appointed Braunau-on-the-Inn to be my birthplace. For that little town is situated just on the frontier between those two States the reunion of which seems, at least to us of the younger generation, a task to which we should devote our lives and in the pursuit of which every possible means should be employed.

Beyond this point, the original manuscript and the printed version parallel each other in good measure, though once again one sees Hitler's attention to the tone and nuance of individual words. In describing his grandfather, he initially writes that he was "a poor, simple wanderer and dayworker"—*Häusler* and *Taglöhner*—but ultimately deletes the latter word from the published version. Hitler's attentiveness to his family background is also suggested by the fact that he writes extensively about his mother and father but makes no mention of his older half-brother and half-sister, Alois and Angela, or his younger full-blood sister, Paula. The only allusion to his siblings can be found in a reference to the grief felt at "our father's death." Paula never forgave her brother the slight; decades later she was still complaining that her existence had been reduced to a possessive pronoun.

Hitler appears to have worked intensely on the manuscript through July and August and into September, by which time he was approaching the end of the book—as well, he hoped, to his time in prison. Hitler's expectations for his opus were high. From his prison window he had watched cars passing on the road and become infatuated with the idea of owning a Mercedes-Kompressor. "I saw one of them in a brochure and knew immediately, it had to be that one!" Hitler later recalled, quoting the exact price. "Twenty-six-thousand marks!"

In mid-September, Hitler wrote to Jakob Werlin at the Benz garage, which shared the same building with the Nazi Party headquarters in

Schelling Street, and ordered his dream car, preferably, Hitler said, "in gray with wire spoke wheels," and ideally with a discount. "The problem for me is that if I am released on October 1," Hitler explained to Werlin, "I will not be able to expect significant income from my book before mid-December, and thus I will be forced to get an advance or take out a loan from someone." Based on the date of his preface, Hitler had the entire manuscript completed by October 16, 1924, but he was still in Landsberg.

Hitler misjudged his release date from prison, and, once again, his publication date. He left Landsberg on December 20 with his book scheduled for publication in March 1925 and in possession of his new Mercedes, thanks to the generosity of Otto and Elsa Bruckmann. His book would not appear until July.

The repeated delays in publication were caused in part by Max Amann's concern about the weak book market and the limited number of sales venues. Beyond the bookshops, beer hall rallies represented a major source for selling books. With Hitler banned from speaking in public, Amann had lost access to much of his target audience. But the main reason for the delay was the editing process. As many as seven different Hitler associates claim to have labored on the book in advance of its appearance, including Bernhard Stempfle, a Bavarian priest who edited the *Miesbacher Anzeiger*, a local anti-Semitic newspaper; Josef Stolzing-Cerny, the theater critic for the *Völkischer Beobachter*; and Adolf Müller, the owner of the printing house for Franz Eher.

Hanfstaengl remembers battling Hitler over the first seventy pages of the manuscript, claiming to have slashed Hitler's "worst adjectives" and his "excessive use of superlatives," and clashed with him over various points of nuance. When Hitler wrote about his "talent" as a painter, Hanfstaengl alleges to have told him, "You cannot say this. Other people may say it, but you cannot say it yourself." Hanfstaengl also noted "little dishonesties," such as Hitler's use of the term "senior civil servant" for his father. Hanfstaengl also complained of the parochial nature of Hitler's intellect that caused him to apply a term such as *world history—Weltgeschichte*—to "quite minor European quarrels." After this initial editing session, Hanfstaengl claims, Hitler never showed him any more of the manuscript.

Rudolf Hess and his wife, Ilse, who worked for a publishing house, also remembered wrestling with Hitler over his manuscript, though with better results than Hanfstaengl. "We struggled for weeks and months with this manuscript, also with Adolf Hitler, who only slowly agreed that we were right," Ilse recalled. The Hesses would work through the manuscript together, and then Rudolf would review the edits with Hitler line by line. Ilse described Hitler's writing style as a form of airborne prose—*Sprech-Deutsch*—that contained oratorical devices that worked well in the smoke and din of a beer hall but merely cluttered the page when committed to paper: *thus, also, of course, but, now, therefore.* And we might add, *"Nein! Nein!"*

We will never know with certainty the degree to which these various editorial claims are justified, since the vast majority of the working drafts have vanished.* What does come through in these various accounts, however, is the sense of ownership Hitler felt for his text, the attention he gave to the tone and content of his book, and the stubbornness he demonstrated in seeking to retain his distinctive authorial voice.

One editorial change that can be credited to a particular individual, and certainly represents the most consequential in the yearlong editing process, was that made by Max Amann when he distilled Hitler's original title to the leaner and pithier *Mein Kampf* (My Struggle).

WHEN HITLER'S BOOK appeared in July 1925 it was greeted almost unanimously with scathing reviews. The *Frankfurter Zeitung* described

---

* The files in the Library of Congress contain an adventurous account of Hans Beilhack's vain attempt to locate the original manuscript.

Mein Kampf as an act of political suicide and headlined its review "Hitler's End." A Berlin newspaper expressed "partial doubts about the mental stability of the writer." One critic observed that Hitler "settled accounts" with everyone except himself.

Even the radical right was hard put to say something positive. Gen. Erich Ludendorff was offended by Hitler's seething anti-Semitism and distanced himself from both book and author. Alfred Rosenberg, author of virtually impenetrable prose who spent nearly a decade getting *The Myth of the Twentieth Century* written and published, offered the glancing observation that the book appeared to be "quickly written." The *Bayerische Vaterland* (Bavarian Fatherland) called it *"Sein Krampf"*(It is Cramp). In some circles, the book became the butt of jokes.

One Nazi Party leader, Otto Strasser, claimed that when he quoted entire passages verbatim from *Mein Kampf* during an informal gathering of Nazi Party leaders at the 1927 Nuremberg rally, he evoked expressions of astonishment from his cohorts. Only after he confessed that he had not actually read the book but only memorized select passages did a round of similar confessions ensue. "General laughter broke out, and it was decided that the first person who came and claimed that he had read *Mein Kampf* had to pay the tab for everyone," Strasser recalled. The first to appear was Strasser's older brother, Gregor, who "answered with a sonorous 'No.' Goebbels shook his head. Göring broke out in a loud laugh."* Though the anecdote belongs to the lore generated by disaffected associates—Otto Strasser fled to Canada in 1933; Gregor was murdered the following year—it does convey an enduring and generally acknowledged truth: the general unreadability of Hitler's book.

Despite the unflattering reviews, and the book's evident deficiencs, Hitler's pride of authorship is preserved in the numerous copies of *Mein*

---

* In his diary entry for October 14, 1925, Goebbels had, in fact, nothing but praise for *Mein Kampf.* "I will finish reading Hitler's book tonight," he writes. "Absolutely fascinating! Who is this man? Half plebeian, half god!"

Kampf inscribed to family, friends, and associates. Alois Hitler remembered receiving a copy, as did Paula and Hitler's former landlord, Josef Popp, whose copy was inscribed "for old time's sake." Emil Maurice received the tenth numbered copy of *Mein Kampf* with a signed inscription from Hitler, "To my loyal and brave shield bearer." For Christmas that year, Hitler sent Goebbels one of the five hundred numbered editions as an expression of appreciation, "For your exemplary method of battle." Hitler continued to inscribe copies of *Mein Kampf* for years to come. I have come across various inscribed editions of *Mein Kampf* in private collections, including three different editions in the Harvard University Rare Book Library with dedications from Hitler, including one of the original collector editions—Number 144—autographed by Hitler as late as November 1942.

Hitler's satisfaction with his first book is most convincingly demonstrated in his decision to write a sequel. By the time *Mein Kampf* appeared in July 1925, he was hard at work on volume two. That spring, Hitler rented quarters on the Obersalzberg, an alpine peak overlooking Berchtesgaden, where he had met with Dietrich Eckart in the months before the Beer Hall Putsch, and set to work in a small hut that became known as the *Kampfhäusl,* or "Battle Hut," whose ruins can be found in a dense thicket of trees. Hitler returned in the summer of 1926 to complete the manuscript, this time taking a room at the Hotel Deutsches Haus, in Berchtesgaden.

"Here I was really spoiled," he remembered. "Every day I would walk up to the Obersalzberg, to the Schatzkehl, and then down again, two-and-a-half hours. Down below I wrote the second volume." His first book had been primarily autobiographical. The second was purely political, four hundred pages in which Hitler outlines his vision for Germany, writing about the need for *Lebensraum* (living space) for the German people, about the infrangible bond of *"Blut und Boden"* (blood and soil), and, most notably, about the danger of the Jews. "If at the beginning of the war and during the war twelve or fifteen thousand of these Hebrew corrupters of the people had been held under poison gas, as happened to hundreds of thousands of our very best German workers in the field, the sacrifice of millions at the front would not have been in vain. On the contrary: Twelve thousand scoundrels eliminated in time might have saved the lives of a million real Germans, valuable for the future."

Hitler finished the manuscript in August 1926, with a dedication to Dietrich Eckart, "who devoted his life to the awakening of his, our people, in his writings and his thoughts and finally in his deeds." Then he turned to a writing project that he had begun considering the previous spring: a book-length memoir of the First World War.

HITLER'S DECISION TO DEVOTE his next literary endeavor to his wartime service is remarkable not only because it appears to have been overlooked by most Hitler biographers but also because it represented for Hitler a conscious turning away not just from political writing but also from the Nazi Party, and away from Franz Eher as his publisher. As Otto Bruckmann said, Hitler did this "in the hope of reaching above and beyond the Party with this unpolitical book." It was Hitler's most explicit expression of interest in being a real writer.

Hitler was almost certainly motivated by a number of factors. For all his aspirations for *Mein Kampf,* not to mention his investment of time and energy in the writing and editing process, the book had done only moderately well, barely selling out its first printing in a year— respectable given the market conditions but hardly commensurate with his inflated ambitions. His expectations for the second volume were certainly more sober. Indeed, while volume one was met with derision and contempt by reviewers, volume two was simply ignored—not only by critics, but by readers, too. It sold fewer than seven hundred copies after a year on the market.

But there were lessons to be learned from his initial experience as an author. Those newspapers that had published excerpts from volume one invariably selected his account of his time at the front, which seemed to resonate. As for Franz Eher, it was clear to Hitler that it was a regional publisher with little access to the market beyond Bavaria. So in the spring of 1926, while he was in the midst of the second volume of *Mein Kampf,* he began talking with Otto and Elsa Bruckmann about his next book project. As the publisher of Chamberlain's *Foundations of the Nineteenth Century,* which by then was in its seventeenth printing, Bruckmann had both conservative credentials and access to the broader reading public.

At the same time, Hitler was immersing himself in World War I literature, inspired in part by Ernst Jünger's *Blood and Steel,* which the author had sent to him earlier in the year, with a personal inscription: "To the national Führer Adolf Hitler." Jünger's three previous books—*Storm of Steel, War as Inner Experience,* and *Copse 125,* in which a German unit is obliterated in a heroic effort to hold their position in a small stand of trees—had established the veteran as the most prominent voice of the frontline soldier. In contrast to the flood of pacifist literature, which would find its consummate expression a few years later in Erich Maria Remarque's *All Quiet on the Western Front,* Jünger's books glorified the German soldier and his sacrifices for the Fatherland, finding grace and nobility amid the carnage. Hitler apparently imbibed Jünger vigorously that spring. "I have read all your writings," he wrote the author that May. "In them I have come to value one of the few powerful conveyors of the frontline experience."

Throughout the summer of 1926, Hitler seems to have been contemplating his own war memoir, for within a month of completing the second volume of *Mein Kampf* in August 1927, he spoke with Elsa Bruckmann about his vision for his next book. "He is already reflecting on the form of his war book, and says it is becoming more vivid and alive in him," Bruckmann wrote to her husband on September 26. "The images are crystallizing around the core which he has conceived and are demanding to be completed." By December, Hitler's war memoir had progressed to the point where Bruckmann had already set a publica-

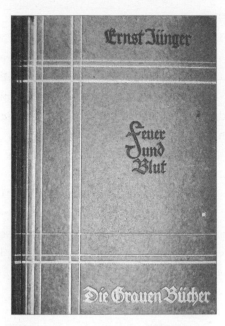

Hitler read this copy of Ernest Jünger's
Fire and Blood *in early 1926 while*
preparing to write his own memoir
of his time at the front.

tion date. When Alfred Rosenberg approached him about publishing a recently completed manuscript, Bruckmann declined the offer with the explanation that "in the spring I am going to be publishing Hitler's war memoirs." But Hitler never delivered the book. Like most of the type-script to *Mein Kampf,* no manuscript has ever been found.

Nevertheless, we can make some informed conjectures about its form and content, not only from descriptions in *Mein Kampf* of battles, but also from the photostats of cards and letters Hitler sent to a Munich friend, Ernst Hepp , that preserve in a tight but even hand the emotions of his baptism by fire as a twenty-six-year-old: the midnight march beneath a star-filled sky, listening to the distant thunder of artillery, the rising tension as the incoming shells fall ever closer, and the gnawing uncertainty of the enfolding clamor, followed by the sudden thrilling release of attack on an enemy emplacement where British soldiers "swarm like ants" from their dugouts. "We run forward like lightning over the fields and after repeated bloody one-to-one clashes throw the chaps from one trench after another," the young Hitler reports. "Many raise their hands. Whoever doesn't surrender is gunned down. And so we clear trench after trench."

In the spring of 1926, Hitler was reminded of these moments in the pages of Jünger's battlefront memoirs, with their near-identical descriptions of nocturnal marches, distant artillery barrages, and the emotional surges that came with the rush into battle. Jünger not only awakened wartime memories and familiar emotions but also inspired emulation, as suggested by Hitler's book negotiations with the Bruckmanns that spring and by the passages I found that the author had highlighted in his copy of *Fire and Blood*.

In the 190-page hardcover, there are repeated penciled intrusions, extended lines beside individual sentences, and paragraphs frequently trailing off in a series of staccato dashes that seem to complement the sporadic rattle of machine-gun fire depicted in these pages. In these penciled marks we can see Hitler following Jünger's reflections and commentaries about the transformative effects of war. Like Jünger, Hitler had experienced the carnage as something ennobling and transformative. "But this is one of the inexplicable riddles that the battlefield constantly poses to us and with which we will continue to occupy ourselves for some time, if we happen to survive," Jünger muses on page 86, with Hitler attentively following with his pencil. "And that is this unflinching dignified composure that a man reveals when confronted by his own extermination, and that we in our paltry everyday existence cannot even begin to imagine."

In paging through this slender volume, I observed that Hitler focused his attention on Jünger's explorations of the emotional and spiritual aspects of war, overlooking the descriptions of battle, except in two places, at the top of page 106 and the bottom of page 107, where he

Tagen während der langen Schwärmbewegungen seine Maschinengewehrkästen nicht mehr tragen konnte und zu weinen anfing? Ja, gewiß, das war sehr lächerlich. Aber, was ich hier sehe, das scheint mir gar nicht mehr lächerlich. Ich sehe, daß er einen breiten Gurt um den Hals trägt, und daß rechts und links neben ihm zwei schwere Munitionskästen liegen. Damals waren sie mit Platzpatronen gefüllt, heute sind sie es mit scharfem Geschoß. Das bedeutet einen großen Gewichtsunterschied, und ich überlege ganz automatisch, daß dieses Kind mit seinen weichen Händen, das vor ein paar Monaten sicher noch in die Schule ging und vor den Lehrern Angst hatte, vorhin während der entsetzlichen Augenblicke des Einschlages an die ihm anvertrauten Kästen gedacht haben muß und sie auch während unserer langen, mühseligen Wanderung nicht im Stiche gelassen hat. Wenn es jeder andere, wenn es einer von den alten Kriegern gewesen wäre — gut. Aber dieser hier — das ist eins von den unerklärlichen Rätseln, die uns das Schlachtfeld immer wieder stellt, und mit denen wir uns noch lange beschäftigen werden, wenn wir davonkommen sollten. Das ist es ja, diese unbedingt vornehme Haltung des Menschen, die sich zuweilen der Vernichtung gegenüber offenbart, und von der wir in dem Krämerdasein, aus dem wir kommen, nichts ahnen konnten.

Aber wir müssen weiter, schon wieder jagt uns ein Einschlag hoch. Von neuem beginnt die Wan-

86

derung durch knietiefes Wasser, das Nasen und Irren im Kreis. Es ist, als ob wir von einem bösen Geist umhergeführt würden. Endlich gehen wir einem Stichgraben nach, an dem wir schon einige Male vorübergekommen sind und entdecken eine gut ausgebaute Linie mit Laufrosten, Postenständen und Stollen, aus denen ein warmer Rauch nach oben dringt. Wir treffen einen Posten und erfahren, daß Teile unseres Bataillons hier liegen, und daß auch die für uns bestimmten Unterkünfte ganz in der Nähe sein müssen. Aber dann geraten wir wieder in verfallene Gräben und sehen endlich die Unmöglichkeit ein, in der Dunkelheit zum Ziele zu kommen. Wir müssen die Nacht draußen verbringen, um die Helligkeit abzuwarten. Wir trennen uns, um uns nicht wieder, dicht zusammengedrängt, einem schweren Treffer auszusetzen. Ich gehe mit Vinke, der auch heil davongekommen ist, zurück zu einer Stelle, an der wir uns erinnern, einige in die Lehmwand eingebaute Munitionsnischen gesehen zu haben. Ich krieche in eine hinein, sie ist lang und eng, mit Wellblech gestützt und von halbkreisförmigem Profil wie einer der Backöfen in den Gärten niedersächsischer Bauernhöfe. Vinke rollt die Decke vom Tornister und breitet sie über mich.

Natürlich ist es ausgeschlossen zu schlafen. Alle Nerven schwingen nach wie die Saiten eines Klaviers, das mit Hammerschlägen bearbeitet worden ist. Ich erinnere mich, daß ich heut nachmittag vor dem Ab-

87

Hitler has marked a passage in Jünger's memoir Fire and Blood *describing how men react when faced with "extermination" (vernichtung).*

marked passages that recall an artillery barrage where "the throttling concussion of the explosions" becomes so intense that everything begins to "shiver and dance like images in a flickering movie." Jünger is paralyzed with sensory overload. "I no longer hear the bombardment, it has transcended the point where it is even possible to hear." Beside these passages Hitler has drawn dense, dark lines.

Mostly, though, his pencil traces Jünger's frontline epiphanies about the transformative effects of slaughter, about the hardening of the heart and soul, of the forging of the human spirit into something "hard and merciless," about the bonding experience of men rushing forward into battle, about the fusion of human life and the state apparatus into the expression of the collective will of a people, about a world beyond all known "borders of human values," where "courage, fear, sympathy—all that no longer exists"—meld to the point where the human will first "speaks through fire, then speaks through blood."

Hitler's pencil follows these articulations in a single-line concurrence with one exception: on page 26, beside a passage in which Jünger speculates on the power of the human will in the face of the "kinetic force" of "monstrous mass production." "The battle is a horrific measuring of competing production," Jünger writes, "and victory is the success of the opponent who knows how best to produce less expensively, more efficiently and the most quickly." Beside this passage Hitler has planted a single question mark, an apparent challenge to Jünger, and an intimation of calumnious calculations to be made on the future battlefields of Europe.

Given what we know from all this, we can only speculate on the dimensions, tone, and direction of Hitler's missing war memoir. Perhaps it was never completed, most likely because it fell victim to Hitler's political career. By 1927, the speaking ban that had prevented Hitler from making public appearances had been lifted in most German states, allowing him to renew his political activity. As he wrote in his letter to Siegfried Wagner, and underscored in his preface to *Mein Kampf,* he was a man of the political act not the written word.

Most likely whatever existed of the manuscript was burned along with most of Hitler's personal papers in the spring of 1945, when he dispatched his adjutant, Julius Schaub, first to his Munich apartment to gather his private papers, then to his residence on the Obersalzberg to collect the rest, and incinerate them. Christa Schröder, one of Hitler's secretaries, was witness to the event and recalls that Schaub first cleared the strongbox in Hitler's second-floor library, then piled diverse letters, files, manuscripts, and books beside the flagpole and "with the assistance of a few canisters of petrol" set the heap of papers ablaze, erasing much of Hitler's private life—but not everything. What Hitler had forgotten, and Schaub could not have known, is that fifteen years earlier, Hitler had placed a carbon copy of his fourth writing project in a strongbox at the Eher Verlag offices in downtown Munich.

THE TWO-INCH STACK of yellowed paper is a carbon copy of a 324-page typewritten manuscript. Time has gnawed the margins of individual pages. In places, entire words have fallen away. At some point, water penetrated the manuscript on pages 18 through 22, giving rise to mildew, which ingested entire tracts of thought.

An accompanying memorandum, identifying the original location of the manuscript at Thiersch Street 11, reads:

> Joseph Berg, who lives at 35 Scheubner Richter Strasse, Munich, and was technical manager of this publication house, gave us a manuscript of an alleged unpublished work by Adolf Hitler. It was written over 15 years ago and locked up in a safe. Mr. Berg had strictest orders that the manuscript could neither be printed nor shown to anybody.

The memorandum is signed by Capt. Paul M. Leake of the Army Signal Corps, and identifies the manuscript as "Target No. 589." With Target No. 589, we not only have our only complete working draft of a book manuscript by Adolf Hitler but also possess a document that preserves his development as an author. By the summer of 1928, the thirty-nine-year-old writer had four years of writing, editing, and publishing experience behind him. There is confidence both in style and form, with none of the waffling and second-guessing we find in his first draft of *Mein Kampf.* When editorial changes are made, they are clearly intended to intensify the prose, to inject greater compression or authority, with an acute ear for nuance. In one case, the plaintive subjunctive "I would like" (*ich möchte*) is replaced with the more deliberate "I want" (*ich will*). In another, the "amount of force" (*Machtgehalt*) is replaced by the "use of force" (*Machteinsatz*). Other changes are stylistic in nature. A syntactical misstep is corrected on page 5, where "eternal hunger" is initially "ful-. filled," then replaced by "satiated." On page 19, "to possess courage" is given greater emotive power with the phrase "to carry courage in one's heart." On page 20, one passage is given entirely new meaning when "biological transformation" is recast as "geological transformation." A reference to "artificial restructuring" becomes "sudden restructuring," and in another passage, circumstances are "determined" rather than "influenced."

In these raw manuscript pages, we see the author's mind at work, processing information, wrestling with his ideas, watching his words appear on the page, gauging style and nuance, occasionally tripping over grammar and syntax, making a quick typed correction, then pressing forward in a relentless torrent of prose. In his opening sentence he writes: "In August 1925, while writing the second volume [of *Mein Kampf*], I laid out the fundamental thoughts for a German National Socialist foreign policy though in somewhat abbreviated form." Hitler says he intends in this book to provide a more detailed vision for Germany's role in the world, in effect, transforming *Mein Kampf* into an integrated trilogy: volume one focusing on Hitler and the Nazi movement, volume two exploring the Nazi Party and Germany, and volume three contextualizing Germany in the world.* This marked a return to political writing and to Franz Eher as his publisher.

AS WITH THE FIRST two volumes of *Mein Kampf*, Hitler resorted to his authorial voice only when deprived of his public one. Just as volume one had been written behind prison walls, and volume two during a ban on public speaking, volume three emerged in a moment of imposed silence. For the previous two years, Hitler had worked relentlessly to

* Hitler also published a monograph on foreign policy, extracted from volume two of *Mein Kampf*, regarding South Tirol, a portion of northern Italy inhabited by a large population of ethnic Germans.

I

Politik ist werdende Geschichte.Geschichte selbst ist die
Darstellung des Verlaufs des Lebenskampfes eines Volkes.Ich
setze hier mit Absicht das Wort "Lebenskampf" ein,weil in Wahrheit jegliches Ringen um das tägliche Brot ganz gleich ob im
Frieden oder Kriege ein ewiger Kampf ist gegen tausend und
abertausend Widerstände,so wie das Leben selbst ein ewiger
Kampf gegen den Tod ist.Denn warum sie leben,wissen die Menschen so wenig als irgend eine andere Kreatur der Welt.Nur
ist das Leben erfüllt von der Sehnsucht, es zu bewahren.Die
primitivste Kreatur [könnte ohne den] kennt nur den Selbst-
erhaltungstrieb des eigen Ichs,für höherstehende überträgt
er sich auf Weib und Kind,für noch höhere auf die gesamte
Art. Indem aber der Mensch auf seinen eigenen Selbsterhaltungs-
trieb scheinbar nicht selten zugunsten der Art entsagt,dient
er ihm in Wahrheit dennoch am höchsten.Denn nur in dieser
des Einzelnen
Entsagung/liegt nicht selten die Gewährung des Lebens für
die Gesamtheit und damit dennoch wieder für den Einzelnen.
Daher der plötzliche Mut der Mutter in der Verteidigung der
Jungen und der Heldensinn des Mannes im Schutze seines Volkes. Der Größe des Triebes der Selbsterhaltung entsprechen
die beiden mächtigsten Triebe des Lebens : Hunger und Liebe.
Stillung
Indem die [Erfüllung] des ewigen Hungers die Selbsterhaltung
gewährleistet,sichert die Befriedigung der Liebe die Forter-
haltung. In Wahrheit sind diese beiden Triebe die Regenten
des Lebens. Und wenn tausendmal der fleischlose Aesthet gegen
eine solche Behauptung Protest einlegt,so ist doch schon die
Tatsache seiner eigenen Existenz die Widerlegung seines Pro-
testes. Was aus Fleisch und Blut besteht,kann sich nie den
Gesetzen entziehen,die sein Werden bedingen. Sowie der
menschliche Geist glaubt,darüber erhaben zu sein,vernichtet
er jene reale Substanz,die der Träger des Geistes ist.

The first page from Hitler's unpublished sequel to
Mein Kampf, *written in summer 1928. Note how few
corrections there are compared with the first manuscript
page of* Mein Kampf. *See the illustration on page 73.*

establish the Nazi Party as a nationwide political force. He traveled
ceaselessly, asserting his personal authority across the widespread and
occasionally faltering movement, and by May 1928 he had positioned the
party to participate in its first national elections. But he found himself
facing a receding political tide.

In the more than four years since the Munich putsch, the Weimar Republic had stabilized thanks to the diplomatic acumen of its foreign minister, Gustav Stresemann. In 1924, Stresemann negotiated the Dawes Plan, lifting the crushing reparation payments that had led to the catastrophic inflation of 1923. The following year, he signed the Locarno Pact, formally recognizing the postwar western borders, and reconciling Germany with its neighbors, in particular France. The effort earned him a Nobel Peace Prize. Stresemann had cleared much of the tinder that fueled Germany's radical right by spring 1928 when German voters went to the polls and delivered Hitler a staggering defeat. Stresemann's party commanded a monumental 30 percent of the vote in a landscape cluttered with political movements. The right wing won a mere 26 percent of the vote. That night, in his Berlin apartment, Goebbels described the election results as *"trostlos"* (hopeless).

That same evening, Hitler glossed over the debacle, observing that the Nazi Party was now the only right-wing movement in Germany. But with less than 3 percent of the national vote, the party tottered on the brink of extinction. "We will continue to work and our goal is that in a few years we will be standing there where Marxism now stands, and Marxism will be where we are today," Hitler said. The following Wednesday, he repeated this conviction in a three-and-a-half-hour speech that, according to a police report, was only "moderately attended." The following day, he retreated to the Obersalzberg to write his book.

Unlike with the two preceding volumes of *Mein Kampf,* Hitler opened this new book—after a brief introduction in which he concedes the Nazi Party's marginalization ("alone and isolated") in German politics—on a decidedly philosophical note. *"Politik ist werdende Geschichte,"* he began, or "politics is history in the making." "History itself is the presentation of the course of the struggle for survival of a people," he continued. "I use the words 'struggle for survival' intentionally because in truth every effort to secure one's daily bread whether in peace or war is an eternal struggle against thousands and tens of thousands of obstacles, just as life itself is an eternal battle against death." The narrative voice is firm and direct, the script is clear and assured, with only occasional corrections. The *ä* key falls unevenly.

"Human beings understand as little about why they are alive as any other beast in this world, but life is filled with the desire to preserve it. The most primitive beast could not . . ." Hitler pauses for the first time, hammers *x*'s across the "could not," and begins anew. "The most primitive beast worries only about survival of the self, while the more advanced transpose this concern to wife and child, and the more advanced still to the entire race." As examples, Hitler cites the courage a mother will show in defending her children, and the heroism of a man in protecting his people. He notes that only through this "renunciation of the individual" is the continued existence of the community possible. In order to achieve this higher state, the individual must transcend the most fundamental animal instincts: "hunger" and "love." "That which consists of flesh and blood," he writes, "cannot escape these laws that determine its being, and if the human spirit believes itself to be superior to this, it exterminates that basic substance that is the carrier of that spirit." The survival of the spirit requires the continuation of the species. It is at heart the Darwinist plaint.

Hitler then extends this paradigm for individual survival to the community—"The communal body is nothing more than the multiplicity of more or less identical individual beings"—and elevates the concept into a philosophy of foreign policy. "These same laws that determine and dominate the life of the individuals are thus also valid for a people," he wrote. "Sustaining the self and procreation are the greatest impetus for every action, as long as the body is healthy enough to do so. The manifestation of these general rules of life will thus be as similar among peoples as they are among individuals." Driven by the need to satiate this "eternal hunger" and this unquenchable desire to reproduce, the myriad species of our planet thus find themselves locked in an eternal *Lebenskampf,* a struggle for survival.

Invoking the concept of *Weltgeschichte* in the most expansive terms possible—with none of the niggling "European quarrels" of which Hanfstaengl complained—Hitler traces the "struggle for existence" to the very origins of our world. He speaks of a geologic *Weltgeschichte* before mankind, when there raged a "battle among the forces of nature" that separated land from sea and forged mountains and plains and oceans, and from which emerged the first forms of organic life, "whose development is marked by an eternal battle of man against animal and even against man." From this battle within the human species has emerged races, tribes, peoples, and eventually nations, an observation that brings Hitler back to his opening thesis. "But if politics is history in the making, and history itself is the depiction of the struggle of men and peoples for survival and procreation," he writes, "then in truth politics is thus the implementation of the life struggle of a people." For Hitler, politics is nothing more—to turn the Clausewitzian maxim—than war in its most refined form. For Hitler politics is the "art" of the struggle for life.

In these opening pages there is none of the emotionalism and personal confession we find in volume one, or the party-specific details of volume two. Here the tone is notably measured, thoughtful, analytical. We find Hitler articulating his views on existence more thoroughly and completely than anywhere else in his published writings, speeches, or monologues. We see him seeking to stitch together his eclectic accumulated knowledge into a philosophical framework, straining for profundity in an odd patchwork that seems to have been cut from the cloth of the likes of Charles Darwin and Max Weber. As usual, Hitler presents his ideas with only meager reference to sources, leaving scholars to speculate with varying certitude on the origins of his ideas, whether they derive from intense and extensive reading or from rummaging through secondary sources and boulevard newspapers. With the two volumes of *Mein Kampf,* which were written over extended periods of time and subjected to repeated editing, we are left to speculate on sources for both their form and content. For Hitler's third book, we know the exact weeks during which it was written and have one of the books we know served as a model.

SIX WEEKS BEFORE Hitler began work on his new book project, he celebrated his thirty-ninth birthday. Among the gifts he received was a 105-page hardcover, *Fichte's German Belief,* written by Maria Grunewald and inscribed to "the revered Führer" by Theodor Lühr, the husband of Maria Lühr, a master bookbinder with a studio on Berlin's fashionable Kurfürstendamm. Bound in forest-green linen with the title and name of the author embossed in gold Gothic script, *Fichte's German Belief* contains a series of lithographs of Aryan maidens and struggling warriors with titles such as "On Beauty" and "Gods of Light Battling the Forces of Darkness." The text itself deals with Fichte's spiritual essays, and though there is no marginalia or other traces of Hitler's intrusion, we find Maria Grunewald's intellectual fingerprints in the pages of Hitler's manuscript.

In explicating Fichte's philosophy of the role of the individual in society, Grunewald identifies a three-stage development: the "lowest form of a personality" is completely self-absorbed, and thinks only of itself; at the next stage of development, an individual extends this concern to the family—the way, for example, a man protects his wife and children; the most elevated personality transcends immediate concerns and extends itself to the "community." As Hitler framed his ideas for his book, Grunewald's words appear to have echoed in his mind and ultimately found their way onto the page. But while Grunewald, in interpreting Fichte, sees this evolution transcending the material world into the spiritual realm and ultimately into a union with God, Hitler detours into the ruthless ethic of social Darwinism. To this point, Hitler's measured pace and progressive logic dissipate into two hundred pages of rambling foreign policy objectives, with particular emphasis on German minorities in northern Italy, spiked with a beer hall–style rant about Jewish and Bolshevik conspiracies before returning to the Clausewitzian axiom with

the Hitlerian twist: "It is the responsibility of politics to fight for the existence of a people and in order to do this it must use whatever weapons
seem most appropriate, so that life is best served," Hitler concludes.
"One does not engage in politics in order to die, rather one allows people to die on occasion, so that a people can live."

Hitler must have finished the manuscript by the second weekend in
July—234 pages in six weeks—for on Monday, July 13, he traveled to
Munich, where he gave a speech, then continued on to Berlin, where he
gave two more speeches, addressing the issue of ethnic Germans in
northern Italy and quoting extensively from his manuscript. The following Monday, his sister Angela and niece Geli joined him, and in the company of Goebbels, who had just completed the finishing touches on his
novel, *Michael,* the party traveled to Helgoland for a week's vacation on
the North Sea. Max Amann returned to Munich with a carbon copy of
the Hitler manuscript and locked it in the safe at 11 Thiersch Street,
where it was to remain for the next seventeen years.

Hitler's renewed political activity may have caused him to abandon
the book or to sequester it. But it's also possible that there was a com-
mercial consideration. After an initial flurry of interest following the
release of *Mein Kampf* in the summer of 1925, sales plummeted. In 1927,
volume one sold fewer than five thousand copies, and volume two a paltry twelve hundred. In 1928, Amann may have been reluctant to enter a
sluggish market with yet another Hitler book. Hitler himself may also
have recognized the inherent flaws in the book's eclectic and haphazard
structure or possibly his limitations as a writer. "What beautiful Italian
Mussolini speaks and writes," Hitler said to his personal lawyer and later
gauleiter Hans Frank. "I am not capable of doing that in German. I just
cannot keep my thoughts together when I am writing." In comparison
with Mussolini's work, Hitler observed, *Mein Kampf* appeared to be an
exercise in fantasizing "behind bars," little more than a "series of feature
articles for the *Völkischer Beobachter.*" "*Ich bin kein Schriftsteller,*" Hitler
told Frank. "I am not a writer."

For Hitler, however, this epiphany did not constitute a creative or existential crisis, an admission of failure, or a nod to ruined ambition. It was merely a statement of fact. He was, in essence, as he repeatedly said, a man of deeds, not words. He recognized not only his limitations as a writer but also the inherent liabilities of the written word. As he told Frank, "If I had had any idea in 1924 that I would have become Reich chancellor, I never would have written the book."

He expressed a similar sentiment about his unpublished manuscript. "I'm certainly glad this volume hasn't been published," Hitler told Ernst Hanfstaengl in the mid-1930s. "What political complications it would make for me at the moment." He noted that Amann had offered him a million-mark advance and that millions more would follow in royalties. As tempting as the prospects were, Hitler felt the political liabilities were too great. "Perhaps later, when I'm further along," he said. "Now it's impossible." Within a year of completing what was to become Target No. 589, Hitler saw his political prospects, so grim in the summer of 1928, change dramatically. On October 3, 1929, Gustav Stresemann suffered a massive heart attack. Three weeks later, the New York stock market collapsed, and with it the German economy. Hitler's popularity soared. No longer idled by political marginalization, Hitler abandoned book writing. In three brief years, he would be chancellor of Germany.

BOOK FOUR

The Lost Philosopher

Each and every irksome Jew is a serious affront to the authenticity and veracity of our German identity.

Passage highlighted in Hitler's copy of
German Essays by PAUL LAGARDE

IN HIS ESSAY ON BOOK COLLECTING, Walter Benjamin suggests that most bibliophiles have read at best 10 percent of their collections and claims to base his estimate on good authority. "Suffice it to quote the answer which Anatole France gave to a philistine who admired his library and then finished with the standard question, 'And have you read all these books, Monsieur France?' " Benjamin recalls that the grand old man of French prose and Nobel Prize laureate deftly replied, "Not one tenth of them. I don't suppose you use your Sèvres china every day?"

Book collecting is an art, Benjamin insists, that matures with time. "For years, for at least the first third of its existence, my library consisted of no more than two or three shelves which increased only by inches each year. This was its militant age when no book was allowed to enter it without the certification that I had read it." As time passed, Benjamin came to appreciate books for other reasons: a particularly handsome binding, enchanting illustrations, a rare antiquarian volume offered at auction, a memory of a particular book on a particular day in a particular bookshop. "Suddenly the emphasis shifted," he says. "Books acquired real value." Possession became an end unto itself. Without this "inflation," Benjamin observes, he would never have acquired enough books to dignify the term *library*.

With Hitler, we see a similar acceleration. During the decade Hitler resided at his modest Thiersch Street apartment, his library grew incrementally, filling first one bookcase, then another, and when both of these had reached capacity, accumulating in random and precariously pitched stacks on top of the bookcases, as evidenced in the photograph taken in early 1925. That year, his book collection was among the few notable possessions he recorded on his tax declaration. Among a meager inventory that included his writing desk and a chair, he listed "two bookcases with books."

During the 1930s, Hitler's collection expanded dramatically. Once again, the tax record testifies to the intensity of Hitler's bibliophilic interests. Hitler's single largest tax deduction after personnel costs and political travel was for books: 1,692 marks in 1930, with similar amounts in the two subsequent years. When insuring the contents of his Munich residence in November 1934 with the Gladbacher Fire Insurance Company, Hitler calculated the value of his possessions at 300,000 marks, with half the amount allocated to his art collection and the rest to books and other valuables. In a typed addendum to the standard policy, Hitler has added the provision *"einschliesslich Bücher,"* "including books."

Word of Hitler's book collection was such that when Janet Flanner wrote a profile of the Nazi leader for *The New Yorker* in 1935, she reported that he possessed a "fine library," which she estimated at six thousand volumes. A few years later, Frederick Oechsner, the Berlin correspondent for United Press International, calculated the Hitler collection at 16,300 volumes. In more recent times, two scholars, Philipp Gassert and Daniel Mattern, studied the remnant Hitler books as well as archival materials, including the acquisition lists for the Reich Chancellery Library, and arrived at the Oechsner approximation.

After January 1933, the steady stream of books entering Hitler's library became a deluge. Among Hitler's books I found numerous mem-

Hitler's policy with the Gladbacher Fire Insurance Company, November 1934,
contained a supplemental provision for his book collection.
Note "einschliesslich Bücher" (including books).

oirs by fellow veterans, who, like Adolf Meyer, had sent Hitler personal accounts of their service, dozens of volumes by local Nazi officials, and hundreds more by distant admirers who hail Hitler as a "messiah" and "savior." There were also reports on diverse official activities. The head of a local association for graves of the war dead sent Hitler an album of photographs with the inscription "To the former frontline soldier, the forger of German unity and pathbreaker to new ascendancy from deep ignominy." The president of the Reich Health Office gave Hitler a report on a 1938 medical convention with the handwritten inscription "Through the health of our people we physicians are battling for high performance in culture and economy and thus for the political strength of the nation." A local Nazi Party member from Leipzig sent Hitler a copy of his publication *Recommendation for the Improvement and Consolidation of Accounting Procedures for Cigar Factories, also a Path to National Socialist Economic Methods.* In an intensification of the Benjamin 10 percent rule, one can assume that Hitler never saw, let alone read, a large portion of these books.

The books from Hitler's minions are a different matter. Here we find volumes and inscriptions that preserve the nature of the personal dynamics between Hitler and some of his closest associates. On the fourth anniversary of the Munich putsch in 1927, Hermann Göring, Hitler's self-absorbed deputy, gave Hitler a copy of a brief personal biography, *Göring, What Were You Thinking! A Sketch from a Life,* which he inscribed in "loyalty and reverence." The SS leader Heinrich Himmler gave Hitler two ideology-infused volumes, *Voices of Our Ancestors* in 1934 and *Death and Immortality in the World View of Indo-Germanic Thinkers* in 1938. In this latter book, a Christmas present, Himmler uses the pagan circumlocution *Julfest*—related to Yuletide—to skirt Christian associations with the holiday season.

For Hitler's forty-fourth birthday, Baldur and Henriette von Schirach presented Hitler with a two-volume antiquarian history of Braunau, the Austrian town where Hitler was born. The inscription reads "To our beloved Führer in celebration. Family Schirach, April 1933." The personal nature of the Braunau history and the confident intimacy of its dedication preserve the special relationship between Hitler and the Schirachs. It also suggests the fragility of such relationships. The Nazi Youth leader entered Hitler's inner circle of associates when he married Henriette Hoffmann, the daughter of Hitler's personal photographer. Hitler, who had known Henriette since she was nine and used to refer to her as "my sunshine," hosted their wedding reception in his Prince Regent Square apartment.

During the war Henriette used a late-night gathering at the Berghof to express her distress after witnessing the brutal treatment of Jewish women in Amsterdam. "I cannot believe you know about them," she told Hitler. "Helpless women were being rounded up and driven together to be sent off to a concentration camp and I think that they will never return." Hitler's face froze. Silently, he rose to his feet. Then he screamed, "You are sentimental, Frau von Schirach! You have to learn to hate. What have Jewish women in Holland got to do with you?" Henriette fled the room and was advised to leave the Berghof immediately. She never saw Hitler again.

Among the most revealing volumes I found from Hitler's close associates are those with inscriptions from the filmmaker Leni Riefenstahl, who directed the 1934 tribute to the Nazi Party, *Triumph of the Will*, and the two-part epic, *Olympia*, the landmark documentary of the 1936 Berlin Olympic Games. Riefenstahl gave Hitler two large-format coffee table books with black-and-white stills from *Olympia*, one for Christmas 1936 and the other for Christmas 1937. The latter volume is particularly handsome.

Bound in red linen, *Beauty in the Olympic Games* highlights the most dramatic moments of the Summer Games—Hans Woellke with eyes pressed shut as he prepares to hurl the shot that was to win him an Olympic gold medal; Gisela Mauermeyer throwing back her head in ecstasy and victory as her discus soars; the strikingly handsome gold medal winner Glenn Morris—whom Riefenstahl took briefly as a lover—gripping his javelin in the decathlon; Jesse Owens poised for a sprint, his fingertips planted firmly on the ground, his eyes fixed intently ahead. The caption to this last image reads "The fastest man in the world."

There are also two close-ups of Hitler—one with his arm raised in a Nazi salute, and another with him in a pensive gaze—and more than a dozen of the famously narcissistic Riefenstahl "at work," studying the Olympic stadium, consulting with her film team, directing a cameraman, sitting in the cutting room amid miles of unedited celluloid. The volume is dedicated to "my Führer in gratitude and loyalty," as is the other Olympic book, *Olympia,* which features sixty-seven stills from the uncut footage and expresses both "inextinguishable loyalty" and "profound gratitude."

Riefenstahl's gratitude was especially well deserved. Hitler had not only given the thirty-four-year-old filmmaker exclusive domain and seemingly unlimited resources to film the Olympic Games in the summer of 1936 but had also personally rescued her from financial ruin that autumn. Despite an unprecedented budget of 1.5 million marks, Riefenstahl was nearly bankrupt by November. When a bank refused to advance her an additional 500,000 marks, Riefenstahl turned to the Nazi minister of propaganda. "Fräulein Riefenstahl came to me in hysterics. It is impossible to work with these wild women," Joseph Goebbels recorded in his diary. "Now she wants another half million for her film and [wants to] make two [films] out of it. Despite the fact that her bookkeeping stinks to high heaven. I remain cold-hearted. She cries. That is the ultimate weapon of a woman. But it doesn't work with me any more." But it did with Hitler. When Riefenstahl sidestepped Goebbels and appealed her case to Hitler, the loan was approved. The two Olympic books stand as testament to her appreciation as well as her cunning.

A third volume of cinematic stills, inscribed to Hitler with "loyalty and reverence" on the occasion of his birthday in April 1944, preserves Riefenstahl's gratitude for an equally extravagant but more sinister proj-

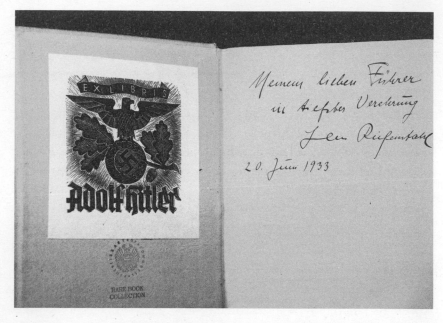

Leni Riefenstahl's inscription to Hitler in volume one of
Johann Gottlieb Fichte's Collected Works.

ect, Riefenstahl's unfinished film *Tiefland,* which this time involved the
use of slave laborers rather than Olympic athletes.

Certainly, Riefenstahl's most valuable contribution to Hitler's library
was a first edition of the collected works of the German philosopher
Johann Gottlieb Fichte. Published in 1848, this handsome eight-volume
set is bound in cream-colored vellum with gold leaf tipping on the pages.
Each spine bears a hand-daubed quadrant in red pastel with the title in
gold and a second quadrant, an inch below, in pastel green. The individual volumes are signified by Roman numerals. On the inside cover of
volume one, in an elegant cursive script, Riefenstahl expresses her "deep-
est reverence" to "my dear Führer." The inscription is dated June 20, 1933.

I was puzzled not only by Riefenstahl's choice of a late-nineteenth-
century philosopher but also by the date of the inscription, which did

not correspond to any immediately evident occasion such as a birthday or holiday. When I came across these Fichte volumes in the spring of 2001, Riefenstahl was one year short of her hundredth birthday. I had communicated with her a few years earlier, while conducting research on the Daimler-Benz corporation—Hitler had once given Riefenstahl a Mercedes-Benz sports car—and now I again wrote to her, asking if she had any recollection of the Fichte books. She remembered the exact circumstances, which she had recorded in precise detail in her memoirs: a beautiful afternoon in the spring of 1933 on the terrace of the Reich Chancellery in Berlin.

Riefenstahl had met Hitler the previous year when she was riding high on the success of her film *The Blue Light*, in which she played a village beauty—her eyes charged with erotic mysticism—who possessed visionary abilities. When Riefenstahl accompanied a friend to hear Hitler speak, she was so mesmerized that she wrote him an admiring letter. Hitler was equally enchanted. Having recently seen the dark-eyed beauty in *The Blue Light*, he invited her for a meeting at the North Sea fishing village of Horumersiel. The two spent several hours walking together along the windswept beach, with Hitler's entourage following at a distance.

In the ensuing months Hitler and Riefenstahl saw each other repeatedly, spawning rumors that they were lovers. Hitler had more pressing issues. His political fortunes fluctuated dramatically. He was soundly defeated in his bid for the presidency in March, and he watched his party surge in parliamentary elections in July only to erode again in November. That autumn the Nazis faced a stark choice: seize the moment and negotiate their way into power with compromises, or remain in opposition and risk political and financial ruin.

When Hitler refused to compromise, Gregor Strasser resigned from the party amid rumors that he had been offered the position of vice chancellor. For Hitler, the betrayal was especially bitter. Along with his brother Otto, Gregor had masterminded the victories of the Nazi movement in northern Germany. Even after Otto left, Gregor remained loyal to Hitler, and in the grim days following the 1927 electoral setback, he inscribed a book to him "in loyal allegiance." It is a handsomely bound edition of Alfred Rosenberg's 374-page tribute to the leading figures of the 1923 Beer Hall Putsch, *Thirty November Portraits,* inscribed to Hitler on November 18, 1927. Now, five years after committing his loyalty to paper, Strasser was cutting a deal for himself.

"These traitors, these cowards—and just before the final victory— these fools," Riefenstahl remembers Hitler saying in a rage the day Strasser submitted his letter of resignation. "For thirteen years we have fought, toiled, and given everything—have overcome the worst crises, and now just before the goal this betrayal!" Riefenstahl listened sympathetically, offered consoling words, then left for three months in Switzerland, where she was starring as a daredevil pilot in the upcoming film *SOS Iceberg,* about a wife who ventures into the Arctic in search of her missing spouse.

Within two months, following a series of backroom deals, Hitler was chancellor. In late May 1933, shortly after Riefenstahl's return to Berlin, she received a call on Hitler's behalf inviting her for tea the following afternoon. On a pleasant spring day beneath a flawless blue sky, the fetching actress, dressed in a stylish white outfit with just enough makeup to "look natural," arrived at the Reich Chancellery in her red coupe. She was escorted to the chancellery garden, where she found Hitler on the sun-filled terrace beside a table set for two.

As they sipped their tea, they talked about the dramatic reversal in Hitler's fortunes, and Riefenstahl recalled that she, much like Henriette von Schirach was to do a decade later, expressed her concern about the treatment of Jews. When Riefenstahl mentioned a number of Jewish friends who had encountered difficulties under the new regime, Hitler held up his hand in protest. "Fräulein Riefenstahl, I know your opinion, which you shared with me in Horumersiel," he said. "I respect you. But I would ask you not to speak with me about a subject that is uncomfortable for me. I respect you greatly as an artist, you have a rare talent, and I would not want to influence you. But I cannot have a discussion with you about the Jewish problem." Despite Hitler's mild reprimand, Riefenstahl said she felt herself go weak.

Hitler quickly turned the conversation to the topic of film. Riefenstahl claims that Hitler offered to make her head of artistic direction for the German film industry. Riefenstahl, flattered, nevertheless declined. She was an "artist," not a "manager." In truth, she despised Goebbels, the propaganda minister, and preferred to remain as far from his realm as possible. Hitler then suggested she direct a film about Horst Wessel, the storm trooper whose death in a barroom brawl had been immortalized in the Nazi anthem, "Raise the Banner!" ("Die Fahne hoch!"). "I can't. I can't," Riefenstahl remembers sputtering in despair.

A morose silence followed. Hitler rose to his feet. "I am sorry that I cannot win you over for my films, but I wish you much luck and success," he said curtly. He signaled to the waiter. "Please accompany Fräulein Riefenstahl to her car."

Riefenstahl departed the Reich Chancellery in a state of extreme distress. When she recounted the fiasco to Arnold Fanck, a close friend who had directed her in *White Ecstasy*, and who had edited *The Blue Light*, he made a suggestion: send Hitler the "valuable first edition of the complete works of Fichte" that his sister had "elegantly" bound in white leather, and that Fanck had given Riefenstahl a few years earlier when he was first infatuated by her. "How about if you parted with them, wrote a few lines and gave them to Hitler as a present?" Fanck said.* The Fanck

*Steven Bach, author of a recent biography of Leni Riefenstahl, advises caution regarding the details of this incident. Bach notes that Riefenstahl was a notoriously unreliable narrator. Nevertheless, the Fichte volumes lend some credence to her account, as does a shooting script for Franz Wenzler's film *Hans Westmar* with the film's original title, *Horst Wessel: A German Fate*. An undated handwritten inscription from the screenwriter, Hanns Heinz Ewers, reads to "Herr Reichskanzler Hitler." The score was written by Giuseppe Becce, who had done the music for *The Blue Light* and the score for the filmed version of *Peer Gynt*, and for Riefenstahl's *Tiefland*. In composing the score for *Hans Westmar*, Becce was assisted proposition was doubly wise: It fed Hitler's bibliophilic ambitions and flattered his philosophical pretensions.

FOR ALL THE TALK of Hitler's exploitation of Friedrich Nietzsche's concepts of the "master race" or Arthur Schopenhauer's notion of the "will to power" that Hitler used to headline the 1934 party rally and Riefenstahl cribbed as a title for her cinematic chronicle of that event, we have little credible evidence of Hitler's personal engagement with serious philosophy. Most of what we know is tenuous and at best anecdotal.

Hitler's confidant Hans Frank claimed that Hitler told him he carried Schopenhauer's central work, *The World as Will and Representation*, with him during the First World War, though it is difficult to imagine the young corporal who left mud stains and candle wax on the pages of Osborn's *Berlin* transporting, let alone reading, Schopenhauer's magnum opus through the trenches of northern France. The claim becomes even less credible when one observes that Hitler, as previously noted, did not even know how to spell the philosopher's name. In scribbled notes for a 1921 speech, Hitler writes "Schoppenhauer."

However, Schopenhauer is listed among the authors of books Hitler borrowed from Krohn's library at the National Socialist Institute between 1919 and 1921, and he makes a brief appearance in *Mein Kampf,* when Hitler references Schopenhauer's infamous anti-Semitic description of the Jew as the "great master" of lies. Schopenhauer also finds his way into Hitler's speeches, but generally finds himself in random company.

On one occasion, Hitler speaks of "Kant, Goethe, and Schopenhauer"; on another "Goethe, Schiller, and Schopenhauer"; on another, Schopenhauer is bundled into a clutch of other nineteenth-century

---

by Ernst Hanfstaengl, who wrote incidental music for the film and had significant involvement in the production, which he describes in detail in his memoirs.

German nationalists that includes Richard Wagner, Paul Lagarde, and Friedrich Ludwig Jahn, the Prussian pioneer of modern gymnastics. These references are made with no intellectual bearing or depth: they are mere catchphrases, and as easily could have been snatched from a passing conversation or casual reading.

Though there is no reason to doubt that Hitler owned copies of Schopenhauer's works, I found only a single Schopenhauer volume among Hitler's remnant books, a 1931 reprint of Schopenhauer's translation of *Hand Oracle and the Art of Worldly Wisdom,* by the seventeenth-century mystic Balthasar Gracián. This inexpensive, ninety-two-page hardcover is so modest in size that Hitler's bookplate fills the entire inside cover. The most solid piece of evidence to the centrality of Schopenhauer in Hitler's life is the bust of the wild-haired philosopher that Hitler displayed on a table in his Berghof study.

Hitler's associations with Nietzsche are equally eclectic and suspect. We know that he visited the Nietzsche archive in Weimar, where he was

*Hitler viewing the bust of Friedrich Nietzsche in
Weimar in the early 1930s.*

received by Nietzsche's sister—a vicious anti-Semite—posed for a photo beside Nietzsche's bust, and came away with the dead philosopher's walking stick. The inventory of the Reich Chancellery library indicates that Hitler owned a first edition of Nietzsche's collected works, an eight-volume set published between 1903 and 1909, but the only extant Nietzsche volume is a book taken from the *Führerbunker* in Berlin, *Nietzsche's Political Legacy,* edited by Eitelfritz Scheiner. It is a slender hardbound book with a quote from Nietzsche scrawled on the inside cover by the editor and dated December 15, 1933: "It was those who created the races and hung them with a belief and with love: thus they were of service to life."

Other sources attesting to Hitler's interest in Schopenhauer and Nietzsche are notoriously unreliable. Ernst Hanfstaengl claimed that Schopenhauer had been Hitler's "philosophical god in the old Dietrich Eckart days"—Eckart himself attributes several Schopenhauer remarks to Hitler in his "Conversation"—but that following the meeting with Nietzsche's sister, Hitler became a convert. "From that day at Potsdam the Nietzschean catchphrases began to appear more frequently—the will to power of the *Herrenvolk,* slave morality, the fight for the heroic life, against reactionary education, Christian philosophy and ethics based on compassion," Hanfstaengl confidently recalled though he mistakenly placed the encounter in Potsdam rather than Weimar. "Schopenhauer, with his almost Buddhist gentleness, was buried forever, and the Gauleiters started to take their inspiration from a savage parody of Nietzsche."

Riefenstahl provides an equally vivid but contradictory account. "I have a great deal to catch up on," Riefenstahl recalls Hitler telling her in the book-lined comfort of his Prince Regent Square apartment. "In my youth I did not have the means or the possibility to provide myself with an adequate education. Every night I read one or two books, even when I go to bed very late." He said that these readings were his primary source of knowledge, the grist from which he derived his public speeches. "When a person 'gives' he also has to 'take,' and I take what I need from books," he said. When Riefenstahl asked Hitler what he liked to read, he allegedly replied, "Schopenhauer."

"Not Nietzsche?" Riefenstahl asked.

"No, I can't really do much with Nietzsche," Riefenstahl recalls Hitler telling her. "He is more an artist than a philosopher; he doesn't have the crystal-clear understanding of Schopenhauer. Of course, I value Nietzsche as a genius. He writes possibly the most beautiful language that German literature has to offer us today, but he is not my guide."

Though unmentioned, Johann Gottlieb Fichte was in fact the philosopher closest to Hitler and his National Socialist movement in tone, spirit, and dynamic. Unlike Schopenhauer, a brooding, bookish man, or the frail, bedridden Nietzsche, Fichte was brash and defiant. In 1808, with French troops garrisoned in Berlin, Fichte defiantly called for Germans to rise against foreign oppression in his landmark *Speeches to the German Nation.* On the eve of the decisive battle against Napoleon at Leipzig, Fichte appeared before his students, armed for battle. He was said to be a mesmerizing speaker who held his audiences "prisoner" with his words. "To action! To action! To action!" he once declared. "That is why we are here."

Like Fichte, Hitler called for the "overthrow of the political elite" through a populist uprising. Fichte spoke of a *Volkskrieg,* a people's war. Like Fichte, Hitler wanted to see the sundered German nation united. When Hitler denounced the political dialogue of parliamentary democracy and called for direct dialogue with the German people, he assumed a distinctly Fichtean rhetorical stance and called for "speeches to the German nation."

Most consequentially, Fichte helped pioneer the notion of German exceptionalism. The Germans were, he claimed, unique among the peoples of Europe. Their language was rooted not in Latin but in a distinctly Teutonic tongue. Germans not only talked differently from other Europeans, but they also thought, believed, and acted differently. Fichte argued that pure German language, free from the corruption of French and other foreign influences, could give expression to pure German thought. The Nazi efforts to purge the German language of foreign elements were grounded in this Fichtean precept, which Hitler articulated when he mused on the concept of the word *Führer*. "The title *Führer* is certainly the most beautiful because it emerged from our own language," he observed, and went on to note with satisfaction that only members of the German nation could speak of "my *Führer.*"

Fichte was also decidedly anti-Semitic. He believed that the Jews would always remain a "state within a state" and thus a threat to a unified German nation. He proposed ridding Europe of their presence by establishing a Jewish state in Palestine. His other solution: "To cut off all their heads in one night, and set new ones on their shoulders, which should not contain a single Jewish idea."

Of all the philosophical stars in the constellation of Nazi ideology, few blazed as intensely during the Third Reich or faded as quickly afterward as this late-eighteenth-century advocate of belligerent German nationalism. Schopenhauer and Nietzsche may have lent themselves conveniently to Nazi-era sound bites, but it was Fichte who provided the philosophical foundations for the toxic blend of Teutonic singularity and vicious nationalism. No one less than Dietrich Eckart identified Fichte, Schopenhauer, and Nietzsche as the philosophical triumvirate of National Socialism. Arnold Fanck acknowledged this fact when he recommended Fichte's works as Riefenstahl's peace offering to Hitler.

Today, the Fichte volumes represent the only serious works of philosophy among Hitler's surviving books. Although there are more than a hundred pages of marginalia in the Fichte volumes, close scrutiny of several intrusions, especially the words *"sehr gut"* scrawled in the margin of page 594 of volume four, suggests an authorship other than Hitler's. In addition, the potentially most revealing volume, which contains Fichte's *Addresses to the German Nation* as well as an essay on rhetorical technique, is missing.

Despite the absence of these seminal works of German philosophy, the remnant Hitler library contains a cache of books that is almost cer-

tainly more central to the shaping of the dark core of Hitler's worldview
than the high-minded musings of Schopenhauer, Fichte, and Nietzsche:
more than fifty volumes inscribed to Hitler between 1919 and 1935 by
Julius Friedrich Lehmann, an individual who has the dubious double
claim to being both the single most generous contributor to Hitler's private book collection and the public architect for the Nazi pseudoscience
of biological racism.

COLLECTIVELY, THE FIFTY-ODD Lehmann books, all but one of them
published by his eponymous press, J. F. Lehmann Verlag, preserve the
National Socialist legacy in the full range of its multifaceted nuance and
mendacity, a veritable compendium of the pervasive moral, ethical,
social, political, legal, economic, and historical absurdities and excesses
we have come to associate with the Nazi era. I found a 1930 treatise, *The
Lawyer's Mission,* inscribed to Hitler as a "contribution to reclaiming
German law," and a book on Weimar democracy titled *Justice in Chains.*
A proposal on health insurance bore the subtitle "Once a Curse, Transformed into a Salvation for the People."

In his handwritten dedications to Hitler, Lehmann repeatedly refers
to these books as "building blocks" for the Nazi movement and, in some
cases, as educational primers for Hitler himself. In the first volume of a
massive, two-part study, *Teachings on Human Heredity and Racial Hygiene,*
Lehmann wrote, "To Mr. Adolf Hitler, as an important building block
for deepening his understanding. Warmly dedicated, J. F. Lehmann." A
1929 manual on sterilization by Otto Kankeleit, *Terminating Reproductive
Capacity for Racial-Hygienic and Social Reasons,* which includes seven har-
rowingly detailed illustrations, has been inscribed to Hitler "in great
friendship."

Like Dietrich Eckart, Lehmann was an early supporter of right-wing
causes and recognized Hitler's nascent potential. The first book Lehmann gave Hitler was the 1919 edition of *German History by Einhardt,* that
Ernst Hanfstaengl recalled seeing among Hitler's early collection, which

bears the inscription "Herr Hitler, as thanks for his work in enlightening the German people." During the 1923 putsch, Lehmann's Munich villa was used to detain the hostage Bavarian government. Mostly, though, Lehmann appears to have supplied Hitler with inscribed copies of his publications, book by book, year after year, for nearly a decade and a half, gradually filling the bookcases in Hitler's Thiersch Street apartment and eventually gracing the shelves of the Prince Regent Square residence. I found a translation of Madison Grant's 1916 classic racist tract, *The Passing of the Great Race; or, The Racial Basis of European History.* Hitler's copy, a fourth edition published in 1925, is "warmly inscribed" by Lehmann.

Along with Grant's *Passing of the Great Race,* the most notable books are those by Hans F. K. Günther, whose works Hitler included among his recommended readings for Nazi Party members. The former literary scholar turned social anthropologist produced a series of infamous studies on racial typology that veritably defined the Nazi discipline of racial anthropology and laid the groundwork for its racial laws and eugenics programs. Günther's efforts earned him the sobriquet "Racial Günther" (*Rassengünther*), and the personal attendance of Adolf Hitler at his appointment ceremony as a professor at the University of Jena.

Four of Hitler's six Günther volumes are copies of *Racial Typology of the German People,* a dense five-hundred-page tome that provides a compendium of Aryan identity. The earliest volume, a third edition published in 1923, is inscribed by Lehmann to "the successful champion of German racial thinking," and is followed by a 1928 edition sent as a "Christmas greeting," a fourteenth edition in 1930, and a copy of the sixteenth edition in 1933 with a handwritten inscription that hails Hitler as "the trailblazer of racial thinking."

This latter volume, bound in simple gray linen with the author and title imprinted in old German script on the cover and an extended appendix of European Jews, shows signs of frequent or sustained study. It opens effortlessly to reveal worn pages and a ragged tear along the inside cover where the spine has begun to come apart.

With this cache of Lehmann books we are in possession of a core collection within the Hitler library and the primary building blocks not only for Hitler's intellectual world but for the ideological foundations of his Third Reich.

In Lehmann's publications, Hitler found in particular the alleged

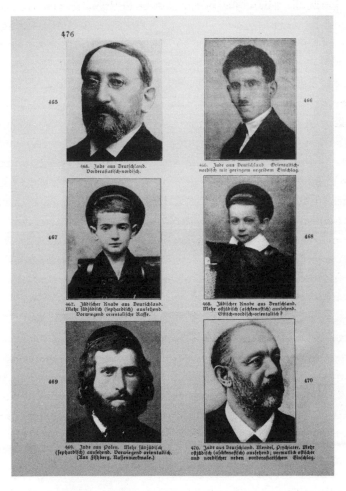

A page from Hitler's copy of Hans F. K. Günther's
Racial Typology of the German People,
depicting Jews from various regions of Germany.

empirical substance he had missed in the racist pamphlets of his Vienna years. As a leading publisher of medical textbooks and handbooks known for the quality and precision of their illustrations, J. F. Lehmann Verlag brought serious scientific credentials to the pseudoscience of biological racism. Even as Lehmann supplied the medical community with indispensable handbooks and reference works, he was serving as the major purveyor of biological racism. J. F. Lehmann Verlag is said to have almost singlehandedly established the discipline of racial science in the Weimar Republic. For his contribution to advancing the Nazi cause, Hitler honored Lehmann with the gold party pin, one of the highest awards in Nazi Germany.

As I rummaged through these solidly bound, richly illustrated volumes, many of them printed on high-quality paper that has retained its suppleness and vibrancy, I calculated that Hitler's Lehmann collection easily doubled the Benjaminian 10 percent reading quotient. Several of the books were well worn, with pages bent and spines well-exercised so they opened leisurely, frequently to pages bearing illustrations. One volume, a 1934 reprint of Paul Lagarde's late-nineteenth-century collection of nationalist and anti-Semitic writings, bore nearly a hundred pages of penciled marginalia: underlinings, vertical strikes, and occasional question marks.

Lagarde's *German Essays* belongs to a handful of "classic" works of German nationalism that found their way into Hitler's collection: several works by Houston Stewart Chamberlain, including one titled *Richard Wagner: The German as Artist, Thinker, Politician;* a reprint of Julius Langbehn's *Rembrandt as Educator,* an awkward plagiarizing of a Nietzsche essay on Schopenhauer; and most notably *The Third Reich* by Arthur Moeller von den Bruck, whose title provided the Nazi movement with its emblematic slogan.*

---

* Moeller von den Bruck met Hitler in 1922 but rejected his "proletarian primitiveness." Nevertheless, the Nazi movement did not hesitate to use select ideas from von den Bruck's theories and most famously plagiarized the title of his book for their movement. Von den Bruck suffered a nervous breakdown and committed suicide in May 1925.

A copy of Arthur Moeller von den Bruck's 1923 treatise
The Third Reich, *whose title provided the Nazi*
movement with its emblematic slogan. This copy was
inscribed to Hitler in November 1924, on the first
anniversary of the failed Munich putsch.

Lehmann appears to have given Hitler two copies of Lagarde's *German Essays,* each with a slightly different dedication. The first is inscribed "to the prophet of the Third Reich, to its creator," and the second "from the old prophet of the German people, to his successor." The Hungarian scholar Ambrus Miskolczy has studied Hitler's marginalia and speculates that the second volume could possibly have been intended for Alfred Rosenberg and mistakenly incorporated into the Hitler collection after the war, but ultimately concludes that both volumes were intended for Hitler. Miskolczy observes that Lehmann would have possessed more "tact" than to "elevate" Rosenberg above Hitler as the prophet of the Third Reich. He also notes that the selection of particular passages as well as the "distinctive fine pencil lines" suggest Hitler's authorship of the marginalia.

In particular, Miskolczy notes the highlighting of a passage that corresponds to Hitler's very specific views on the theory of revolution and the state. Miskolczy observes that on page 44 Lagarde writes, "All the power of Germany shall be expressed in state actions, and the state that ought only to be the nation's servant, shall become the lord of the nation's surrogates," with Hitler's pencil following in apparent concurrence. On the previous page, a question mark beside a passage about creating a single religion for Germany leads Miskolczy to the conclusion that "it would be more typical of Hitler" to challenge such a proposition since he remained ambivalent or at least noncommittal on spiritual matters, while Rosenberg advocated militantly for the fusion of state and religion. The highlighting of passages related to a strong-willed leader, Miskolczy further observes, also suggesting Hitler's hand.

On page 72 of Lagarde, for example, there is a line beside a passage discussing the sense of alienation experienced by "great men" who shape the destiny of their societies, a sentiment echoed in marked passages in Hitler books I found at Brown University.* The nature of these intrusions seems to support the Miskolczy thesis, as does Hitler's own theory of reading as detailed in *Mein Kampf.* He compares the process of reading to that of collecting "stones" to fill a "mosaic" of preconceived notions. He studies the table of contents or even the index of a book, then gleans select chapters for "usable" information. On occasion, he reads the conclusion first, to determine what to look for in advance. He

---

* The two books are Carl Ludwig Schleich's *The Wisdom of Happiness*, published in 1924, and Ernst Schertel's *Magic: History, Theory, and Practice*, published in 1923.

recommends that a reader hone the skill of "instantly" discerning information that is useful to his personal needs or general knowledge.

"Once the knowledge he has achieved in this fashion is correctly coordinated within the somehow existing picture of this or that subject created by his imagination, it will function either as a corrective or a complement, thus enhancing either the correctness or the clarity of the picture," Hitler wrote. "Then, if life suddenly sets some question before us for examination or answer, the memory, if this method of reading is observed, will immediately take the existing picture as a norm, and from it will derive all the individual items regarding these questions, assembled in the course of decades, submit them to the mind for examination and reconsideration, until the question is clarified or answered."

Through this technique Hitler was able to commit prodigious amounts of information to memory with virtually instant recall on a seemingly endless array of subjects, from tank production to works of drama. One evening after listening to Hitler compare the respective qualities of works by Friedrich Schiller and George Bernard Shaw, Goebbels returned home and scribbled in his diary, "The man is a genius."

As Hitler told Riefenstahl, he read nightly, a habit that appears to date back to his early years in Linz and Vienna, where August Kubizek observed his intense passion for books. "Books, always more books! I can never remember Adolf without books," Kubizek recalled. "Books were his world." Another early Hitler associate, Rudolf Häusler, who shared quarters with Hitler in Vienna and later in Munich, recalls his roommate reading dense tomes until two or three in the morning. According to Kubizek, this passion for books had nothing to do with leisure or pleasure. It was "deadly serious business."

From my own conversations with surviving Hitler associates, it appears that Hitler's nocturnal reading habit was still in place decades later. Margarete Mitlstrasser, one of Hitler's longtime housekeepers, recounted a nightly regimen that included his reading glasses, a book, and a pot of tea. Hitler read intensely, even fiercely. The Berghof estate manager, Herbert Döring, recalled an evening when Eva Braun intruded on one of these late-night reading sessions and was dispatched with a tirade that sent her hurtling red-faced down the hallway. Döring himself exercised extreme caution. Each night before closing the Berghof, he would walk outside to wait until Hitler's reading light was extinguished. On more than one occasion, dawn was breaking on the horizon. Anni Plaim, a Berghof maid, remembered a sign outside Hitler's second-floor study that read ABSOLUTE SILENCE.

In the summer of 2001, when I spoke with Traudl Junge, Hitler's last surviving secretary, she mused on the morning breakfasts when Hitler would reprise his previous night's reading in extensive, often tedious detail, a habit that was insightfully observed by Christa Schröder, another of Hitler's secretaries, when she explained in her memoirs that he would discuss "a topic that he had read about numerous times in order to anchor it more permanently in his mind." Schröder noted the "compartmentalized" nature of Hitler's mind, which permitted him to recall complete passages from books.

The corresponding analogue to this compartmentalization process is preserved among Hitler's books in a twenty-volume, leather-bound deluxe edition of the *Great Brockhaus Encyclopedia*, a massive compendium of facts and information designed to be retrieved with maximum efficiency and effectiveness, the ultimate resource for the self-educated man and, by all accounts, Hitler's preferred source of reference and affirmation.

Christa Schröder remembered how Hitler would discuss the length of a river or the size of a city and then turn to his encyclopedia. "Hitler, excessively exacting in all things, would then look it up in two encyclopedias in order to be entirely certain," Schröder recalled. Traudl Junge related an identical process, recalling an evening debate on the exact height of Napoleon Bonaparte, when Hitler left the room and returned with the corresponding volume of his encyclopedia. Both Junge and

Schröder spoke of Hitler's preference for *Meyer's Encyclopedia*, a set of which is visible in a photograph of a Berghof bookcase, but the presence of *The Great Brockhaus Encyclopedia*, in an edition published between 1928 and 1934, with a supplemental volume from 1935, and the Hitler ex libris bookplate pasted on the inside cover of several volumes, preserves in tangible form the physical structures that come closest to reflecting the inner dimensions of Hitler's intellectual world.

IN THE LAGARDE VOLUME, we can observe the application of Hitler's reading technique in all its selective intensity, sense the pencil hovering beside the book as the eye scans the page for any information that is "useful," then striking the page, underlining a single passage or an entire sentence, then double striking the margin to highlight the importance. Occasionally there are exclamation points and sometimes question marks, but mostly there are a series of focused and sporadic lines indicating a plundering of the volume for facts that can be fit into his preconceived "mosaic" of ideas.

This process is especially evident in passages relating to the Jewish question, which are repeatedly highlighted throughout the 520-page tome, beginning on page 41, where Lagarde adopts the Fichtean stance that the Jews, now numbering two million, can never be assimilated. There is a pencil line beneath the passage recommending their "transplantation" to Palestine, with two dense vertical lines in the margin. The pencil continues to trace Lagarde's references to Jews, pausing at a passage where Lagarde asserts that Germans are incapable of competing with the Jews. The Germans, Lagarde claims, are made of "inferior material" (*zu weiches Material*) compared with the Jews, "who have been hardened in the forge of Talmudic training." Lagarde draws the only natural conclusion, which is underscored with a particularly dense marking: "Because I know the Germans, I cannot wish that Jews be allowed to live with them."

Two hundred and fifty pages later, on page 292, when Lagarde again addresses the fundamental irreconcilability between Germans and Jews, the entire passage is highlighted: "Despite their desire to be placed on equal terms with Germans, the Jews continually emphasize their foreignness in the most obvious manner through the style of their synagogues. What is that supposed to mean, to lay claim to the honorable German name while constructing the most sacred sites one has in a Moorish style in order not to forget that one is a Semite, an Asian, a foreigner?" The passage is indicated with thick pencil lines, twice struck in the right-hand margin. On page 370, an even more ominous passage is highlighted: "Each and every irksome Jew is a serious affront to the authenticity and veracity of our German identity." The pencil lines track Lagarde's words across the page as he insists that "Jews will remain Jews" and that it will ultimately be left to the German people to resolve the "Jewish question." This is the last marked passage in the volume.

These marginalia bring little that is new to our understanding of Hitler per se or the Nazi movement in general. The belligerent sentiments and rhetoric are familiar to us from Hitler's speeches and writings during the previous fifteen years. They are redundant mosaic pieces being fit into a redundant pattern. What is new and notable is the context. Since Lehmann never dated his inscriptions, we rarely know the exact date when Hitler received a particular volume, with the exception of the occasional holiday gift, though the pattern suggests that Lehmann inscribed and dispatched the individual volumes in the same year they were published. With Lagarde, we can place a bit more certainty around the time frame and context. We know that *German Essays* was published in 1934 and that Lehmann died in March 1935, making this volume one of the few books Lehmann inscribed to Hitler after his appointment as chancellor.

When this copy of Lagarde entered the Hitler book collection in 1934 or early 1935, Hitler was no longer the leader of a radical right-wing party that was frequently in crisis or on the verge of dissolution. He was now a head of state, who, following the burning of the Reichstag in March 1933, declared a state of emergency, suspended democratic process, and assumed the dictatorial powers he was to retain for the next twelve years. Guided by a hand imbued with dictatorial powers, Hitler's penciled intrusions resonate differently than they did before 1933.

When Lagarde writes about the responsibilities of being German on page 164, and Hitler frames the paragraph with a phalanx of three dense lines to the left and three equally intense lines to the right, the markings resonate ominously with the words: "Germany is the totality of all those Germans who feel German, who think German, who long to be Germans: each and every one of us is a traitor to the nation if we do not realize and respect our personal responsibility to the existence, the happiness, the future of the fatherland in every moment of our lives; each of us is a hero and a liberator when we do."

These are no longer the marginalia of the marginalized. A penciled mark can become state doctrine. The Lehmann volumes had become the building blocks the publisher had always intended them to be.

BOOK FIVE

Book Wars

*Hasn't National Socialism also brought the German people a good, worth-
while idea so that the support of the movement by people with a positive religious attitude is not only desirable but is absolutely necessary?*
                    From the introduction to *Foundations of National*
                    Socialism by BISHOP ALOIS HUDAL, July 11, 1936

WITH ITS TITLE AND AUTHOR whispered in muted gold across
a linen cover that appears to be of a hue halfway between the
shrill brown of a storm trooper uniform and the rich chocolate tone of a
Franciscan cassock, Hitler's copy of the *Foundations of National Socialism*
hardly seems like a conspiratorial tract, just as the full-page glossy photograph of its forty-nine-year-old author, with his gentle, bookish, even
boyish look, more quizzical than calculating, hardly seems like the
image of an architect of a Vatican-based plot to fracture the Nazi movement from within, to leach it of its anti-Semitic toxins, to infuse it with
Christian beneficence, and to awaken in Adolf Hitler the latent Roman
Catholicism that the plotters were certain lay dormant within his soul. It
was a plan that seemed as naïve as it was ambitious, but for a few hours
in November 1936, when Hitler received the book, it appeared to totter
on the brink of success, a one-man conspiracy initiated two and a half
years earlier, on the afternoon of February 7, 1934, by a scholar of the Old
Testament.

On that particular afternoon, Hitler received Cardinal Karl Joseph
Schulte, the bishop of Cologne, in his Reich Chancellery office. Schulte,

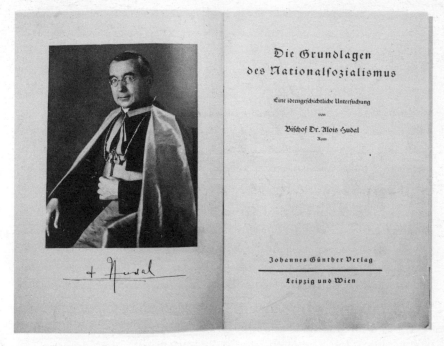

The copy of Alois Hudal's Foundations of National Socialism *handed to Hitler in November 1936 as part of a plot to split the Nazi movement*

responsible for the spiritual lives of the huge number of Roman Catholics in the German Rhineland, had come to Berlin to express his concern over the growing anti-Christian agitation among local Nazis, and, in particular, Hitler's recent appointment of Alfred Rosenberg as his "chief ideologue" in charge of the "spiritual" welfare of the German people.

Rosenberg was among the most militantly anti-Christian Nazis, his book *The Myth of the Twentieth Century* a compendium of heresies including the advocacy of polygamy, forced sterilization, and the propagation of a "fifth Gospel" that allegedly revealed the true nature of Jesus Christ. According to this "lost Gospel," Jesus was not the embodiment of forgiveness and beneficence whose identity was defined by suffering and crucifixion. Instead, he was a raging prophet bent on destruction and vengeance. In the book, Rosenberg claimed that Saint Peter, working as a Jewish agent, changed his name from Saulus to Paulus, and obscured this fifth Gospel as a means of enslaving the peoples of Europe.

Rosenberg spoke of a "Jewified" Christian ethic, and envisioned the emergence of a new religion. "The horrific crucifixes of the Baroque and Rococo eras, which display emaciated limbs on every street corner, will gradually be replaced by monuments to fallen soldiers," Rosenberg predicted. "They will bear the names of those men who, as a symbol of the eternal myth of blood and will, gave their lives for the noblest cause: for the honor of the German name."

In October 1933, the Vatican had formally protested the inclusion of Rosenberg's *Myth* in school curricula, but to little avail. In January, the Prussian ministry of education included the book on a list of "recommended" titles for school libraries. The bishops sounded the alarm. "Recently, I heard that the two books *Mein Kampf* and *The Myth of the 20th Century* were supposed to be included in the school libraries of the middle schools," one bishop complained. "There is nothing to object to in this first book, but Rosenberg's book does not belong in such a library; if anything, it belongs on the Index [the Vatican's *Index Librorum Prohibitorum,* the legendary list of banned books]."

Now Schulte was raising the issue with Hitler himself. Schulte was responsible for the spiritual welfare of seven million Catholics, he reminded Hitler, who had initially welcomed the Nazi seizure of power and the concordance that had been forged with the Vatican. Schulte said he had noticed an unsettling increase in anti-Christian and anticlerical rhetoric among many Nazi leaders, a trend that was only aggravated by Rosenberg's appointment as "deputy" for "ideological and spiritual" instruction. Not only did the monitoring of religious instruction violate the terms of the Vatican agreement, but Rosenberg was a known militant critic of the Church, a fact that was abundantly clear in his *Myth.* At the mention of the Rosenberg book, Hitler stopped Schulte.

"I don't want that book," Hitler barked. "Rosenberg knows it. I told him that myself." Hitler said he wanted nothing to do with "these heathen things."

"You cannot talk like that about Rosenberg and his book anymore, Herr Reich Chancellor," Schulte shot back.

"And tell me why not?"

"Because a few days ago you officially appointed this same Herr Rosenberg as ideological instructor of the Nazi Party and thereby as instructor to a large portion of the German people," Schulte reminded him. "Henceforth, whether you like it or not, you will be identified with Herr Rosenberg."

"That's right, I identify myself with Herr Rosenberg but not with the author of the book *Myth*," Hitler said. How then, Schulte pressed, did Hitler intend to make this distinction clear to the German people?

Hitler ignored the question. He confirmed that Rosenberg was indeed the Nazi Party's chief ideologue. He repeated his conviction that the Rosenberg appointment had nothing to do with *Myth*. The book, Hitler again insisted, was a purely private matter. Then he added derisively that if anyone was to be held accountable for the book, it was the Catholic Church. "The bishops are the ones who have made Rosenberg's book so well known," Hitler said. "Without them no one would have paid any attention to the book."

Schulte was stunned. "What, the bishops are to blame?"

"Yes, the bishops," Hitler repeated. "Wasn't it the Cardinal of Munich who talked about it in his sermons and tried to destroy the ancient German ideals in our young people?" When Schulte told Hitler he was "twisting" things, Hitler changed the subject. The meeting sputtered to a conclusion.

Hitler was showing himself as chancellor to be master of the rhetorical dodge, the dialectical diversion, the off-kilter counterpoint thesis that sent an argument careening into a tangential direction, never to return to the original point. And he did so with the ease and confidence of a head of state. Seated in the office once occupied by Otto von Bismarck,

Hitler no longer needed to dodge or duck. He evaded with beneficence and lied with magnanimity. He had come a long way in twelve months.

In February 1933, when Paul von Hindenberg appointed him the sixteenth chancellor of the Weimar Republic, Hitler was just the next politician to take his place in a notoriously shaky seat from which fifteen predecessors had toppled since 1919, an average of one per year. A cache of right-wing newspapers from February 1933, found in the Berlin *Führerbunker* in the spring of 1945, hint at the "insecurity" Franz von Papen then sensed in Hitler. In one yellowed newspaper, Hitler has highlighted several passages in an article—"Herr Chancellor! Just a Few Questions"—needling him about his campaign promises, and in another asserting that he has fallen into a "Jewish trap" laid by von Papen. Here Hitler has underlined part of a sentence that says he could only see Hindenburg when von Papen was present. The passage of ten months had brought a total change.

The chancellor of the troubled and turbulent Weimar Republic was now the Führer of the Thousand-Year Reich. The books he received that December reflect not only his new circumstances but also Germany's. A collection of "wit and wisdom" gleaned from Goethe's writings is dedicated "respectfully" to the "Führer, founder and first chancellor of the Third Reich." A copy of *Wagner's Resounding Universe* is inscribed by its author, Walter Engelsmann, to "the steward and shaper of the descendents of Siegfried upon the earth." On the following page, Engelsmann has written triumphantly, "Wotan's dream of the man-god is fulfilled."

In June 1934, Hitler would give final shape to this new Germany. Having dismantled the democratic structures of the Weimar Republic, and with them any effective political resistance, he turned on his own men. On the night of June 30, 1934, in an operation code-named "Hummingbird" but better known as the "Night of the Long Knives," Hitler had eighty Nazi Party leaders, including his close associate Ernst Röhm, arrested and executed. Hitler now commanded absolute authority, and the ruthless nature of his regime was evident to all.

But even as Hitler eliminated dissent within his country and his own party, Alois Hudal's plot to undermine the Nazi movement was already under way. On the same afternoon that Hitler sparred with Schulte over Rosenberg's *Myth,* an assembly of cardinals known as the Sanctum Officium met in Rome to take a decision that set Hudal's ambitious designs in motion.

ON THE AFTERNOON OF February 7, 1934, the Vatican newspaper *L'Osservatore Romano* published a news item reporting that the Sanctum Officium had recommended that Rosenberg's *Myth* be placed on the Vatican's Index. The list of banned books was most catholic in the literal sense of the word, and its thousands of titles included Galileo's *Sidereus Nuncius,* Gustave Flaubert's *Madame Bovary,* and Charles Darwin's *The Origin of Species.* Generally, books were placed on the Index with no explanation or commentary, but in this case, the Sanctum Officium felt compelled to make its reasoning public. *L'Osservatore Romano* reported:

> The book scorns all dogmas of the Catholic Church, indeed the very fundamentals of Christian religion, and rejects them completely. It argues for the need for the founding of a new religion or a Germanic church and proclaims the principle: "Today there is awakening a new faith, the myth of the blood, the faith in defending with blood the divine being of man; the faith that embodies the absolute knowledge that the northern blood represents that mystery that has replaced and overcome the old sacraments."

The appearance of Rosenberg's *Myth* on the Index transformed this bizarre, overwritten, and by general consensus impenetrable eight-hundred-page tome into an overnight sensation. A book that had taken seven years to write and another six to find a publisher—it was taken on by Hoheneichen Verlag, Dietrich Eckart's former publishing house, after being rejected even by Hanfstaengl and Bruckmann—was sud-

Hitler once described Alfred Rosenberg's The Myth of the Twentieth Century *as impenetrable. This 1940 edition contains Hitler's ex libris but shows no signs of having been read.*

denly one of the most talked about books in the world, featured in head-lines in Paris, London, and New York. Its indexing led to a public debate in Germany and made Rosenberg a cause célèbre in the Nazi press.

Six months after *Myth* was proscribed by the Vatican, German theolo-gians published a major study dissecting the book line by line, exposing not only its religious but also its historical, geographic, and ortho-graphic transgressions, which they published anonymously—for fear of Nazi reprisal—in a two-hundred-page book titled *Studies of Myth.*

Beyond the substantive issues, they observed that the Hadrian IV mentioned in the book was in fact Hadrian VI, that one church historian was named "Merx," not "Merk," that another, Eusebius, was not a eunuch, as Rosenberg claimed, and that the assembled "monks" Rosenberg described as gathering in Nicaea were in fact bishops. When Rosenberg inquired with Hoheneichen about removing all the errors from future editions, his editor advised against it. It would require excising 60 percent of the book's content.

Instead, Rosenberg counterattacked. He replied with his own two-hundred-page polemic, *The Church's Shadowed Men*, which defended *Myth* by insisting that the book laid claim to a truth that went deeper than historical or theological accuracy. "That which I maintain in my *Myth of the 20th Century* and see as absolutely necessary for our epoch," Rosenberg said, "would endure even if all the historical evidence contradicted every detail of it." *Shadowed Men* was immediately placed on the Index beside *Myth*, much to Rosenberg's delight.

By the end of 1934, *Myth* had sold more than 150,000 copies. *Shadowed Men* sold twice that number. Within a year, sales of *Myth* itself had doubled. By 1935, the book was into its seventieth edition, with 353,000 copies in print.

For all Rosenberg's profit and pleasure, Hitler was very possibly annoyed by the scandal. He disliked *Myth*, considered it unreadable, and said he had managed to read only a small portion of it. As an author, he may have been chafed that *Myth* had received so much serious critical attention, unlike *Mein Kampf.* He wouldn't have been pleased that the public attention elevated *Myth* to a position where it was viewed as an ideological companion to *Mein Kampf.* Rosenberg had repeatedly lobbied Hitler to accord *Myth* official status, which he had refused to do, but the book had risen to de facto official status on the tide of its proscription. It eventually sold more than two million copies, making it second only to *Mein Kampf* as the best-selling book of the Third Reich.

Of more serious consequence for Hitler were the religious implications. According to paragraph 47 of the updated ecclesiastical law of 1900, "the penalty of excommunication is forthwith incurred by all, who, though conscious of law and penalty yet read or keep or print or defend books of heretical teachers or apostates maintaining heresies." It now became a sin punishable by automatic excommunication for millions of Roman Catholics, including students, to read or own the Rosenberg book.* Not only were the millions of German Roman Catholics whom Hitler had attempted to appease through a concordance with the Vatican suddenly confronted with a choice between competing claims of church and state, but Hitler's own party colleagues were forced to take sides in the Rosenberg debate, which is exactly what the Austrian bishop Alois Hudal had intended.

IN THE NEGOTIATIONS leading up to the concordance in the spring and summer of 1933, Hudal had identified two distinctive camps within the Nazi movement: the "conservatives" such as Göring and Goebbels, who were concerned mainly with political power, and the party "radicals" such as Rosenberg, who promoted a bizarre cultish Aryan ideology. As a complement to the indexing of Rosenberg's *Myth*, Hudal recommended a public relations campaign to expose these divisions and force Hitler to take sides.

"In *L'Osservatore Romano* and all other possible newspapers abroad, and also in speeches, yes, even speeches, the expectation and hope should be emphasized that Adolf Hitler and Franz von Papen would like religious reconciliation," Hudal proposed in an internal Vatican memorandum. He urged that this "be repeated again and again—in different variations." Hudal believed that public expectation could compel Hitler and Papen to distance themselves from the radicals and embrace fully

---

* Hitler's library contains two copies of Rosenberg's *Myth*, both relatively late editions, published in 1940 and 1942, and most likely perfunctory acquisitions for his Berlin library. As a registered Roman Catholic, Hitler himself would also have been subject to paragraph 47.

the terms of the concordance as part of their "duty to the happiness" of the German people. "Thus and in this sense, the position of the Vatican and all possible Catholic papers abroad must be the identical demand in the identical spirit: Papen and Hitler, Hitler and Papen!" Hudal thumped. "Only in this manner can a potentially beneficial mood be created."

By recommending the indexing of *Myth* and the launching of a press campaign, Hudal intended not only to expose and aggravate a public schism within Germany, but also to bolster his own credibility within the Vatican in anticipation of a second and even more consequential phase to his plan. Once the Nazi movement had been polarized, the "radicals" alienated on the extreme left and the "conservatives" lured into the Christian camp, Hudal intended to propose a theological blueprint for the melding of Roman Catholic belief with National Socialist doctrine. Hudal saw great potential here.

In his study of National Socialist ideology, Hudal recognized a number of fundamental alignments between Catholics and Nazis. Both shared a common belief in blind obedience to authority. The Nazi notion of the *Führerprinzip* was little more than a secular rendering of papal infallibility. Both Nazis and Catholics shared a deep-seated antipathy toward Jews. Hudal noted that as early as the thirteenth century, Saint Thomas Aquinas had in his treatise *De regimine Judaeorum* warned of the attempt by the Jews to rule the world. If the Nazis could be persuaded to abandon "anti-Semitism" in favor of "anti-Judaism," that is, hating the Jews as a religious rather than a racial community, Hudal believed that the Germans could create a catechized form of fascism that would represent the most powerful political and social force on the Continent and serve as a bulwark to the greatest common threat to Europe: the spread of Bolshevism. Hudal spoke of a "Wehrmacht of the spirit," and noted that the Soviet foreign minister, Vyacheslav Molotov, had himself declared that the greatest threat to communism was a fusion of fascism and Roman Catholicism.

———

IN THE AUTUMN OF 1934, Hudal traveled from Rome to Germany to assemble a comprehensive library of books on National Socialist ideology. He then returned to Rome to begin work on the theological architecture for his plan. When Hudal outlined his strategy during a private audience with Pius XI, the pope listened patiently then told the Austrian bishop that he had misjudged Hitler and his movement by assuming that National Socialism represented a belief system. "There you have made your first mistake. You cannot talk about anything spiritual in this movement," the pontiff told Hudal. "It is a massive materialism." To Pius's mind, there was no desire on the part of the Nazis to compromise with Christianity, and there never would be. The movement was about tactics and power, not faith or belief. At the end of the audience, Pius told Hudal that he did not believe in the "possibility of an understanding" between Nazis and Catholics, but he wished Hudal "good luck" with his enterprise. Hudal disregarded the papal counsel. He had read *Mein Kampf* and had noted the passages in chapter one in which Hitler talked about his time as a choirboy at the Benedictine monastery at Lambach and its impact on his person. "Since in my free time I received singing lessons in the cloister at Lambach, I had excellent opportunity to intoxicate myself with the solemn splendor of the brilliant church festivals," Hitler had written on page 6. "As was only natural the abbot seemed to me, as the village priest had once seemed to my father, the highest and most desirable ideal." Though Hitler's interests migrated with time, those early years left an indelible impression. One need only look at the swastika carved into the keystone of the Lambach monastery or listen to Hitler's music instructor, the aging pater Bernard Grüner, talk about his former pupil. "The swastika here in our abbey impressed itself upon the child, and the little Hitler dreamed of it endlessly," Grüner told one journalist in the summer of 1933.

For Hudal, the residual impact of these years manifested itself everywhere in Hitler's later life, from the black "twisted cross" on the white

host-shaped background set against the blood-red banner to the "cathedral of light" at the annual party rally in Nuremberg, to Hitler's frequent
allusions to biblical and liturgical rhetoric in his public speeches. "And
the power and the hope and the glory of the Fatherland," Hitler concluded one address in raging crescendo, then gasped a brief, seemingly
reflexive denouement, "Amen." As an Austrian Catholic, Hudal felt he
"knew" Hitler.

In the spring of 1935, when Hudal approached Papen with his proposal for a Catholic-Fascist fusion, Papen instantly saw the potential and
believed it would appeal to Hitler, not just for tactical reasons but also
because of its deeper resonances with his Austrian-Catholic upbringing.
"That a prelate of such stature, a native German from the old Danube
Monarchy would devote himself to the German question with 'burning
passion' would have to make a strong impression on Hitler," Papen
reasoned.

As vice chancellor, Papen over the last two years had spent time with
Hitler on a regular basis, and on several occasions had engaged with him
in religious discussions. Like Hudal, Papen felt he knew Hitler. That
spring, when he discussed Hudal's proposal a number of times with
Hitler, he was encouraged by the "great interest" Hitler showed in the
idea. Papen advised Hudal not to publish his opus until he had had an
opportunity to share it with Hitler personally and secure his personal
endorsement. Hudal agreed to wait.

On June 8, 1936, during a meeting with Hitler and Goebbels, Papen
presented Hudal's draft manuscript, extolling its ability to bridge the
gap between Catholic theology and Nazi ideology, which would form
a bulwark against the Bolshevik threat. As Hudal anticipated, Hitler
seemed amenable to the idea. Goebbels remained skeptical. He took the
manuscript and said he would review it. A week later he sent Papen a
list of seventeen points of serious contention. "Book of Bishop Hudal
forbidden. Papen lobbied hard for him," Goebbels scribbled in his diary.
But Papen did not relent. He shared Goebbels's response with Hudal,
and recommended the bishop make the suggested amendments. Then

he wrote to Hitler urging him to endorse Hudal "in order to keep this man capable of fighting for us and not to expose him to the clique of cardinals who are his superiors and can silence him forever if his upcoming book is officially banned." The deliberations dragged on into the autumn.

As intended, the Hudal manuscript seeded dissension among the Nazi elite. Papen, of course, pressed hard for publication. Rosenberg was outraged that a bishop would "dictate" terms to the party. In early October, Hitler, tired of the posturing and infighting over the Hudal manuscript, said he would "determine whether or not that book will appear in the Reich, and that is that." He "endorsed" the book. Hudal's *Foundations of National Socialism* was published that month by Johannes Günther Verlag, in Vienna. The fissures among the Nazi Party elite were clear, the lines hardening, but the alignment appeared to be tilting in Hudal's favor. "If I had not acted resolutely, the book would still not be published, since Goebbels still has not given his *official* 'yes,' while Göring, Hitler, Hess and Neurath are for you," an inside source of Hudal's reported, then enthused, "We will reach our goal!!! Even against Rosenberg."

By October 1936, Hitler had wearied of the incessant public scuffles with the Church and even more so of Rosenberg's *Myth.* He dismissed it as the product of a "narrow-minded Balt who thinks in horribly complicated terms." According to Hitler, even the title was wrong. The Nazi movement was based on modern science, not a "myth." As a National Socialist, Rosenberg should have known better. He should have called his book *Knowledge of the Twentieth Century,* a title that would have underscored the empirical advancements of human understanding in the twentieth century. Further, Hitler hardly knew a Nazi leader who had read the book, let alone understood it.

In September 1935, Hitler had already publicly distanced himself from the party radicals. "His speech is a singular rejection of Rosenberg and Streicher," Goebbels noted in his diary. "And both of them applaud the loudest." But Hitler was also tiring of Goebbels. For nearly two years, the minister of propaganda had orchestrated a series of "indecency trials," exposing sexual abuses among the clergy. Goebbels had headlines splashed across the daily papers until the public grew weary. On October 25, Goebbels wrote of the end of his campaign against the clergy, and Hitler's desire to resolve differences with the church. "Trials against the Catholic Church temporarily stopped," Goebbels noted in his diary. "Possibly wants peace, at least temporarily. Now a battle with Bolshevism. Wants to speak with Faulhaber."

Hitler's desire to speak with Michael Faulhaber was significant. As archbishop of Munich and Freising, Faulhaber was not only the spiritual steward to the largest Catholic community in Germany, but also one of the fiercest critics of Nazi ideology. Jews, Protestants, and Catholics alike had packed the Munich Cathedral to hear his Advent sermons in December 1933, when he patently rejected Nazi ideology and embraced the German Jews as "brothers." When the government demanded a list of Jews who had converted to Christianity between 1900 and 1935, Faulhaber complied by informing them that 331 "Israelis"—138 men, 178 women, and 15 children—had been baptized in Bavaria. Nazi officials demanded the names, but Faulhaber refused to provide them or even the specific years of conversion. They were now Roman Catholics; they would not be abandoned or betrayed by their church. "National Socialist ideology adheres to its law on blood and race, 'A Jew remains a Jew,' whether he is a baptized Jew or not," Faulhaber stated. But "from the perspective of the bishops in which the former Jew according to the word of Paul from 2 Corinthians 5:17 becomes a 'new-born being,' a true child of God, through baptism, we hold out our hand to him as does any other diocese in this confirmation. With this the baptized Jew has received a right from the Church authorities to be treated as a Christian and no longer as a Jew and at least not to be handed over to anti-Semitic enemies."

Faulhaber was as principled as he was imperious, both intellectually

and spiritually. Like Schulte, he had hailed Hitler's appointment as chancellor for the stability and promise it brought to Germany, especially in the fight against Bolshevism, but he was not to be moved on matters of faith, morals, or principle, especially when it came to the more radical aspects of Nazi ideology. As early as the spring of 1930, Faulhaber had warned of the dangers of Rosenberg's *Myth* at a bishops' conference in Fulda, where he had cited and critiqued extensive passages. Hitler had alluded to this gathering in his meeting with Cardinal Schulte when he blamed the "bishop in Munich" for popularizing Rosenberg's book.

During Faulhaber's first Advent sermon in December 1933, the Munich bishop had assailed the Rosenberg-style radicalism that was penetrating German society. He did not mention Hitler's chief ideologue by name but the allusions to Rosenberg's work were obvious. Faulhaber noted that racial research, "in itself a neutral matter in regard to religion," had been "assembled for battle against religion and was shaking the very foundations of Christianity." Faulhaber spoke of a necessary response on the part of the church. "When it comes to such voices and movements the bishop cannot be silent," he stated. Faulhaber was no less direct when he arrived at the Berghof on the morning of November 6, 1936.

The Obersalzberg was shrouded in mist. An autumn drizzle fell, chilling the Alpine air. Hitler led Faulhaber to the privacy of his second-floor "study" in the company of Rudolf Hess. No sooner were they seated than Hitler told Faulhaber he was going to say things that the cardinal was not going to like but that needed to be stated openly.

Echoing Hudal's thesis, Hitler said that Bolshevism was a threat not only to Germany but also to Christianity. He noted the emergence of the left-wing Popular Front movement in France, the rising threat in Czechoslovakia, Poland, and other countries, and especially in Spain, where at that very moment, the fascists were fighting communists for control of Madrid. "The Catholic Church must not allow itself to be deceived," Hitler said. "If National Socialism does not become the master over Bolshevism, then it will be over with Christianity and the Church in Europe."

Hitler then turned to the matter at hand: the relationship between National Socialism and the Catholic Church. "Christianity is insolubly bound to our people and to the Occidental culture by a thousand-year-old history," he told Faulhaber; he also said that in his briefcase he had 380 cases regarding priests who had been accused of preaching against National Socialism. The Catholic Church needed to abandon this "ridiculous bagatelle" against the state. With the looming Bolshevist threat, both Catholics and fascists had greater worries. However, "if the Church continues to oppose National Socialism and continues the battle, then National Socialism will have to continue without the Church," Hitler told Faulhaber. He went on for nearly an hour.

Faulhaber listened patiently and then responded. No one needed to lecture him about the Bolshevik threat, he said. He had been preaching vehemently and repeatedly against Bolshevism for a decade and a half. He cited his speech at the Catholic gathering in Salzburg in 1921, when he denounced Bolshevism as "the greatest affliction of our time." He said he had spoken out similarly again in 1921, in 1922, and in 1930. Hitler could rest assured that the Church had long recognized the danger of communism. The Church supported the national government and respected the head of state. But Hitler needed to understand, in no uncertain terms, that the Church did not do this out of "tactical considerations." The Church was willing to obey the laws of the state as long as they did not violate fundamental principles. "I believe that in no religion is the notion of authority emphasized more strongly than in the Catholic Church," he told Hitler. "But certainly when your officials or your laws offend the Church dogma or the laws of morality, and in so doing offend our conscience, then we must be able to articulate this as responsible defenders of moral laws."

The Nazi government, Faulhaber charged, regardless of what it said, had waged war for the last three years on the Catholic Church. Not only were Nazi youth events scheduled on Sunday mornings to keep young people away from communion, but more than six hundred religion teachers had lost their jobs in Bavaria alone, and the number would soon rise to nearly seventeen hundred. Worse still, the state had introduced policies the Church could never endorse, including the sterilization of criminals and people with genetic defects.

Faulhaber lectured for a solid hour, with Hitler listening mostly in silence. However, when Faulhaber complained about radicals, and recalled recent plays, handbills, and speeches calling for the "eradication of Christendom," Hitler protested. He told Faulhaber that "when there was peace between National Socialism and the Church, all that will stop. We have nothing to do with this movement!" Hitler insisted, "I have always told my political party chiefs that I do not want to play the role of the religious reformer," Hitler insisted. "I do not want to do that and I will not do that."

Then they came to Rosenberg, and Hitler revived the argument he had used on Schulte: the Church was to blame for the Rosenberg success. "It wasn't until the bishops' conference in Freising issued a warning about the book, and then the Church placed the book on the Index, that the sales of the book begin to climb, and that it began selling in the hundreds of thousands," Hitler said. Faulhaber said that before the Rosenberg indexing, *Myth* was being promoted across Germany. Equally matched in force of will and conviction, neither man would stand down, with Hitler raising both voice and hand and Faulhaber punctuating his objections with a thunderous *"Herr Reichskanzler!"*

After three hours, Hitler seized the final word. "Herr Cardinal, you should speak to the other leaders of the Church and consider in which way you will support the great task of nationalism not to allow Bolshevism to reign, and how you will come to a peaceful relationship with the state," he threatened. "Either National Socialism and the Church will be victorious, or they will both be destroyed. I am telling you: I will remove all the small things that intervene in peaceful cooperation, like the trials against priests and the German religious movement. I don't want to engage in horse-trading. You know that I am an enemy of compromise, but it should be a last attempt." Then, Hitler's tone softened. He grew reflective.

Anyone, he told Faulhaber, who looked at his own life had to know that at one point each and every person had to face his own mortality: Michael Faulhaber the cardinal, Alfred Rosenberg the best-selling author, and yes, even Adolf Hitler the Führer. "Every individual is nothing," Hitler said. "Everyone will die. Cardinal Faulhaber will die, Alfred Rosenberg will die, Adolf Hitler will die. This makes one introspective and humble before God."

The men rose from the sofa and went downstairs into the dining room, where they sat in a niche overlooking the Untersberg and had a small lunch. They chatted about economic affairs. Faulhaber was impressed by Hitler's capacity to remember facts and details. At two o'clock that afternoon Faulhaber prepared to leave. The rain and fog had dissipated and the sun appeared through the clouds. Faulhaber was reminded of Psalm 29: First there is a storm over Lebanon, but in the end, *Dominus benedicet populo suo in pace*—the Lord will bless his people with peace. Back in Munich, Faulhaber reflected on the day. In a confidential memorandum of the meeting, he wrote that he was convinced Hitler was a man of serious spiritual conviction.

A few days later, Hitler reported to Goebbels on the meeting. He told him that he "had really let him have it." Either they would fight together against Bolshevism or it would be war against the Church.

THAT SAME WEEK in October, the first copies of Hudal's book came off the press. Sitting at his desk on November 3, 1936, Hudal, with a series of elegant flourishes, inscribed the first copy to "the Führer of the German resurrection" and "the Siegfried of German hope and greatness," then forwarded it to Papen for presentation to Hitler. On Saturday, November 14, Papen met with Hitler, along with Goebbels and Martin Bormann, in the Reich Chancellery to press for a final decision on the Hudal book. Papen handed Hitler the handsome brown volume with its gold embossing and personal dedication. Hitler took the book and told Papen he would be certain to read it.

Hudal's *Foundations,* Papen said, had arrived at a time when both the Church and the government were ready for peace between them. He urged Hitler to allow the widest possible distribution of the book in Germany. It offered a chance to bridge the divide that had opened between Germany's National Socialists and Roman Catholics, to heal the public wounds caused by the trials against priests and the debates over *Myth.* Hudal's book embraced the common values of Nazis and German Catholics alike—it recognized the preeminent role of Germany on the Continent, the inherent dangers of Bolshevism, and, though admittedly in moderated form, the centuries-old threat of the Jews. Coming from a senior prelate in the Vatican, *Foundations* also bore a credibility that few other ideological treatises could have. The Hudal book represented a singular opportunity to forge a lasting and meaningful bond between Nazis and Catholics.

Goebbels and Bormann both disagreed with this vehemently. By injecting Roman Catholicism into National Socialist ideology, they argued, Hudal diluted the essence of National Socialism, its grounding in scientific racism. Papen argued that at the very least, a public debate about the book would provide an opportunity to explore the potential for common ground. Goebbels and Bormann said that Hudal's book would be divisive, dangerous, subversive. The debate went on for several tense hours. Each time Papen seemed to have Hitler convinced, Bormann would intervene and pull him back. Ultimately, the party "radicals" prevailed. "In the end, I succeeded in securing the import for two thousand copies with the understanding that these would be distributed to leading circles in the party," Papen later recalled. "The attempt for a serious discussion was ultimately sabotaged." "Hudal's book shot down again," Goebbels wrote in his diary.

When Hudal learned of the result, he was devastated. For all the ambition he had for his book, it had been relegated to a circle of individuals who were unlikely to read, let alone understand, it. *Foundations* had become a footnote.

At roughly the same time, the Vatican distanced itself from Hudal's book in an official statement: "As the author himself has said to an Austrian agency, and based on various solicited remarks, it is declared: namely that in writing his book, he was inspired by no one else and received no official assignment to do so." As the rector of the seminary of Santa Maria dell'Anima, as a prominent bishop with twenty years of service in the Vatican, Hudal was as insulted as he was hurt by this snub. When he complained to a cardinal about this public reprimand, he was told he had gotten off lightly. According to the cardinal, Pius XI had been furious with *Foundations,* and had argued for placing it on the Index. Had it not been deemed "inopportune" to do so, Hudal would have been the first bishop ever to be "indexed." When Hudal attempted to address the matter with the pope himself, he was refused an audience. The Catholic bishops in Germany were equally harsh. They called him a "Nazi bishop." Faulhaber dubbed him Hitler's "court theologian."

Hudal never recovered from the debacle. After the war, he was forced to leave his post in the Vatican, and was relocated to an isolated monastery. The embattled bishop may have taken solace in the Latin verity *habent sua fata libelli*—books have their own fate.

Hudal was spared one final disappointment. When I spread the copy of *Foundations* that Hudal had inscribed to Hitler, I was struck by two quotations on the second flyleaf, clearly intended to bolster Hudal's argument for a "baptized" Nazi movement. One was the quote by Molotov, dating from 1934, claiming that the greatest threat to Bolshevik expansion would be an alliance between the "Catholic and fascist internationals." The second is an extended passage from pages 124 and 125 of *Mein Kampf:* "He who believes that he can move from a political organization to a religious reformation only shows that he has absolutely no idea about the origins of religious faith let alone religious teachings and their theological impact."

This particular volume contains no marginalia, though the first sixteen pages fall open easily as if having been exercised limber by a careful reading. The remainder of the book is held taut by the binding, clutching a message that never made it beyond these tightly bound pages.

BOOK SIX

Divine Inspiration

The human intellect is thus never a prime mover, but rather a result of the interaction between body and soul.

MAXIMILIAN RIEDEL, "Law of the World"

IN THE EARLY 1930S, when the journalist Edward Deuss asked Hitler about the single most revealing sentence in *Mein Kampf*, Hitler answered that it was a short passage on page 11 in which he talks about his interest in history. He then went on to say that an equally consequential influence was his religious upbringing. If Hitler said anything more about the matter, Deuss did not record it. In chapter one of *Mein Kampf*, Hitler speaks only in passing about the "intoxicating" influence of Roman Catholic ritual.

However, Hitler's uncorrected manuscript of *Mein Kampf* suggests a more intense and sustained interest in religious ambition. In the surviving draft pages, Hitler describes his wish to become an abbot as his "highest and most desirable ideal," without the qualifier "for a time, at least, this was the case" that appeared in the published version. Similarly, in these draft pages Hitler's "aspirations" to a high religious station are untempered by the qualifying adjective "temporary." Friends and family also provide witness to Hitler's early obsession with Roman Catholicism. Helene Hanfstaengl recalled that Hitler spoke extensively of his early devotion to Roman Catholicism, how he used to drape a tablecloth over his shoulders, stand on a kitchen stool, and deliver extended sermons to his assembled siblings. Paula recalled her brother once telling her, "I believe the good Lord holds a protective hand over me."

In his after-dinner monologues delivered to his close circle of associates during the Second World War, Hitler returned repeatedly to issues of faith and the spirit, speaking of his attempts to square the rote catechisms of religious teaching with those of biology class—"I confronted the professor of the second hour with what I had learned in the first hour so that the teachers were driven to desperation"—and his gradual alienation from formal religious instruction. It appears to have been left to Dietrich Eckart to spike doubt with hatred, which was recorded in the "Conversation," and which Hitler was echoing two decades later. "The worst blow ever suffered by mankind is Christianity," Hitler observed in one of his evening rants. "Bolshevism is the illegitimate son of Christianity. Both are an outgrowth of the Jew. Through Christianity the world has been filled with the conscious lie in the questions of religion."

The residual Roman Catholicism that Hudal and Papen detected in Hitler was little more than an empty shell, void of meaning. The Nazi rituals, with their twisted crosses and cathedrals of light, were a plagiarized sham, as were his speeches so resonant with biblical allusion; his invocation of the divine was little more than faux spiritual rhetoric full of sound and fury, to quote from volume six of Hitler's collected works of Shakespeare, signifying nothing, rhetoric as empty of meaning as the reflexive or rehearsed—it doesn't matter which—"amen" at the end of that one famously impassioned speech.

What remained of Hitler's vacated spiritual life was the inner architecture that had emerged in his youth, once filled with the intoxicating impressions of the "solemn rituals," and that Hitler spent a lifetime seeking to fill with meaning. It wasn't belief itself he sought but that more fundamental human impulse, the need to believe, to understand, and to explain the deeper forces that move and shape our world.

"There exists in every human being the intuitive capacity to comprehend the forces that we call God," Hitler once observed. "The church exploited this inner capacity by threatening to punish those who did not believe what was supposed to be believed." According to Hitler, the Church had crippled this intuitive capacity and instrumentalized it for partisan purposes. How was it, he wondered, that there were two billion people on earth and 170 major religions, each praying to a different deity? "A hundred and sixty-nine of them have to be wrong," he declared, "because only one of them can be right." It was a cynical observation to be sure, but one rooted in the sentiments of the searching agnostic rather than the confirmed atheist, and one to which Hitler returned repeatedly during his monologues.

Traudl Junge, one of Hitler's longtime secretaries, was present for many of these extended musings on man, nature, religion, and God. When I visited her in her Munich apartment in the summer of 2002, she confirmed Hitler's preoccupation with matters of the spirit, not only in his monologues but also in his nighttime readings. Though she refused to ascribe to Hitler a particular spiritual conviction—"How can we know what another person truly believes?"—she was certain he believed in the existence of a deeper force that moved the world as evidenced in the laws of nature, of the presence of a deeper intelligence, or, as he himself said, of a "creative force" that gave shape and meaning to the world.

THE SURVIVING BOOKS in Hitler's library on spiritual and occult matters, of which there are scores, are perhaps the most articulate witnesses to Hitler's lifelong preoccupation. Many of the books were acquired in the early 1920s, and others are from the final years of his life. Among them are Peter Maag's *Realm of God and the Contemporary World,* published in 1915, with "A. Hitler" scrawled on the inside cover, but without date or place-name; an undated reprint of *Anulus Platonis,* an eighteenth-century mystical classic on occult sciences, inscribed to "Adolf," with two pages of handwritten alchemical symbols; more tendentious books, such as a 1922 account of paranormal phenomena, *The Dead Are Alive!,*

which features examples of "occultism, somnambulism and spiritualism" in various European countries, and provides sixteen photographs
as "incontrovertible proof" of supernatural moments. One grainy black-
and-white image shows four people at a 1909 séance in Genoa levitating
a table. Another reveals "the ghost" of a fifteen-year-old Polish girl, Sta-

This reprint of a seventeenth-century alchemical
treatise, Secret Sciences, *belongs to a cache of*
occult books acquired by Hitler in the 1920s
and 1930s.

sia, being consumed by a "luminous, misty substance." A picture of a stately looking Englishman is captioned "The Phantom of the English writer Charles Dickens who died in 1871 and is buried in Westminster Abbey. He appeared in 1873 and was photographed." The earliest such book is a 165-page treatise called *The Essence of Creation: Research About This World and the Afterlife, About the Essential Truths of Nature, About the Substance of the Soul and the Resulting Conclusions,* published in 1914, with an undated handwritten inscription to "Mr. Adolf Hitler" by the author.

Several of these early books found their way to Berlin and ultimately into the *Führerbunker,* where they were discovered after Hitler's suicide, and today are in the rare book collection at Brown University. Others were taken from his Berghof library, including a 1934 German translation of *Body, Spirit and Living Reason,* by Dicaiarchos Carneades, a handsome, leather-bound tome that explores the complex of interactions—"philosophy, history, religion, monoism, dualism, pleiadism and myriadism"—underlying the human decision-making process. And still others were discovered among the crated volumes taken from the Berchtesgaden salt mine that are now at the Library of Congress.

A number of these books contain marginalia that correspond to similar marked passages in Hitler's books at Brown University, suggesting a common authorship. Despite the absence of handwritten comments that would permit definitive attribution, there is a notable alignment between these marginalia and ideas expressed in Hitler's monologues and other recorded comments. Like footprints in the sand, they do not necessarily reveal the purpose of the journey, but they do allow us to see where his attention caught and lingered, where it rushed ahead, where a question was raised or an impression formed. In these books one finds Hitler's pencil repeatedly drawn to passages related to the connection between the scientific and the spiritual, between the material and immaterial worlds. In one book, on the "future state," published in 1910 but with no indication when Hitler may have acquired it, he has written his last name on the inside cover in pencil, in carefully articulated script.

On page 391, pencil markings indicate the passage "Whoever goes far enough in science, becomes accustomed to going from miracle to miracle, without ever coming to an end," a sentiment echoed in Hitler's monologues. "That which distinguishes the human being from the animal, possibly the most remarkable proof of the superiority of the human being is that he has comprehended the existence of a creative force," Hitler observed. "You need only to look through a telescope or a microscope: There you can understand that the human being has the capacity to comprehend these laws."

In Hitler's copy of the 1924 collection of essays by Carl Ludwig Schleich, I found a series of penciled markings in a chapter exploring the relationship between cellular biology, immortality, and human knowledge. "What I physically succeeded in creating in this life through struggle, exertion and suffering, I give back a billion-fold with my immortal cells, just like this small spark of life I call myself returns to the organic property of the earth, my spiritual self belongs to the universe," Schleich observes, with the pencil following in the margin. "There it will find new forms as it slowly rises until it achieves equality with the collective soul of the world, and will rejoice at the opportunity to nourish a star with a being that is based upon my purified effigy."

We find near identical passages marked in a 1923 handbook on the "history, theory and practice" of the occult by Ernst Schertel. In this handsome, red-linen volume bearing the Hitler bookplate and Schertel's "respectful" dedication, Hitler has marked a passage in which Schertel cites Schleich, quoting almost verbatim from him: "Our body presents a collection of potential and kinetic world energies and extends beyond to other lineages through animals, plants and crystal down to the very beginning of things." Hitler's pencil traces the passage in the margin. "In our body rests the entire history of the world, beginning with the birth of the first star. Through our body flows the energies of the universe, from the eternal to the eternal. And these drive the mills of our existence." Hitler recast this same pantheistic vision in his own words one

-3-

V o r w o r t

Vorliegendes Buch, in welchem erstmals das

G e s e t z d e r W e l t

veröffentlicht wird, hat den Zweck, den grossen Umbruch der
Weltanschauung des 20.Jahrhunderts in einer zeitlosen Sach-
lichkeit der natürlichen Ursachen und Gründe zu erklären.
       Der Inhalt dieses Buches stützt sich in keiner
Weise auf eine zeitliche Politik oder Konfession, sondern
stellt lediglich die Tatsachen und n a t ü r l i c h e n
Wahrheiten fest, welche die Grundlagen jeder Politik und
Religion bilden.
       In verständlicher Form beginnt dieses Buch mit dem
~~Anfang des~~ Ur - Geschehens, um bei dem wahren praktischen
Wert der gegenwärtigen Weltanschauung zu enden.
       Als wesentlich N e u bringe ich Klarheit über
die   n a t u r g e s e t z l i c h e   D r e i e i n i g k e i t
des Daseins- und Gottbegriffes und deren Erkenntnis durch die
z w ö l f menschlichen Sinne. Weiterhin, den ursächlichen
und zusammenhängenden Beweis für die Richtigkeit der not-
wendig gewordenen neuen Weltanschauung der Gegenwart.
       Möge dieses Werk all denen ein Wegweiser sein,
welche sich aus den bestehenden Teilwerten unseres Wissens
und Empfindens kein k l a r e s Weltbild machen können.

München, den ~~21.Juni~~ 1939   *1937/*

Maximilian Riedel
München – Grünwald
oberhachingerweg 1

z.Zt. Feldpost - Nr. 37513 A

*The cover page to an unpublished manuscript titled "Law of the World,"
sent to Hitler by Max Riedel in August 1939.*

evening in December 1941, while musing on suicide. "Even if you take
your own life, you simply return to nature as much in substance as in
spirit and soul," he said, repeating the theme a few days later and arriving at the same conclusion drawn by Schleich and Schertel. "The notion
of eternity is fundamental to our nature," he said. "Spirit and soul defi-

nitely return to a collective reservoir—like the body. As the substance of life, we thereby fertilize the foundation from which new life emerges."

Unquestionably, the most interesting of the works I found among the esoteric volumes is an unpublished treatise called "Law of the World," by Maximilian Riedel, which includes a two-page diagram outlining the linkages between the physical and spiritual worlds, describes the techniques by which one accesses the deeper wisdoms embedded in the natural world, and bears repeated penciled intrusions in passages related to the relationship between the natural and spiritual worlds.

Today, this somewhat battered, 326-page typewritten manuscript, mimeographed and bound and subtitled "The Coming Religion," is catalogued in the Library of Congress as BR856.R49. The preface is dated June 21, 1939, with the year 1937 written above it in blue pencil, possibly suggesting that the text was two years in the making. The word *manuscript* has been scrawled across the cover page in bold red letters, with an additional scribbled blue-pencil notation: "Appeal for the recognition of the existence of God." It is clearly a work in progress. Accompanying the manuscript is a typewritten letter addressed to Hitler and dated August 7, 1939, claiming that this "new discovery" provides "incontrovertible scientific evidence" of "the concept of the trinity of God as a natural law."

WHEN RIEDEL ENTRUSTED his unpublished manuscript to Anni Winter, the housekeeper at Hitler's Prince Regent Square apartment, in August 1939, Hitler was summering at his Alpine retreat on the Obersalzberg. He had spent the previous week in Bayreuth, where he attended performances of *Tristan and Isolde*, *The Flying Dutchman*, and the entire *Ring of the Nibelungen*, including the monumental climax, *Twilight of the Gods*, in which the Nibelungen empire crashes into ruin and the waters of the Rhine rise to cleanse the earth of greed and failed ambition.

Hitler's cultivated leisure activity belied the tensions of that politically overheated summer, as Europe tottered on the brink of war. On his return to the Berghof on August 4, Hitler found a terse message from the Polish government bluntly rejecting his proposals to resolve escalating antagonism between Poland and Germany. On August 7, the day Riedel posted his manuscript, Hitler summoned Alfred Forster to the Berghof to discuss the growing crisis.

As Hitler's "man in Danzig," this former storm trooper had spent the last nine years building the party structure in that city and fomenting unrest among its three hundred thousand German residents. He exhibited the steely, rough-edged belligerence Hitler liked to see in his top lieutenants. When the League of Nations delegated Carl J. Burckhardt to the free city as its high commissioner, Forster welcomed the cultivated Swiss diplomat with disarmingly easy ungraciousness: "So, you are the representative from this Jewish-Freemason gossip club in Geneva!"

Hitler spent much of the day with Forster, discussing the situation in Danzig and the appropriate German response to the Polish missive, then sent him back to Danzig only to recall him three days later, this time in the company of Burckhardt. On August 11, Forster and Burckhardt boarded a two-engine Douglas aircraft in Danzig and flew to Salzburg. There they were met by a car that transported them to Berchtesgaden, and from there to the Obersalzberg, past the Berghof, then up a series of dramatic, serpentine switchbacks hewn into shear rock that brought them to the Kehlsteinhaus, a massive stone house perched atop a knife's-edge cliff. They were greeted by a stunning vista of snowcapped peaks cast against a flawless blue sky and Adolf Hitler, dressed in a formal blue suit.

"I hope you had a comfortable flight," Hitler said in welcoming Burckhardt with casual graciousness. "My Condor aircraft is not as fast as the Douglas, but it is more solid and useful as a military aircraft." He then added ominously, "It holds up better under gunfire."

Hitler told Burckhardt that he knew it had been a stressful week. He talked about Forster's efforts to ameliorate the situation, of German patience, of growing Polish intransigence. Forster was a patient man,

Hitler said, and so was he, but they had their limits. Hitler expressed particular annoyance at the belligerent tone of the missive he had received from Warsaw upon his return from Bayreuth. "Last Friday I would have been satisfied with a telephone call from them," he said. "The Poles knew that talks were possible. They did not have to send a note."

The two men spent the next several hours discussing both the politics and "technicalities" of the failed peace negotiations, with Hitler repeatedly billowing into a rage. He refused to be served ultimatums. He would not be ridiculed in the press. He would not be accused of having lost his nerve. "If the slightest incident occurs," Hitler said threateningly, "I will smash the Poles so completely that not a single trace of Poland will be found afterwards. Like a lightning bolt I will strike with the full power of my mechanized army, the power of which the Poles have no idea. Mark my words."

Burckhardt sought to calm the Nazi leader, expressing sympathy for his concerns but also cautioning that an armed conflict with Poland would necessarily ignite a larger war. "If I must lead Germany into war then I would rather do it today than tomorrow," Hitler said, again with rising temper. "I will not lead it the way Wilhelm II did. He let pangs of conscience keep him from throwing in his armed forces completely. I will fight to the very last."

"A new war will usher in the end of civilization," Burckhardt warned. "That is a great responsibility to bear for the future." He suggested it was better "to live in honor" than to burden oneself with the responsibility for war. "The stronger one is, the longer one can be patient," he counseled. "The more honor a man has, the more attacks he can fend off. Someone once said to me that Germany's strength lies in being patient when it comes to the Polish and Danzig questions." Hitler brightened and told Forster to note the remark for his foreign minister. They continued to discuss details of the crisis. At one point, Hitler rose from his chair and suggested they go for a walk. Leaving the massive stone building, they walked onto the craggy ridge to gaze across the towering peaks that even in late summer were still blanketed in white. Hitler paused to take in the view. "How happy I am when I am here," he said. "I have had enough trouble. I need my rest."

"You are expressing the sentiments of the entire world," Burckhardt said, then underscored Hitler's singular role in the world. "You more than anyone have the chance to give the world the peace and quiet it needs."

As they strolled, Hitler grew meditative. He spoke about the singular nature of the German people. They were a true nation-state— *Volksstaat*—unified by blood and soil, he said. That is what made the Germans different, say, from the British, who commanded an empire cobbled together from different races, a mongrel assemblage of peoples. Burckardt responded that all peoples were essentially the same, that human nature was universal, united by a common desire for peace. *"Paix, Pax, Pacts,"* he informed Hitler. "These words all have the same root." He reminded Hitler that the German word for "peace," *Friede,* derived from the same linguistic root as that for "happiness," *Freude.*

Hitler let the remark pass and returned to his wounded pride, to the insults he had endured, to his determination to protect German interests in Poland at any price. His mood darkened yet again. "I am not bluffing," he told Burckhardt. "If even the slightest incident occurs in Danzig or anything happens to our minorities, I will strike hard."

By any measure, this isolated cliff in the Bavarian Alps, five thousand feet above sea level with a dramatic snowcapped panorama, was an unlikely place for a high commissioner of the League of Nations to meet a head of state to discuss alleviating tensions in a Baltic port city, not to mention averting "the end of civilization." But it was the sort of theatricality that Hitler preferred to underscore his place in politics and the world, similar to the power conveyed by the Colosseum on the ancient Romans, or the fabled domes of the Kremlin on the rulers of Russia, whether tsarist or communist, or the mirrored galleries of Versailles, which the French used to impress their allies and awe potential opponents and, in 1919, to humiliate the Germans.

In Berlin, Hitler had constructed representational spaces such as the

New Reich Chancellery, and had plans for grander spaces yet, but he chose this mountain in the Bavarian Alps for conceiving and engineering many of his most momentous acts of governance. It was at the Berghof, halfway down the slope from the Kehlsteinhaus, that he had sparred with Cardinal Faulhaber on matters of the spirit, browbeat the Austrian chancellor Kurt Schussnig into annexing Austria to Germany, charmed Neville Chamberlain into dismembering Czechoslovakia, and was now orchestrating the ethnic unrest that would serve as the prelude to the invasion of Poland. He would stand with a guest before the massive picture window, with its view of the Untersberg, as if to say, This is my realm, this my power. When weather permitted, the window could be retracted, permitting an unobstructed view of the imposing stone face. He claimed to have designed the entire Berghof with this view in mind.

Hitler sought both refuge and inspiration in the natural world. Ever since that morning in the spring of 1923 when he had stood on the balcony of the guesthouse Pension Moritz and looked across the valley at the snowcapped mountain, the Untersberg had exercised a magnetic power over him. "A view of the Untersberg, indescribable!" Hitler recalled. "The Obersalzberg became something magnificent for me. I fell completely in love with that landscape."

When Helene Bechstein offered Hitler a piece of property on another, sunnier part of the Obersalzberg, he declined her generous offer. He preferred the view to the Untersberg. He would eventually code-name the invasion of the Soviet Union, the largest land assault in history, "Operation Barbarossa," after the medieval German emperor whose spirit was said to reside within the Untersberg. The very geography of his second-floor study spoke to the centrality of this mountain in his life. Seated at his writing desk in the center of the book-lined room, with its overstuffed armchairs and brass lamps, Hitler looked through a pair of French doors, flanked by oil portraits of his parents, with a view of the Untersberg and the rolling hills of Austria beyond, a sight line that at a glance represented a personal fusion of "blood and soil," his personal genealogy linked to his native soil. "Yes, I am closely attached to

The Berghof guestbook, designed by Frieda Thiersch
and inscribed by numerous visiting dignitaries.
It was taken at the end of the war by a French officer.

this mountain," Hitler once observed. "There is much that happened there, that came and passed. They were the most wonderful times of my life." He was particularly attached to the original house around which he constructed the Berghof. "All my great plans were conceived here," he claimed.

Surviving members of the Berghof staff—Anni Wilkins, Hitler's housekeeper in the old Haus Wachenfels before its conversion into the Berghof; Herbert Döring, the Berghof estate manager; Gretl Mittl-strasser, who ran the Berghof after Hitler's sister departed—recounted numerous stories of Hitler's private "communing" on the property: when the guests and entourage had departed; when he paced hour-long circles in the garden, his head bowed, his arms locked behind his back; when he held late-night vigils on the Berghof balcony, watching the Untersberg bathed in moonlight; when he let the ethereal strains of Wagner's *Lohengrin* fill his study as he watched the jagged cliffs peek through the enfolding mists. They described symmetries of mood and spirit between Hitler and this mountain. With its patches of green mead-ows, its sheer cliffs, and a mantle of snow that draped its summit for most of the year, the Untersberg could be ominous and threatening at

Hitler sitting at the window of his Alpine retreat on the Obersalzberg. He once said that his "great plans" were conceived here.

one turn, as on the afternoon of the Schussnig visit, and deceptively comforting and reassuring at another, as it was when Cardinal Faulhaber watched the cloud cover lift and was reminded of the storm that cleared over Lebanon and—*Dominus benedicet populo suo in pace*—the Lord had seemed to bless the world with peace.

In August 1939, the Untersberg played center stage in a natural drama that reflected the ominous political mood of those weeks when the night sky along the northern horizon was illuminated by a particularly intense display of the aurora borealis—as was widely reported in the press—that washed the cragged mountain in a turquoise hue that gradually transformed into a deep violet that became an "eerily beautiful" red glow. "At first we thought it was a large fire in one of the towns north of the Untersberg," recalled Nicolaus von Below, who watched the display with Hitler on the Berghof terrace, "until the red light engulfed the entire northern sky and it became evident that this was an unusually intense display of the northern lights, a natural phenomenon that rarely occurred in southern Germany." Awed by the eerie scene, Hitler's adjutant suggested that it was perhaps a sign of an imminent and bloody war. "If it has to be, then as quickly as possible," Hitler replied. The longer wars lasted, he said, the bloodier they became. By then, Maximilian Riedel's "Law of the World" had been waiting for Hitler at his apartment in Munich for nearly three weeks.

RIEDEL MADE A SMART tactical move when he entrusted his manuscript to Anni Winter. By August 1939, most of the hundreds of books sent to Hitler were intercepted by either Albert Bormann, who ran Hitler's office at the Reich Chancellery in Berlin, or Bormann's older brother Martin, who oversaw Hitler's affairs on the Obersalzberg. Manipulative, self-serving, power-mongering, and riven by sibling rivalry, the Bormann brothers filtered all but the most important queries, requests, complaints, appointments, and gifts from Hitler's life. Only books from close

Hitler associates made their way into his hands. The chances of his see-ing a typewritten manuscript by a distant admirer were negligible. Anni Winter therefore proved to be a convenient back door to Hitler. Few people had as intimate and proximate access.

Winter had been resident in Hitler's Munich apartment for nearly a decade. During the war, she locked the basement air raid shelters, and told the building's residents that if she had fifty gallons of petrol she would not hesitate to set the building on fire with them in it. Her neigh-bors, unsurprisingly, found her "vulgar" and "disagreeable"; Hitler liked her spunk as well as her discretion. When his niece, Geli, committed sui-cide in the apartment in September 1931, Winter called Hitler before giv-ing a brief and terse deposition to the police, and never discussed the matter again. Bonded with Hitler by tragedy, Winter became family. Hitler left her a lifelong stipend in his handwritten will from May 1938, a commitment he repeated seven years later in his "bunker testament." Beside Eva Braun, Anni Winter was the only other beneficiary men-tioned by name.*

It is unclear when Winter passed Riedel's "Law of the World" to Hitler, but his schedule in the overheated days of August 1939 had him traveling directly to Berlin and from there to Poland, where he remained for most of September and much of October. He returned to Munich on November 8, when he attended the annual commemoration of the Beer Hall Putsch, and again on November 11, when he was briefly back in town. He most likely saw the Riedel manuscript during a two-day stay later that month, from November 25 to 26, when he spent an overnight at his Prince Regent Square apartment.

Riedel's cover letter would have spoken to him:

---

* In the early 1950s, Winter was arrested for attempting to sell a suitcase full of Hitler's per-sonal documents, including his passport, his gun permit, a number of watercolors, and photographs of his parents, for a hundred thousand marks on the black market. In her defense, Winter claimed Hitler had given them to her. The cache of material is now in the Bavarian main state archives in Munich.

My Führer!

Based on a new discovery I have been able to prove with incontrovertible scientific evidence the concept of the trinity of God as a natural law. One of the results of this discovery is, among other things, the seamless relationship between the terms: Truth-Law-Duty-Honor. In essence, the origins of all science, philosophy and religion. The significance of this discovery has led me to ask Frau Winter to hand to you personally the enclosed manuscript.

Heil my Führer!

Like Carneades's *Body, Soul and Living Reason,* with its chapters on the "Quantitative and Geometric Definition of Material," "Chemical, Biological and Psychological Knowledge and Science," and the "Aristotelian, Immaterial Dualistic Definition of the Spirit," Riedel seemed to be promising Hitler insights into the spiritual world based on the sort of "scientific evidence" Hans Günther had provided for understanding the superiority of the Aryan race. It was just the sort of thing Hitler liked. Through extensive scientific research, Riedel had determined that beyond the five known senses, the human being possessed additional perceptive capacities that had gone unrecognized and that existed in a vestigial state. By identifying and cultivating these untapped cognitive abilities, a person was able to access reserves of knowledge and insight, to connect to the deeper forces that moved the world, those universal "reservoirs" of knowledge described by Carl Ludwig Schleich and Ernst Schertel. To support his thesis, Riedel provided definitions and descriptions, detailed lists that charted various relationships between the physical and spiritual worlds, and a two-page foldout diagram that charted his theory with a series of intersecting spheres linked by a spiderweb of connecting lines—soul, space, reality, present, past, possibility, transformation, culture, afterlife, humanity, infinity—and included a series of Aristotelian progressions: solid-liquid-gas; hate-love-devotion; fact-knowledge-wisdom.

In this densely written treatise, Riedel establishes the groundwork for his "new religion," replacing the "trinity" of the Father, Son, and Holy Ghost with a new tripartite unity, the *Körper, Geist, und Seele*—body, mind, and soul. He argues that the traditional five senses—sight, sound, taste, smell, and touch—relate only to physical perceptions, permitting us to interact with the material world but blinding us to the more profound dynamics underlying our relationship to other human beings and to the deeper forces of the universe, a position Hitler himself advanced. "We will at best learn about the laws that determine the nature of life, or at the very least apply this knowledge to make the laws of nature serve us, but why these laws have the power they do we will never know," Hitler once observed. "Our position in the world does not allow us to look into other levels. Therefore the human being has invented the wonderful concept of the almighty whose powers he reveres."

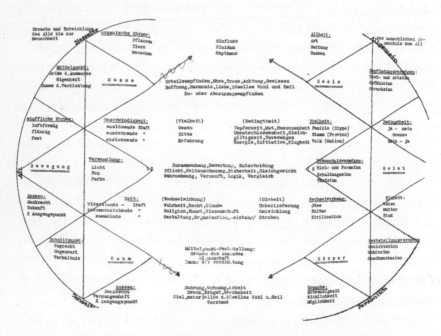

*Linkages between the physical and spiritual worlds as outlined by
Max Riedel "Law of the World."*

Based on the penciled intrusions in "Law of the World," Hitler was particularly taken with the chapter in which Riedel discusses the human being's seven additional perceptive capacities, identified by Riedel as those that transcend the superficial perception of the world and touch on deeper universal knowledge. On page 43, Hitler highlights a passage affirming what he had previously encountered in his readings of Schleich and Schertel: "The body, mind and soul do not belong to the individual, they belong to the universe." By cultivating our emotional perceptions, our emotional "sense" of others, our "sense" of racial belonging, our "sense" of nature, we can develop a cognitive emotional intelligence that transcends the pure objective logic driving most people's decision-making. In affirmation of Riedel's thesis, Hitler marks a passage on page 45: "The human intellect is thus never a prime mover, but rather a result of the interaction between body and soul"; and another on page 47, where Riedel expounds on the limited cognitive value of relying on the five recognized human senses and the misleading notion of "objectivity" that results: "The problem with being objective is that we use objective criteria as the basis for human understanding in general," Riedel writes and Hitler affirms, "which means that the objective criteria, that is, the rational criteria, end up serving as the basis for all human understanding, perception, and decision-making." By cultivating and engaging the additional seven senses identified by Riedel, a person is able to tap the deeper forces of the world, and is thus able to achieve that unity of body, mind, and soul.

In these marked passages we find echoes of similar highlighted sentences and paragraphs from Hitler's copies of the books of Schleich and Schertel. In a Schleich essay on "genius and talent" from *The Wisdom of Joy,* Hitler has repeatedly marked passages related to individuals of exceptional talent, underlining a sentence about genius as a "singular creation"; double-striking a passage in which Schleich describes genius as "the materialization of the divine" that is both "incomprehensible" to and "unrecognized" by the common man; highlighting a paragraph that explores the relationship between genius and politics in which Hitler underlines a sentence; and once again double-striking passages on pages 26 and 27, in which Schleich talks about the relationship between politics and genius and the fact that "genius belongs to all mankind."

We can follow Hitler's pencil tracing Schleich's edifying musings on genius into Schertel's "handbook" on the occult, where Hitler again marks a passage by Schleich linking the biological and the spiritual with the political:

> Everything of the mind and spirit, whether right or wrong, infects like a bacillus, it transcends the rhythm of thoughts viscerally; therefore ideas have won such great power over the masses. Ideas are infectious and those which emerge from the individual as incontrovertible observations, as concentration of the spirit, can lead to explosive, dynamite-like constructions that can be released like an avalanche begun by the footsteps of a bird on packed snowflakes.

Hitler draws a thick line beside this passage on page 69 of Schertel's book *Magie,* then traces Schertel's reflections on Schleich's observations. Schertel notes, with Hitler's pencil in train, that the great cultures of the past would be unthinkable without the grand ideas that were willed into existence by individuals of "imaginative power," who were not "slaves" to empirical realities, who could imagine a world and then will it into existence through the force of their personality. Schertel describes this creative genius as the "truly ektropic," an energizing force possessed of demonic qualities that is capable of shaping the course of the world.

Like Riedel, Schertel underscores the limits of rational thinking and calls for a deeper perception of the world that permits one to sense its "predetermined fate" and thereby help shape the course of events. "Every man of genius possesses this power and all nations whose histories have not simply 'run their course' have possessed this," Schertel writes, Hitler's pencil following along as Schertel outlines his notion of the "demonic" forces inherent to the "ektropism."

In contrast to Riedel, Schertel posits the notion of the modern "European human type" who has become "calcified" by rational thinking, who has given over to the "thoughtless form of thinking," to an empty form of European rationalism. "One has always said that the European has the capacity for a particularly well-developed 'sense of reality,' 'sense for facts,' etc.," Schertel writes. "But a closer look shows that he looks right past 'reality' and 'facts,' and that what he holds in his hands are empty images. The entire materialism and rationalism of our era is in complete contradiction to the deeper sense of reality and facts." Beside this passage, and in the paragraphs that follow, Hitler has drawn a series of extended dense lines.

Schertel writes of a "mollified" and "castrated" European who had lost the will to determine the course of events, of the need for the "ektropic," powers "beyond good and evil," that can break the constraints imposed by modern society and give birth to a new world, against which society is powerless to resist. Schertel admits that such forces are often perceived as "antagonistic," even "evil," but that they in fact create their own systems of norms. With the "ektropic" dynamic there is no such thing as "real" or "unreal," as "true" or "false," as "right" or "wrong." Only when this completely irrational, amoral, apersonal force has consumed us can we perceive these values.

Here we glimpse at least a portion of Hitler's essential core. It was less a distillation of the philosophies of Schopenhauer or Nietzsche than a dime-store theory cobbled together from cheap, tendentious paperbacks and esoteric hardcovers, which provided the justification for a thin, calculating, bullying mendacity.

It was Schertel's "ektropic" man, not Schopenhauer's genius of will, or even Nietzsche's "new man" born beyond good and evil, who greeted Carl Burckhardt on that airy crag above the Obersalzberg in early August 1939, who seemed to possess the ability to "usher in the end of civilization," and it was this same "ektropic" man who stood two weeks later in the great hall of the Berghof, framed against the imposing face of the Untersberg, and told his generals of his decision to go to war.

On Tuesday morning, August 22, 1939, Hitler assembled his general staff, fifty men in two rows of chairs, in the great hall and informed them that the time had come for the invasion of Poland. Before detailing the plans for his military operation, he made it clear that the outcome of the upcoming war was ultimately to be determined not by military equipment or carefully weighed strategies but by the force of personality. With a calculating perceptiveness of the current political scene, Hitler enumerated the qualities of the personalities to be considered in the coming conflict. Mussolini was a force with which to be reckoned, and could be considered an ally. In Spain, Franco had his own war and would remain neutral. "On the other side, a negative picture, as far as decisive personalities are concerned," Hitler said. "There is no outstanding personality in England or France." He had negotiated with them. He knew they were no match for him. "Our enemies have men who are below average," Hitler declared. "No personalities, no masters, no men of action." Hitler himself was the protean force, the man who by his very will and personality would determine the course of events. "Essentially, it depends on me, my existence, because of my political activity," Hitler said. "Furthermore, the fact that probably no one will ever again have the confidence of the whole German people as I do. There will probably never again be a man with more authority. My existence is, therefore, a factor of great value."

Hitler then provided explicit and detailed instructions on the strategy, tactics, and timing of the invasion. As Hitler spoke, he invoked words he had read in Anton Drexler's *Awakening* back in the autumn of 1919, and had repeated frequently in the intervening decades. The generals and other officers listened dutifully. Hitler had given instructions that no notes were to be taken, but Franz Halder, the German army chief of staff, ignored Hitler's request and recorded the proceedings, as was his habit at all military briefings. Halder was a stocky, humorless, taciturn man with steely blue eyes. He disliked Hitler intensely and had assumed his position the previous year, in his words, to prevent Hitler from doing "any more damage." He now found himself writing notes like none he had ever before taken:

> Goal: Extermination of Poland—Elimination of its living existence. It is not about achieving a specific line or a new border, rather it is the extermination of the enemy that must be sought through ever new and repeated means.
>
> Excuse for attack: Any reason will do. The victor is never questioned whether his reasons were justified. It has nothing to do with having good cause. Only victory matters.

For a general such as Halder—from a proud lineage of three hundred years of military tradition, who had trained under his own father in the Third Royal Bavarian Field Artillery Regiment Prince Leopold and gone on to serve with distinction in the First World War, earning an Iron Cross First Class in the early months of the fighting—it was clear, as it was to the assembled military staff, that this would be a war without precedent, an armed conflict the likes of which the world had never seen, conducted by a man who seemed to have no regard for military convention, not politically, not strategically, not tactically, not ethically, and certainly not rationally.

BOOK SEVEN

Frontline Reading, 1940

That Wilhelm II could bear to hear the truth and also valued it is evident
from a statement he made on the deathbed of his longtime general adjutant,
Field Marshal Wilhelm von Hahnke, on February 8, 1912. "The only man
who always told me the truth."

Schlieffen: A Study of His Life and Character
for the German People, by HUGO ROCHS, 1921 .

THIS SLENDER, NINETY-TWO-PAGE VOLUME, by Alfred Graf von
Schlieffen's personal physician, was evidently designed to impress,
with its solemn Teutonic dignity. The name "Schlieffen" is printed in
bold crimson Fraktur type across an amber field of textured linen with
the author's name and subtitle rendered, also in Fraktur, in rich forest
green. Published in 1921, *Schlieffen* is a "character study" of the legendary
Prussian count known as much for his humane wisdom as for his strategic genius. When urged to bombard Paris during the Franco-Prussian
War, Schlieffen declined, refusing to subject civilians to unnecessary
harm for military purposes.

Schlieffen also cautioned Germans against a two-front war, and was
an advocate of strategic retreat; sometimes it was necessary to sacrifice a
province temporarily to save a country. Most notably he authored the
"Schlieffen Plan," which provided for the invasion of France by the stun-
ningly effective flanking maneuver through the Low Countries, the
blueprint for Germany's dramatic early advances in 1914, one year after
his death, and again in modified form in 1939, to even greater effect.

Hitler's copy of Schlieffen *by Hugo Rochs*

Along with providing a brief biography of his former patient, Hugo Rochs intended his book to serve as a "character study for the German people" by presenting the stately, monocled count as the embodiment of Prussian virtues: diligence, modesty, humanity. Rochs recalls that Schlieffen, after his victory at Königgrätz, bowed to the surrendering Austrian generals in recognition of a battle well fought. His operative aphorism was "Be more than you appear to be, achieve much, boast little." As if to underscore this point, Rochs dispenses with Count von Schlieffen's aristocratic signifier in the book's title and text.

Schlieffen is a hagiography to be sure, but one whose intentions are noble: a "character profile" intended to instill pride, to inspire and to instruct, to remind German readers of the essential humanity and dignity at the core of the Prussian military traditions. It thus seems disconcertingly out of place to open this slender volume of moderated militarism and find the following inscription scrawled across the inside cover:

Meinem Führer gewidmet
Motto: "so-oder-so"
Sieg Heil, Kannenberg, 19.5.1940

Everything about the inscription by Artur "Willy" Kannenberg offends. The crude, haphazard scrawl of the letters, the glaring red of the grease pencil, the implied ruthlessness of the motto, *"so-oder-so"* ("one way or another")—regardless of the means, the costs, or the consequences—and especially the ideologically charged closing saluta-

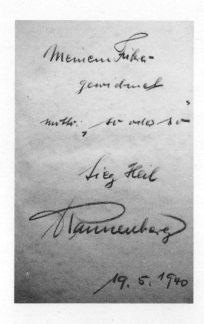

tion, "Sieg Heil," that emblematic greeting of the Nazi movement, military in tone but political in intent.

Most handwritten inscriptions in Hitler's books are scripted in a practiced hand and designed to embody the admiration, even reverence, they convey in form and content. Leni Riefenstahl expresses "deep admiration" in a hand as feminine and alluring as her person. Heinrich Himmler avers his "loyal obedience" in careful, practiced script. Hermann Göring offers a biography of himself "to my Führer" in both "loyalty and admiration."

In contrast, Kannenberg's inscription is casual, jocular, mildly presumptuous. The motto belongs not to him but to Hitler, a catchphrase he frequently invoked to express his single-mindedness of purpose. Whether in politics or personal affairs, through kindness and generosity or deceit, bribery, and brutality, whatever it took to get things done: *so-oder-so*. Another favored Hitler adage: *"wenn schon, denn schon."* If you do something, then do it without hesitation or consideration, fully, vigorously, ruthlessly.

Kannenberg quotes Hitler to Hitler with the same casual confidence, the same easy intimacy, with which he scrawls his own name, simply "Kannenberg." And when Kannenberg writes "my Führer," he means exactly that, in the most proprietary sense of the word, his friend the Führer.

Kannenberg did not belong to the clutch of lieutenants and confidants such as Goebbels, Göring, Bormann, Speer, and Himmler, or to the half dozen other close associates whose company and informal counsel Hitler kept. He belonged instead to that intimate inner circle who knew Hitler as *der Chef*, or "the boss": his valets and adjutants such as Otto Günsche, Julius Schaub, Heinz Linge, and Hans Junge; his quartet of secretaries, Johanna Wolf, Gerda Daranowski, Christa Schröder, and Traudl Junge; his private pilot, Hans Baur; and his chauffeur, Erich Kempka.

These are the handsome figures who populate the periphery of period photographs, nameless and meaningless to history, but individuals whom Hitler considered "family," into whose personal lives he constantly inquired and occasionally interfered. He insisted that his Berghof manager, Herbert Döring, marry a maid who was carrying Döring's child. He urged Traudl Humps to wed Hans Junge, and he served as best man at the wedding of Erich Kempka. He treated them like family but could fire them on the spot. Among this tight, incestuous, and cloying circle, Kannenberg was unique.

As the *Hausintendant* of the Reich Chancellery, the director of Hitler's social affairs, Kannenberg was responsible for orchestrating gala events for state visits and artistic receptions, but his purview was in fact much broader. In 1936, when Hitler expelled his half-sister, Angela Raubal, as his housekeeper and resident hostess at the Berghof, he regularly brought in Kannenberg and his wife to prepare the Alpine residence for visits by dignitaries. At Christmas, Hitler dispatched Kannenberg to scour the finest shops in Berlin for gifts, which Kannenberg then displayed for review on the dining room table in Hitler's Reich Chancellery apartment.

Kannenberg was a heavyset, thick-necked, ruddy, middle-aged man possessed of casual arrogance, a disarmingly ingratiating manner, and a quick wit. His coquettish, dark-haired beauty of a wife ran a flower shop in Berlin's fashionable Adlon Hotel. Hitler first met Kannenberg in the early 1930s, at Uncle Tom's Cabin, a small restaurant Kannenberg ran near Berlin's Anhalter train station and which was frequented by Göring and Goebbels. Hitler was so taken with the vegetarian cuisine and Kannenberg's easy style that he hired him to help run the Nazi Party headquarters in Munich and, after the seizure of power, installed him in Berlin to orchestrate the grand receptions and state dinners. Kannenberg's attention to detail was legendary: He once sent an airplane to Dresden for a single goose, and he matched the flower arrangements, supplied by his wife, to the artwork on the walls. He was possessed of an easy confidence, and was as comfortable in a tuxedo as he was in an apron. He also knew how to hold a room. He would interrupt Hitler with a quip or comment, bring an audience to laughter with a joke, or fill a room with gaiety with his songs.

"Kannenberg was not only an excellent cook but also an excellent one-man-show who was literally blessed with that Berlin wit and humor," Christa Schröder once recalled. "He charmed his audience through his rounds of folk songs and clowning which he often accompanied on the accordion." Schröder compared him to a court jester possessed of the "freedom of the fool"—*Narrenfreiheit*—in Hitler's presence. "Evening with the Führer for dinner," Goebbels once wrote in his diary. "We argue about military-political questions. Kannenberg tells his war stories. They are very strange." Hitler liked the Kannenberg style, though. He also trusted Kannenberg's judgment implicitly. When Kannenberg complained about one of Hitler's adjutants, Hitler fired the man on the spot. When Hitler's chief adjutant, Wilhelm Brückner, protested, insisting that Kannenberg's complaints were unjustified, Hitler fired Brückner, despite more than a decade of loyal service.

Kannenberg could be arrogant, garrulous, calculating, and ruthless but never imprudent. He knew when to interrupt and upstage Hitler, but also when to pander. Thus when Kannenberg inscribed the Schlieffen book to "my Führer" and quoted Hitler to himself, he guilefully repeated *their* "motto," this time in blue grease pencil, in the same crude hand, on the last page of the book, after underlining Rochs's closing sentence: "You will find your way again, you German folk, and a great man from the realm of genius will again become your leader—from darkness into light—all will be well." It was Kannenberg's way of letting Hitler know that he was fully aware of his place in Hitler's life and of Hitler's place in the world.

IN HIS SURVEY of Hitler's private library, Frederick Oechsner reported that nearly half the Nazi leader's collection, "some 7,000 volumes," was devoted to military matters. According to Oechsner, Hitler had books on the "campaigns of Napoleon, the Prussian kings, the lives of all German and Prussian potentates who ever played a military role; and books on virtually all of the well-known military campaigns in recorded history." Oechsner notes that the books on Napoleonic campaigns "are extensively marginated in his own handwriting," and that a collection of "400 books, pamphlets and monographs on the United States armed forces" given to Hitler by Gen. Werner von Blomberg also appear to have been studied. Specifically, Oechsner mentions the presence of Theodore Roosevelt's account of the Spanish-American War and a book by Gen. Friedrich Wilhelm von Steuben on his experiences training George Washington's troops during the American Revolution. "There are exhaustive works on uniforms, weapons, supply, mobilization, the building-up of armies in peacetime, morale and ballistics," Oechsner says. "In fact, there is probably not a single phase of military knowledge, ancient or modern, which is not dealt with in these 7,000 volumes, and quite obviously Hitler has read many of them from cover to cover."

By Hitler's own account, his interest in military matters dates from his youth, when he came across a copy of Heinrich Gerling's two-volume illustrated history of the Franco-Prussian War, as Hitler explains on page 7 of *Mein Kampf*:

> Rummaging through my father's library, I had come across various books of a military nature, among them a popular edition of the Franco-German War of 1870–71. It consisted of two issues of an illustrated periodical from those years, which now became my favorite reading matter. It was not long before the great heroic struggle had become my greatest inner experience. From then on I became more and more enthusiastic about everything that was in any way connected with war or, for that matter, with soldiering.

Hermann Esser, one of Dietrich Eckart's early recruits for the Nazi cause, remembered that during the 1920s, Hitler's book buying changed, especially after his release from Landsberg Prison. "In these years Hitler

spent more money than previously to acquire books on military history . . . not only of Prussian history, but also in particular Austrian military history and French," Esser recalled. "He sort of bought up just
about anything that was available in Munich, whatever he heard about
or happened to find in the bookstores he passed on his occasional strolls
or walks to the Café Heck." In those years before the Nazi Party established its Schelling Street headquarters in Schwabing, Munich's student
quarter, Hitler rarely if ever visited the countless bookshops near the
university, preferring instead to browse the antiquarian bookstores near

Hitler's well-thumbed copy of Hiegl's 1935
manual on tanks. His library contains
numerous manuals on military vehicles,
naval vessels, and aircraft.

the Café Heck. Hitler had a particular passion, Esser recalled, for annual "almanachs" of military equipment. "He bought them for every year," Esser noted. "Then for comparison he had the English, then the French and Russian."

Today, the Hitler library preserves this specialized passion of Hitler's in nearly a dozen "almanachs" on naval vessels as well as aircraft and armored vehicles—several published by Julius Lehmann. Some date from these early years, such as a 1920 edition of *The Conquest of the Air: A Handbook of Air Transport and Flying Techniques*, with an introduction by Count Ferdinand von Zeppelin; some are later acquisitions, such as a 1935 copy of *Hiegl's Handbook of Tanks*, which provides both a detailed analysis of the "origins" of armored vehicles as well as an "identification guide"; several books on naval vessels, including a 1935 handbook, *The Navies of the World and Their Fighting Power*, with an introduction by retired admiral Walter Gladisch; and a 1940 edition of *Weyer's Handbook of War Fleets*, written by Alexander Bredt. This latter volume is especially well thumbed.

Hitler's oldest extant military volume is a 111-page appeal to militant nationalism, written by the early German patriot Ernst Moritz Arndt, and published in 1815, titled *Catechism for the Teutonic warrior and defender, in which is taught how to be a Christian warrior and how to enter battle in the company of God*, with a personal inscription to Hitler from Arndt's great-granddaughter. There is also a well-worn 1902 history of the fortifications of Strasbourg, "from the reconstruction of the city after the great migrations to the year 1681."

The Hitler library also contains a few biographies, including a 1921 profile of Julius Caesar by Matthias Gelzer and a dozen or so books on Frederick the Great, and those of two Prussian military heroes from the Napoleonic era, Karl von Stein and Friedrich Wilhelm von Bülow, though not a single book on Napoleon or his campaigns. A collection of essays by Karl von Clausewitz, *War and State*, subtitled *War Philosophy and Political Writings*, in a 1936 edition, is inscribed to Hitler by the editor, but appears never to have been perused. In Hitler's one book on Helmuth von Moltke (the Elder), the pages remain uncut. Similarly, a book on Alfred von Schlieffen by Karl Justrow, *The Field Marshal and the Techniques of War: Studies on the Operational Plans of the Count von Schlieffen and Lessons for Our Rearmament and National Defense,* published in 1933, also shows no sign of having been read. However, another book on the legendary Prussian general, the one given to Hitler by Kannenberg, has not only been read but also bears extensive marginalia.

IN THE EARLY morning hours of Friday, May 10, Hitler journeyed to the *Felsennest*—translated variously as the "craggy eyre" or "nest on the cliff"—a wooded, hilltop command post deep in the forests of the Eifel, twenty miles southwest of Bonn and a dozen or so miles from the Belgian border. He arrived there after an intentionally diversionary nighttime train ride—the train set off north from Berlin toward Hamburg then, shortly before midnight, reversed course toward the southwest, arriving in the town of Euskirchen, near the Belgian border, at 4:25 a.m. He was met there by a column of military vehicles, which then drove half an hour to the *Felsennest*. The post, a cluster of wooden huts and underground bunkers, looked more like a summer camp than a military headquarters. The "situation room" was a one-story wooden structure with a peaked, camouflaged roof, a small terrace with a wooden balustrade, and a room-length shuttered window that could be opened for natural light when the weather permitted. Hitler was quartered in a low-lying subterranean bunker with a grass roof and an angled entrance that opened outward like cellar doors.

An interior photograph of Hitler's bedroom shows a cramped, spartan space furnished with a striped sleeping sofa and a simple writing table. An electric heater shares wall space with a four-legged wicker stool. A clutter of more than thirty books in several piles takes up room at the far end of his bed; two orderly stacks, one with four volumes and

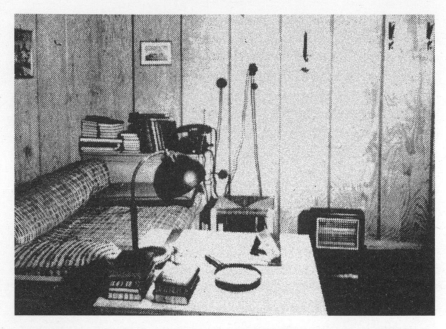

Hitler's quarters near the Belgian border, with nighttime reading. In an adjacent Field Marshal Keitel could hear Hitler turning pages through the thin walls.

another with three, are at the near end. A large magnifying glass lies on a side table. Field Marshal Wilhelm Keitel remembered that the interior walls were so thin—*hellhörig*—that he could hear Hitler turning pages at night.

At exactly 5:35 a.m. on the tenth, the invasion began. Gathering his entourage before his bunker, with birds chirping in the surrounding trees, Hitler announced, "Gentlemen, the offensive against the Western allies has just now begun." For the next nine days, Hitler monitored the progress of the military operation, often in the open air, tracking one German triumph after another.

By Sunday, the nineteenth, there was "good news" on all fronts. "After the elimination of final resistance on the island of Walcheren, all of Holland including its islands is now in hand," the daily log for the German High Command records. "In north Belgium our troops, who have already captured Antwerp as reported earlier, are pressing the remaining enemy troops who are still fighting ever farther to the west." West of Antwerp, the German forces had crossed the Schelde River, and had reached the east bank of the Dendre River, west of Brussels. The news from northern France was equally encouraging. The Oise and Sambre rivers had been crossed. Le Cateau and Saint-Quentin were in German hands. Along the Maginot Line, the French had surrendered a major stronghold, Position 505, northwest of Montmédy. "The numbers of prisoners and captured weapons continue to rise," the log concludes. "Until now 110,000 captured without counting the Dutch army and numerous artillery pieces up to 28 caliber." Kannenberg punctuated the spirit of that Sunday with his triumphant salutation, *"Sieg Heil!"*

WHEN KANNENBERG INSCRIBED the Schlieffen biography, Hitler was a few weeks short of being hailed by the Wehrmacht's chief of staff, Wilhelm Keitel, as the "greatest field marshal of all time." In seven brief months, Hitler had unleashed a series of lightning attacks against Poland and Scandinavia, and now France, Belgium, and the Netherlands, snatching Luxembourg along the way. His dramatic victories left friend and foe alike in awe of the German juggernaut and half of Europe under Nazi domination.

At first glance, Kannenberg's Sunday inscription can be seen indeed as a salute to German victory, a nod to his boss's battlefield prowess, but it may also smack of Kannenberg's famously subtle mendacity, a hint at the undercurrent of tension chilling the hilltop euphoria that weekend. On Friday, Hitler had clashed with Franz Halder after doing something he had never done before: intervening in a tactical military decision. Until then, Hitler's role in the battlefield operations had been primarily decorative. He was omnipresent on the battlefield and in the public eye, especially when the newsreel cameras were whirring: conferring with his generals, studying maps, surveying the battlefield, touring the front lines, chatting with war-wearied but jubilant soldiers. But when it came to operational matters, the generals either ignored or resisted his involvement.

In the summer of 1938, Hitler had clashed with Halder over the draft invasion plan for Czechoslovakia. Instead of a concerted assault on Prague, as Halder recommended, Hitler proposed dividing the German army for twin attacks on Prague and Pilsen. Halder argued that the German forces were not strong enough for a two-pronged assault. When Hitler insisted, Halder handed him the maps and told him to make the changes himself. Hitler returned to Berlin, made his amendments, and forwarded the revised plan to Halder. A few weeks later, Hitler inquired of Halder about the changes. He was told they had arrived too late to be incorporated into the plan. Hitler was furious, and summoned Halder and his senior staff. The men battled over the plan for the next several hours. Halder would not relent. Finally, toward three o'clock in the morning, Hitler had had enough. He ordered Halder to make the changes. With icy composure, Halder took his leave.

"What does he want?" Halder fumed to Keitel in the hallway.

"If you haven't figured that out," Keitel replied, "I feel sorry for you."

The Munich Agreement rendered the disagreement moot, but four months later, when Hitler announced his intention to invade Poland, Halder and his staff again resisted, responding to Hitler's suggestion with an "iron phalanx" of skepticism. Once the fighting began in Poland, Hitler almost never intervened. "I recall only two such cases," Keitel later noted. "Once when Hitler ordered reinforcements for the north flank which was attacking from East Prussia, and a second time when he intervened into the operations of Blaskowitz's army because he had serious concerns. Otherwise, Hitler restricted himself to exchanging opinions and meetings with the chief of staff, as well as suggestions, without ever interfering with actual orders."

When Hitler did attempt to intervene, his generals resisted. Immediately after the fall of Poland, Hitler ordered Halder to turn west and invade France. Halder said no. The German soldiers were exhausted, he told Hitler, and their equipment in need of repair. He also said that Hitler's proposed invasion plan was "an unimaginative knockoff"—*ein fantasieloser Abklatsch*—of the Schlieffen Plan, whose deficiencies had already been demonstrated during the First World War.

Hitler's general staff responded with their own revised plan. The final version did, in fact, use Schlieffen's flanking route through the Low Countries, but with two significant enhancements: an invasion of the Netherlands to block any British landings and a drive to the French coast instead of toward Paris. By late autumn, the only unresolved question was the date of execution, which was left to Hitler. He postponed the invasion fifty-eight times throughout the winter and spring, checking the weather charts—and some say the astrological charts—daily, waiting for the perfect moment.

The period became known as the *Sitzkrieg*—the sitting war. The general staff was dismayed by Hitler's indecision until the morning of Friday, May 10, when the German war machine was again set in motion. "My operation is running like a well-cut film," Halder wrote to his wife that Monday. "By the undeserved grace of God."

Initially, Hitler was content with monitoring the progress of battle, posing for Heinrich Hoffmann's publicity stills, and engaging in his habitual late-night reading. But as he watched the dramatic German advances on the maps, he grew nervous. He worried that the panzer divisions were overstretching themselves. Halder, who was commuting daily to the front, assured Hitler that all was well. The Germans were making solid advances, and it would take the French a full week to mobilize a counterattack. Halder invoked General von Moltke, who during the decisive battle of Königgrätz, had calmly sat smoking a cigar as the fighting unfolded. A good battle plan did not need amendment.

But a week into the campaign, Hitler panicked. Fearing a counterattack from the south, he ordered the Twelfth Panzer Division, which was in a headlong drive for the coastal town of Dunkirk, to stop dead in its tracks. His intervention paralyzed the German High Command. That evening, shortly after eight o'clock, Halder received a call with explicit orders from Hitler to keep the Sixteenth Army in reserve. "[Gen. Walther von] Reichenau has the order to join the corps with the 4th Army via Mons," Halder noted in his diary on the evening of May 17. "This is only possible by attacking. Now, he does not know what to do." By the next morning, confusion had turned to chaos.

With the German flag flying over the city hall in Antwerp, the British systematically withdrawing from Belgium to establish a defensive line farther south, and the French still not able to mobilize their reserves effectively, Halder knew his assessment of the situation had been correct and that the Germans needed to press forward with all due speed. Every hour was "precious." That morning, in a ten o'clock briefing, Halder clashed with Hitler, who had developed an irrational concern for the southern flank. "He rages and yells that we are on the way to ruining the entire operation and are setting ourselves up for defeat," Halder noted that morning. "He does not want the continuation of any operation to the west, let alone to the southwest."

While Goebbels's propaganda machine could trumpet Hitler's military prowess to the German people and to the world, within the tight circles of the general staff, Hitler remained an intruder, an outsider, and, worst of all, a dangerous dilettante. The experience of the frontline corporal that had served him so well in his political career was a liability on the battlefield. "He lacked the thorough training of a military leader that allows one to take a high risk in an operation because he knows he is capable of mastering it," one general later observed. Halder agreed. "The self-assuredness of the field marshal who can leave his subordinates the freedom of action in the context of a well-planned undertaking—a secret of the Moltke leadership style—was absent in Hitler." Invoking a vocabulary that echoes across Hitler's career and embeds itself in much of his reading, Halder spoke of an "inexperienced novice," of a "will driven by dark intuition," and, most notably, of an unmistakable "inner insecurity."

Two decades earlier, when confronted with the dismissiveness of those better educated, better trained, and demonstrably more competent than he, Hitler had to turn and run. But now he held his ground. He had read his Clausewitz's classic, *On War*, which had been among the books in his first apartment on Thiersch Street. During his 1924 trial, Hitler invoked Clausewitz in the closing remarks of his defense. "It is better if a people perish in an honorable struggle, for only after such a collapse can there be a resurrection," he blustered, citing the Prussian general verbatim. "But woe to the people who willingly subject themselves to the shame of a dishonor and slavery! Such a people are lost."

In the final chapter of *Mein Kampf,* when Hitler writes about the fall of Carthage, he invokes the Clausewitzian notions of the "stain of cowardly submission" and of rebirth through an "honorable struggle." He had not only imbibed the wisdom of Clausewitz, Moltke, and Schlieffen verbatim, but he had also gleaned vast quantities of technical data from the annual "almanachs" of military equipment. "He had an exceptional knowledge of weaponry," Otto Dietrich, his press secretary, once observed. "For example he knew all the warships in the world in so far as they were listed in . . . reference works. He could give in detail from memory their age, their displacement and speed, their armor strength, their towers and weaponry. He was thoroughly informed about the most modern artillery and tank construction from every country." Even a critic as harsh as Halder grudgingly conceded to Hitler's exceptional recall. "A reference to the material strength of the Russian army, in particular the high number of 10,000 tanks, unleashed a more than quarter-hour retort from Hitler, in which he cited from memory the Russians' annual production for the last twenty years," Halder remembered.

Hitler had also mastered the writings of Karl May. Unlike his generals, he had studied May's adventure stories of the American West, taking close note of the tactical skills and cunning of Winnetou, May's Native American hero, who combined stealth and surprise to outwit and overcome his opponents. Weary of his generals' "eternal doubts" about his "great ideas," and struck by their own dearth of imagination and boldness, Hitler recommended to them May's books as a means of sharpening their battlefield prowess, and issued a special field edition for the soldiers at the front. "Hitler was wont to say that he had always been deeply impressed by the tactical finesse and circumspection that May conferred upon his character Winnetou," Albert Speer later noted. "And he would add that during his reading hours at night, when faced by seemingly hopeless situations, he would still reach for those stories, that they gave him courage like works of philosophy for others or the Bible for elderly people."

WHEN KANNENBERG INSCRIBED the Rochs biography to Hitler nine days into the blitzkrieg against the West, he indicated those passages he wanted Hitler to read. On the opening page of chapter four, Kannenberg has framed the chapter title, "The Schlieffen Battle Plan for the Two-Front War," which warns of the dangers to Germany of fighting on dual fronts, with one vertical and one angled line, like a mansard roof. Kannenberg bracketed the following passage with a thick line:

> But then again: as long as Schlieffen stood at the head of the general staff, the defense of the Reich lay in good hands. Schlieffen believed that he and his army were equal to any coalition. Rightfully so! As [Adjutant Otto von] Gottberg emphasizes, behind his mask of controlled self-discipline, his fiery spirit hid the recipe for the success of his yet unknown plan. Schlieffen possesses the rare faith in victory that derived from the irresistible, invincible force that is shaped by the effect of a true leader—Führer—who, like a force of nature, crushes all resistance.

In the right-hand margin, Kannenberg has highlighted the following sentence with a second, smaller bracket: "What are the missteps and mistakes of a few subordinate officers in the context of his expansive plan that in itself is a guarantee of victory?" Hitler followed Kannenberg's lead. In a series of marginalia, Hitler ambles through the text, his pencil catching and marking individual sentences or entire paragraphs. One would think he read the book within days of Kannenberg's inscribing it, because what he chose to focus on informed the very issues he was then grappling with on the battlefield.

Here we see Hitler gathering the "mosaic" pieces to help justify ex post facto his invasion of the Low Countries. "Since the French eastern front was considered too strong, as was confirmed in the war against France, the route through Luxembourg and Belgium needed to be taken," he marks on page 47. On page 52: "Schlieffen's plan to go through Belgium was simply a commandment for self-preservation if one did not want to face defeat of the campaign from the outset." There are other markings on page 53, where Rochs talks of English conspiracies against the Continent.

"But the [First World War] had further shown that Great Britain, in agreement with the Belgian government, had long prepared for military occupation of Belgium; for military purposes this came too late," Rochs wrote, with Hitler's pencil following attentively. "Thus, for anyone who has seen the harbor facility at Zeebrugge with the adjacent roads and the extensive railway network, it was clear that this massive facility in the proximity of Antwerp could only have been built with the intention not of trade but for the military purpose of an English landing."

These marked passages either complemented or completed his vision of reality and history, but in other pages, we also find him highlighting issues of more immediacy, as on page 63, where Rochs talks about the strategic importance of a small coastal town near the Franco-Belgian border. "Schlieffen frequently noted with particular pleasure that even Frederick the Great, though in a somewhat different context," Rochs writes, "had spoken, in his proposals for a war against France, of the idea of a northern encirclement and siege of Dunkirk with the right wing over Abbeville." Hitler has drawn a thick line beside this passage.

That Dunkirk should attract Hitler's attention in these days is not surprising since, as we've seen, on May 17 he had ordered the Twelfth Panzer Division to halt its advance toward Dunkirk at Abbeville. The German military leadership knew he had made a mistake.* Hitler offered another explanation. "When the news came that the enemy had launched an attack along the entire front, I could have wept for joy," Hitler later recalled. "They had fallen into the trap! It was right to let the attack begin in Luttich. They were led to believe that we were sticking to the old Schlieffen Plan. Two days after arriving at Abbeville the offensive could be directed southward." While the Germans idled, more than three hundred thousand Allied troops were evacuated.

BY MY COUNT, there are thirty-two penciled intrusions on the twenty pages that constitute chapter four of the Schlieffen biography, most of which reflect in one way or another on the campaign in France. While these markings suggest some of the historical and strategic issues that occupied Hitler's thoughts in those days, they are virtually all retrospective in nature. If there is any marginalia of potentially historical significance it would be several marked passages on pages 60 and 61 where Rochs discusses a two-front war.

Schlieffen saw Germany caught between two major military threats: France and England to the west, and Russia to the east. He felt that Germany needed first to secure its western borders before dealing with Russia. For Schlieffen, the defeat of England and France was of such paramount importance that he was willing to make strategic territorial sacrifices in the east, and invoked the memory of Frederick the Great to bolster his argument: "In the end one will have to sacrifice, as the great

* General Halder suspected that Hitler wanted to deprive the army of the victory to spite his generals, and hand the job of destroying the encircled British Expeditionary Force to his crony Hermann Göring's air force as a propaganda ploy.

Excerpt from Schlieffen, *with marginalia marking a passage*
cautioning against Germany's fighting a two-front war.

king taught us, even a province as rich as East Prussia in order to concentrate all one's strength where a decisive victory is needed." There are two parallel strikes accompanied by an exclamation point beside this passage, and a series of underscorings of individual phrases in the paragraphs that follow: "reckon with the entire Russian army as an additional enemy" and "political and sentimental emotions" and "in the face of a Russian deluge," before the pencil finally drove down hard on the margin to highlight the following paragraph:

If the lands east of the Weichsel [River] could not be retained in the face of overwhelming force, Schlieffen was willing to sacrifice these areas

temporarily, as was repeatedly emphasized above. Once the situation in
France has been decided, the French-English army destroyed, and Ger-
many stands victorious on the Seine, everything else will—according to
Schlieffen—follow on its own accord.

Though Hitler had long talked about expansion to the east and the
need for Lebensraum, he had never addressed the issue of a war with
Russia. These markings represent the earliest recorded evidence of
Hitler's plan to invade the Soviet Union. Keitel recalls that Hitler first
spoke to him of a major offensive in the east in late July 1940, an intention he repeated to Halder and his senior military staff the following
month. By that autumn, Hitler had his generals drafting a plan of attack.
The following June, Hitler would unleash Operation Barbarossa on the
eastern front. By this time, Hitler had taken complete operational control of every decision relating to the planning and implementation of the
military operation. The propaganda machine trumpeted Keitel's claim
of Hitler as the "greatest field marshal of all time."

Hitler's pencil seems to have strayed only once from the parameters
of chapter four, to a footnote at the bottom of page 41, at the end of the
preceding chapter. The footnote refers to a passage in which Rochs discusses Kaiser Wilhelm II's infamous dismissal of Bismarck in 1890, a radical decision taken on poor counsel that abruptly ended the career of
Germany's legendary statesman. Schlieffen observes that Wilhelm was
blinded not only by his youth and arrogance and court intrigue but also
by his inability to see into the true nature of his advisers. "Insight into
the human being and other things, into the very heart of a matter, into
the very essence of existence—that was the kaiser's great failing," Rochs
writes. "The result was not only the frequently incomprehensible choice
of the individuals in his closest circle but the constant vacillating in his
decision-making and his actions." To underscore his point, Rochs wrote
the following footnote:

That Wilhelm II could bear to hear the truth and also valued it is evident from a statement he made on the deathbed of his long-time gen-

eral adjutant, Field Marshal Wilhelm von Hahnke, on February 8, 1912. "The only man who always told me the truth." A statement that honors the master as well as the servant, but sounds remarkably bitter in the mouth of a monarch after nearly 24 years of rule.

Beside this passage, Hitler has placed a single emphatic exclamation point.

BOOK EIGHT

Hitler's History of the Second World War

This war will go down in history as President Roosevelt's war.
SVEN HEDIN, *America in the Battle of the Continents*

H ITLER'S COPY OF SVEN HEDIN'S *America in the Battle of the Conti-nents* has vanished, but its intellectual shadow can be found in a three-page letter Hitler sent to the author on October 30, 1942, after having read the two-hundred-page political treatise the previous night. Hitler signed the letter in the increasingly abbreviated form he began using after 1933, a stylized capital *A* for his given name, and an embel-lished *H* for his surname, with the remaining letters trailing off in a scrib-bled downward line, like unraveling thread, an orthographic idiosyncrasy strikingly similar to his father's signature a half century before.

The letter is typed on Hitler's personal letterhead, with his name in the upper left-hand corner in bold caps beneath a Nazi eagle clutching a swastika wrapped in a laurel wreath. Unlike the eagle on Hitler's ex libris, this one is more formal and stylized, a product of the steel plate of the modern era rather than the soft-edged primitivism of the wood-cut. The letter is addressed to "Professor Dr. Sven von Hedin" at Norr Mälarstrand 66 in Stockholm, Sweden, with the return address and date typed in the upper right-hand corner: Führerhauptquartier, den 30.10.1942.

Unlike Hitler's official Reich Chancellery office at 77 Wilhelm Street

BERLIN, DEN

Führerhauptquartier,
den 30.10.1942.

ADOLF HITLER

Sehr verehrter Herr Doktor Sven von Hedin !

Sie hatten die Freundlichkeit, mir Ihr im
Verlage F.A. B r o c k h a u s, Leipzig neuerschienenes
Buch

"Amerika im Kampfe der Kontinente"
mit einer persönlichen Widmung zu übersenden. Ich danke
Ihnen herzlich für die mir damit erwiesene Aufmerksamkeit.

Ich habe das Buch bereits durchgelesen und
begrüße es ganz besonders, dass Sie so ausdrücklich auf die
von mir bei Beginn des Krieges den Polen gemachten Angebote
eingegangen sind. Wenn ich heute an diese Zeit zurückdenke,
dann liegt das alles so ferne und es erscheint mir so un-
wirklich, dass ich mich geradezu selbst anklage, mit meinen
Vorschlägen soweit gegangen zu sein. Denn in diesem Falle
haben wieder einmal jene Menschen, die es böse zu machen
gedachten, Gutes getan.

Herrn Professor Dr. Sven von Hedin
S t o c k h o l m /Schweden
Norr Mälarstränd 66.

Hitler's letter to Sven Hedin, dated October 30, 1942.

in Berlin, or his private office in the Nazi Party headquarters in Brown House at 45 Brienner Street in Munich, the *Führerhauptquartier* was a "place" without a permanent locus. During the invasion of Poland, the *Führerhauptquartier* moved from battlefront to battlefront in a specially equipped train. For the blitzkrieg in the west, it was of course first

located at the *Felsennest;* then a few weeks later in a cluster of brick farm
buildings near Brûly-de-Pesche, south of Brussels; and during the invasion of the Soviet Union, Hitler commuted between the military headquarters called the Wolf's Lair, in the north, and the Werewolf, a
thousand miles to the south. The *Führerhauptquartier* was by its very
nature as much temporal as geographic. It followed Hitler's itinerary.
The date was the address.

When Hitler dictated his three-page letter to Hedin, he was recovering from a head cold so severe that it left him bedridden, his mind so
blurred that he later told Otto Dietrich that his memory no longer
seemed to be fully intact. He was fifty-three years old but felt a decade
older. Adding to his misery was his self-imposed isolation following a
series of bitter confrontations with his general staff.

Since late summer, he had been living in Ukraine at the Werewolf
headquarters, a cluster of concrete bunkers and one-story wooden huts
from which he had commanded the German offensives along the eastern front. In the heat-soaked, mosquito-infested woods that August,
Hitler had grown ever more irritated with his chronically skeptical and
increasingly belligerent generals, in particular, Franz Halder.

Halder had advised against Hitler's planned invasion of the Soviet
Union in the spring of 1941, and protested Hitler's intention to attack
Leningrad and Stalingrad, the symbolic centers of Bolshevism, rather
than seizing Moscow, the center of Soviet communication and industry
and a nexus of railway connections. Hitler dismissed Halder's objection
as "technical," the product of "calcified brains caught in the ideas of past
centuries." Initially, Halder's caution had proved misplaced. But following Hitler's initial successes in the summer and autumn of 1941, the German advances stalled in the vicious cold of the Russian winter. Hitler
then turned south with a renewed drive on Stalingrad and an ambitious
panzer-driven thrust to the rich oil fields of the Caucasus and the Black
Sea port of Sebastopol. There was talk of invading Iran, and plans for
reaching the Persian Gulf. When the drive into the Caucuses faltered,

however, Halder confronted Hitler. He said he could no longer endorse Hitler's plans in good conscience. There were increasingly ominous signs of impending Soviet counterattacks. Hitler dismissed Halder's concern.

"The Russian is dead," he said. "He exhausted his last reserves with the winter offensive. It is just a matter of pushing him a bit harder till he falls." Hitler spoke of fanaticism and heroism. He quoted from Clausewitz and Nietzsche. Generally, Halder quietly endured the former corporal's wearisome lectures to his generals, but on this occasion he intervened. He cited statistics indicating that the Soviets were in fact producing twelve hundred tanks per month and had mobilized as many as an additional million and a half men. Hitler looked at Halder, then exploded. With "foam in the corners of [his] mouth," he went after the generals with "clenched fists," Halder recalled. He forbade such "idiotic gossip." But Halder was not going to back down. "It does not require any prophetic gift to predict what will happen if Stalin sends the million and a half soldiers against Stalingrad and the Don [River]," he said.

Hitler grew more furious still. This "constant battle" with his generals, he raged, had cost him half of his emotional reserves. It was no longer worth it. With the challenges that now faced the army, it was not a question of "technical skill," he insisted; what was needed was the "passion of National Socialist faith." The meeting ended in a mood of annoyance and discomfort that lingered over the weeks that followed. On September 7, when Hitler was informed of the deteriorating situation in the south, he again exploded. This time, he accused his generals of disobeying his commands. He believed his efforts were being intentionally undermined.

That same day, Hitler ordered a team of stenographers dispatched from Berlin to the Werewolf. They were to record every word he spoke in briefings. Afterward he immediately withdrew to his private quarters on the periphery of the Werewolf complex, where he ate with his secretaries and select members of his entourage. When weather permitted, they sat at a round table beneath the trees.

To bolster Hitler's spirits and provide a pleasant distraction, Martin Bormann decided to bring Hermann Giesler for an extended stay. Giesler was an architect whom Hitler had engaged for various projects, including the redesign of his hometown of Linz.* Giesler had accompanied Hitler, along with Albert Speer, on a tour of Paris monuments in the summer of 1940. "You will build my burial place," Hitler murmured to Giesler before Napoleon's tomb.

Hitler welcomed Giesler's arrival. He spoke to him not only about their architectural plans for Linz and about the residence Hitler intended to build there, but also about the intolerable situation among his general staff. "I live and work in the depressing certainty that I am surrounded by treason," Hitler confided. "Whom can I trust with any surety, and how can I make decisions, give orders, how can I lead with any certainty when there is such distrust created through deception, falsified reports and obvious betrayal, when with justified caution such uncertainty arises, when I need to be so distrustful from the outset?" In particular, Hitler noted, his relationship with Halder had become intolerable. "It just doesn't work any longer," Hitler told Giesler. "I can't stand it when I look into his face and see such hatred and arrogance, something that is completely unjustified in a man of such mediocre intelligence."

On September 24, 1942, Hitler relieved Halder of his command. "My nerves are shot, and his are not much better," Halder scribbled in his diary that night. But Halder's dismissal did little to remove Hitler's sense of isolation, his concerns about betrayal and deceit, not to mention unsettling reports about the mounting enemy pressure in the Caucasus, around Stalingrad, and, toward the end of October, at a village in Egypt called El Alamein. "The bitter fighting in Egypt has intensified on this fifth day of the defensive battle," the log from the German High Command recorded on October 29. "Despite relentless attacks and unusually

* Among Hitler's remnant books at the Library of Congress is an album with architectural sketches and photographs chronicling Giesler's various projects in Weimar, including the rebuilding of the Hotel Elephant and the construction of the "Adolf Hitler Square."

high expenditure of ammunition the enemy was unable to secure any successes against the courageous German defense."

The report for that day records fighting across Hitler's empire: in the Caspian Sea, where the German Luftwaffe sank two enemy tankers and damaged five freighters; in the western Caucasus, where German troops repelled "enemy attacks" along a series of mountain strongholds; in the industrial outskirts of Stalingrad, where repeated Soviet tank attacks were repulsed "with as usual heavy enemy losses"; on the Mediterranean island of Malta; on the southeast coast of England, where German planes attacked industrial, transport, and harbor facilities. On the day in late October, the German armies were defending an empire that extended across two continents.

THE ARRIVAL AT WEREWOLF of Sven Hedin's latest book that day was more than a welcome distraction in Hitler's bunkered isolation. Hedin was one of the few real heroes of Hitler's life. In his youth, he had followed the adventures of the Swedish explorer with the same rapt attention he brought to Karl May novels. Hedin was a rugged, larger-than-life figure who entered some of the most severe, uncharted regions of the world and returned with stories of high adventure and, even more important, discoveries of consequence, charting some of the last unexplored regions of the earth. In an age before Everest had been scaled or the Atlantic traversed by air, Hedin was one of the most famous men on earth. In his legendary expedition across the Gobi Desert, he lost two-thirds of his eighty-man team to the bitter climate of the high plateau but emerged four months later emaciated yet triumphant. This was the sort of superhuman effort that fired Hitler's imagination in his youth and drove his convictions in later life: the ability of the individual to defy seemingly insurmountable obstacles and emerge triumphant.

In October 1933, eight months into his own assertion of individual will, Hitler had dispatched a telegram to the aging Swedish explorer to congratulate him on the fortieth anniversary of the Gobi triumph. When Hitler learned that Hedin would be in Germany for a speaking tour, he invited him to the Reich Chancellery. Hedin returned, once again on a special invitation from Hitler, as a featured speaker at the 1936 Berlin Olympics. Many visits were to follow, and Hedin regularly sent Hitler copies of his publications.

As with Eckart, Hitler showed respectful deference to this older man. When Hedin visited Hitler in his office in the New Reich Chancellery, Hitler would take him by the arm and show him to "his chair" in the small seating area beneath the portrait of Bismarck. With an easy intimacy, Hitler would chat with Hedin about adventure, politics, achievement, and personal concerns and ambitions. On one occasion, Hitler confessed to Hedin that he did not expect to see the completion of his lifelong "project" of establishing Germany as the world's leading power. Hitler said that this task would be left to others to finish. "Keep in mind that I am over fifty years old," Hitler said, to which Hedin replied dismissively, "I am seventy-five!"

"Yes, but you are an exception," Hitler returned.

"Fifty is nothing at all," Hedin insisted. "When you are as old as I am, Herr Reich Chancellor, you will feel just as fresh and energetic as I do."

"Oh no, no, I will be exhausted long before that."

Mostly, though, Hitler and Hedin talked about politics, in particular Germany's relations with the Nordic countries, and frequently Russia, a country Hedin had visited more than forty times. Like Hitler, Hedin feared the "Bolshevization" of Europe, an apprehension he and Hitler discussed shortly after the invasion of Poland, a conversation Hedin, much to Hitler's chagrin, shared afterward with the press, as Goebbels recorded in his diary in October 1939. "Afternoon with the Führer," Goebbels wrote. "He is angry about an interview that Sven Hedin gave with the *News Chronicle* about their talk together. He trumpets Germany as an enemy of Russia. It will be denied immediately. Hedin will also have to issue a denial." Russia and Germany, of course, were allies then.

As a lifelong Germanophile who had traveled with the German

armies during the First World War and subscribed to the notion of racial superiority, though he did not embrace anti-Semitism, Hedin was more than happy to assist the greater German cause, as an emissary to Scandinavia, as an informal spy in Asia, and as a pro-isolationist agitator in the United States. In this latter role, he wrote a book-length appeal to the American people to keep out of the war, for the sake of Europe and America alike.

Hedin had undertaken three major lecture tours in America, in 1923, 1929, and 1932, traveling the continent from Boston, where he was treated briefly by Harvey Cushing, one of the leading surgeons of the day, to California, where he visited Yosemite and the observatory on Mount Wilson. In Stockholm, he had met Theodore Roosevelt. As a friend and admirer of the United States, he wrote in his book, which he finished in the autumn of 1941, he was acting in the best interest of its people. He reminded them that Frederick the Great had endorsed the American Revolution, and that during the Civil War, while France and England supported the Confederacy, Bismarck had provided loans to the Union. He argued that it was Roosevelt, not Hitler, who had plunged Europe into war, and he detailed Hitler's repeated efforts to avert war in the summer of 1939. Hedin also warned that war with the German juggernaut would lead ultimately to U.S. defeat. He appealed to Americans, for their own sake, to recognize the real forces behind the war in Europe. "It is this satanically subtle propaganda that appeals to the Christianity, idealism, humanity and loyalty of the American people that is leading us into war," Hedin wrote. When the Japanese bombed Pearl Harbor the book became irrelevant, and Hedin turned to his German publisher in Leipzig. They published it in October 1942 under the title *Amerika im Kampf der Kontinente* (America in the Battle of the Continents), and dispatched a personally inscribed copy to the German chancellor.

AS HITLER SETTLED IN TO his private quarters with his personally dedicated copy of *America in the Battle of the Continents,* he found himself

reading a history of the outbreak of the war as he believed it would ultimately be recorded for posterity. Three years earlier, when he gathered
his generals in the great hall at the Berghof for his lecture on the imminent invasion of Poland, he reminded them that ultimately it was left to
the victor to write the history of wars. "The victor will not be asked
afterwards whether he told the truth or not," Hitler told them. "When
starting and waging war it is not right that matters, but victory." In the
months and years that followed, Hitler's army had marched from one
victory to the next, extending Gemany's reach to unprecedented dimensions. As Hitler sat down with Hedin's book, he was confident that the
war he had conceived and launched was on the verge of being won.

In that hour, his empire—which stretched from the Channel Islands
off the English coast to the shore of the Black Sea, from the Arctic Circle to the Tropic of Cancer—was proving remarkably resilient, at least
based on that day's battlefront reports, to the onslaught of enemy armies.
It seemed a good occasion to begin reading a history of how this war had
begun.

"No question is more easily understandable than why a new catastrophe came so quickly after the First World War," Hedin began. "Many
people were quick to give an answer: the culprit was once again Germany. This 'once again' by itself shows how quickly people have forgotten the turn of events in the short span of time between 1919 and 1939
even though they themselves lived it." Hedin reminded his readers that
the origins of the Second World War lay not in German annexations
of Austria or the Sudetenland, or even in the subsequent invasion of
Poland, but in the punishing terms of the Treaty of Versailles and the
miseries they visited on the German people—deprivation, humiliation,
starvation—coupled with a British foreign policy agenda that established a single-issue position on Germany: *Delenda est Germania,* "Germany must be obliterated."

Hedin devotes a chapter to Hitler's alleged attempts to counter
British machinations to provoke another war with Germany. He cites a

speech on May 21, 1935, as the onset of Hitler's four-year peace campaign. "A healthy social policy can provide a people in a few short years more children by promoting childbearing than one can by conquering and subjecting foreign peoples," Hitler explained to the German Reichstag, declaiming an emphatic *"Nein!"* to war. He went on to say, "National Socialist Germany's desire for peace is based on deeply held ideological convictions."

According to Hedin, Hitler spent the next four years in an attempt to reach reasonable accommodations with his European neighbors, only to find himself confronted by subterfuge and arrogance. "All of Adolf Hitler's offers were arrogantly dismissed and declared insincere from the outset," Hedin writes. "They were always viewed as a threat, never as an attempt to reestablish a great but long-humiliated people as an equal in the circle of other great nations." Hedin focuses on Hitler's repeated efforts in the summer of 1939 to avert war, in particular, the eleventh-hour peace proposal that was hand-delivered to the British embassy in Berlin the night before the outbreak of the conflict.* Hedin cites the nine-point proposal in its entirety, and observes, "It is rare to find among the diplomatic files of recent history a document that equals this proposal in its restraint, rapprochement, and understanding for the needs of a country."

As Hitler sat in his armchair in the rustic wooden hut in that isolated Ukrainian forest, he was certainly comforted and cheered by Hedin's words. Hitler had built a career on deluding others with his lies, illusions, and false promises, but by age fifty-three he had also mastered the art of self-delusion—Halder spoke of *Selbsthypnose*—so much so that he could take comfort in believing that the current borders of his empire were as fixed as the history of his empire upon the page. The following morning, Hitler wrote to Hedin:

* There is an extensive Nazi historiography of the Second World War, in particular in Nazi-era schoolbooks, that detail Hitler's alleged peace initiatives and alleged Polish efforts to "exterminate" German civilians living in Poland.

Most Honorable Herr Doctor Sven von Hedin!*

You were kind enough to forward to me a personally inscribed copy of your book *America in the Battle of the Continents,* which was recently published by the FA Brockhaus Verlag Leipzig. I thank you warmly for the attention you have shown me. I have already read the book and welcome in particular that you so explicitly detailed the offers I made to Poland at the beginning of the war. When I think back on that time, it all seems so far away, and seems so unreal to me that I almost blame myself for having been so forthcoming with my proposals.

Hitler expressed relief that Poland had rejected his repeated attempts at finding a peaceful solution, for had he not gone to war in 1939, he told Hedin, Germany would have been lulled into a false sense of security and turned its attentions to cultural instead of military matters, while the Soviet Union would have continued to prepare itself for war. "And even if we had not neglected armaments, they would have remained within normal limits, which would have left us a few years later in a position of helpless inferiority before the Asian colossus," Hitler claimed. "Under these circumstances, the fate of Europe and with it thousands of years of culture would have found its end."

Hitler envisioned Europe being overrun by "millions of warriors as fanatic as they are brutal," equipped with an "unimaginable array of weapons." Fortunately for Europe, fate had determined that Hitler should go to war. Europe had been spared. Germany had emerged as the final bastion before the Bolshevik hordes.

Then Hitler turned to the central thesis of Hedin's book: Franklin Delano Roosevelt. "Without question, the individual guilty of this war, as you correctly state at the end of the book, is exclusively the American president Roosevelt," Hitler wrote. "Ironically, by starting this war, he and his cronies have unintentionally and unwittingly awakened this con-

---

* Hedin did not hold a doctorate nor did he have any claim to the aristocratic "von" in his name.

tinent just in time and allowed it to confront with open eyes a danger that a few years later could not have been held in check."

Hitler did not doubt for "a second" that the Germans and their allies would triumph over the Soviets. He reaffirmed his "unshakable determination" not to lay down weapons until all Europe, east and west, was "rescued" from the Bolshevik threat. "I use this occasion, my esteemed Herr Sven von Hedin," Hitler concluded, "to extend my best wishes for your health and for your continued welfare, I remain most heartily yours. Most humbly, Adolf Hitler." Hitler signed and dispatched the letter. The following day, he departed for his headquarters at the Wolf's Lair in East Prussia. He never returned to the Werewolf.

The last page of Hitler's letter to Hedin.

———

IN THE DAYS TO COME, Hitler continued to muse on Hedin's book and
talked about it the following week, during his annual address commem-
orating the Beer Hall Putsch in Munich. But during that week much had
changed. On the morning of November 9, 1942, word came that American troops had landed on the coast of North Africa and established a
beachhead. As he spoke, Hitler was not himself. "We are fighting in the
far reaches to protect our homeland so that we can keep the war far
away in order to spare us the fate we would suffer if it were closer—the
way a few German cities are now experiencing and having to experience," Hitler said in the opening moments that evening. "It is therefore
better to keep the front a thousand or if necessary even two thousand
kilometers from our homeland than to have the front on the border of
the Reich and have to defend it there." Hitler urged the roomful of party
stalwarts to vigilance and fortitude, in the knowledge that their cause
was a just one, and to remember that they represented the bulwark of
European civilization.

"In these days, Sven Hedin published a book in which, thankfully, he
cited word for word the proposal on Poland that I submitted to the English," Hitler said. "I felt a chill when I reread this proposal and can
only be thankful that destiny saw fit that things should go differently."
Expanding on the observation he had made to Hedin the previous Friday, Hitler said that had the Germans devoted the last decade to financing their schools, beautifying their towns, and building streets and
apartments instead of building up their military, the results would have
been catastrophic for Europe. "And one day the storm from the East
would have been unleashed and swept across Poland before we would
have even noticed and stood less than a hundred and fifty kilometers east
of Berlin. That this did not happen is to the credit of the gentlemen who
rejected my proposal back then."

For the next two hours, Hitler talked about Jewish conspiracies,
Napoleon's defeat in 1812, the German defeat in 1918, and the inevitabil-

ity of disaster for the Americans. Plagiarizing Hedin's prediction that the Americans could never develop military capacity equal to that of the German army, with its centuries-old traditions, that the current U.S. soldiers who were training with plywood guns and cannons and cardboard tanks were no match for the battle-hardened veterans of the Wehrmacht, Hitler derisively dismissed the American war machine. He chided the Americans about their "herring boats" mounted with cannons. He dismissed the notion of U.S. "secret weapons." And he assured his audience, quoting Hedin almost verbatim, that the war would be won not with wealth and weaponry but by the force of will. "What we have is a holy conviction and a holy will, and in the end that is a thousand times more decisive than gold in the struggle between life and death." The war was not to be won by mass production or equipment, or even by the size of the armies, but by the iron will of titan figures. This was a battle of wills among Hitler, Stalin, Churchill, and Roosevelt.

"When Roosevelt attacks North Africa today with the observation that he has to protect it from Germany and Italy, it is not worth wasting a single word on the lying phrases of this old gangster," Hitler said. "He is without doubt the most hypocritical in that entire club that opposes us." Hitler denounced the American president as a "freemason," as a "puppet of the Jews," as an enemy of freedom and true democracy, as the *Oberstrolch,* or chief rogue. "And when this *Oberstrolch von Roosevelt*—there is no other term for him—comes here and declares he must rescue Europe with American methods, I can only say: The man should worry about saving his own country!"

Quoting from Hedin, Hitler observed that Roosevelt was using the war in Europe as a means of distracting American attention from the thirteen million unemployed at home. He contrasted American materialism with European values, and tallied the alliance that had assembled itself in defense of European culture—Italy, Romania, Hungary, Finland, Slovakia, Croatia, and Spain. "Think about this, everyone, every man and woman, that in this war it will be a question of existence or obliteration of our people," Hitler concluded. "And if you comprehend that, then every thought and every action you take should represent a prayer for our Germany!"

The speech ended with polite but subdued applause. There were no chorus chants of *"Sieg Heil!"* Hitler departed the hall and withdrew immediately to his Prince Regent Square apartment. Max Domarus, the great chronicler of Hitler oratory, claimed that it was the most "miserable" speech of Hitler's political career. In contrast, Goebbels had found Hitler in "admirable" form that evening, but could not overlook the portentous developments along the battle fronts. "Everyone knows that if things can be forced into a particular direction," he observed in his diary that evening, "we are at a turning point of the war."

The American landings that morning in North Africa were clearly on everyone's mind, as was the accumulating evidence that the course of the war was beginning to shift measurably. Two days earlier, the British had shattered the German defenses at El Alamein, dispatching Erwin Rommel's Afrika Korps into headlong retreat. Pressure was mounting on the German Sixth Army at Stalingrad. That same week, halfway around the world, American marines had captured Japanese positions on a small island called Guadalcanal, the first significant U.S. victory in the Pacific.

On Tuesday, November tenth, the day after Hitler's beer hall speech, Winston Churchill also reflected on recent developments. He expressed cautious optimism following the German defeat at El Alamein. "Now this is not the end, it is not even the beginning of the end," he said. "But it is, perhaps, the end of the beginning."

BOOK NINE

A Miracle Deferred

Pious people say, the darkest hour is nearest the dawn.
THOMAS CARLYLE, *History of Friedrich II*
of Prussia, Called Frederick the Great

O N SUNDAY EVENING, March 11, 1945, Joseph Goebbels called on
Hitler, who was working late in his office in the New Reich Chancellery. Goebbels wanted to report on his two-day inspection of the German defenses in East Prussia and to present Hitler with an abridged
German translation of Thomas Carlyle's 1858 biography of Frederick the
Great. Hitler himself had just returned from the front, now a mere hundred miles east of Berlin, where he had spent the day visiting emplacements, shaking hands with soldiers, and conferring with generals—all in
the presence of propaganda units.

Since coming to power twelve years before, he had fashioned this second Sunday in March, traditionally reserved as a day of national mourn-
ing, into National Hero Day, an occasion for flaunting German military
muscle—on this date in 1935 he declared his intent to rearm Germany,
and in 1941 he triumphantly paraded captured enemy weaponry through
the streets of Berlin—but this year there was little to celebrate. Advanced
units of the American 101st Airborne Division had seized the railroad
bridge at Remagen after the German commander refused to detonate
the bridge in order to allow fleeing civilians to cross it. Hitler had five
officers executed on the spot, but the damage had been done. The Amer-

An antiquarian "history" of
Frederick the Great is one of several
surviving books Hitler owned on
his Prussian hero.

icans had their first foothold east of the Rhine. That Sunday, they spanned the river with three pontoon bridges.

In recognition of the grim news from the front, Hitler set a tone of resoluteness for National Hero Day 1945. "There has never been a great historical state of the past that did not find itself in a similar situation," he announced in a message to the frontline troops. "Rome in the second war against the Carthaginians, Prussia in the Seven Years' War against Europe. Those are only two of many examples," Hitler wrote in his missive. "It is therefore my unalterable decision, and it must be the immovable will of all, not to set a worse example than those before us have done." The humiliation of 1918 could not be allowed to repeat itself. It could not be forgotten that the Allies were intent on nothing less than the "extermination of the German nation." The words of Frederick the Great had to be remembered: "Provide resistance and attack the enemy until in the end they grow tired and collapse!"

Hitler had returned to Berlin that evening in noticeably good spirits "emotionally and intellectually," as Goebbels observed when he called on him in his office. Before Goebbels could give his report on conditions at the front, the conversation focused on a discussion they had begun a few weeks earlier. At the time, Goebbels had mentioned that he had been rereading the biography of Frederick the Great by Thomas Carlyle, and was struck by the courage that the Prussian king had shown in times of adversity. Goebbels and Hitler had talked about the historic stature Frederick had achieved over time, and about their own need to comport themselves in such a manner so that in centuries to come they, too, could serve as "examples of heroic resilience."

Now Goebbels was giving Hitler a copy of Carlyle's book, an appropriate gift for the day of national heroism. Visibly pleased, Hitler recalled Carlyle's theory of "exceptional personalities," individuals who not only leave their mark on history but also provide inspiration for future leaders. "It must also be our ambition to set an example for our own time," Hitler said, "so that future generations under similar crises and pressure can look upon us just the way we today are looking upon the heroes of our own past history."

Goebbels agreed and gave Hitler a case in point. In East Prussia, he had watched Ferdinand Schörner, the forty-five-year-old general commanding the Third Panzer Division, resist a series of Soviet assaults and stabilize a stretch of crumbling front. Yes, Hitler said, he knew Schörner to be an exceptional commander. Goebbels said that Schörner embodied the ruthless determination that it took to win wars. For example, he told Hitler, in order to stem the growing tide of desertions, Schörner

Hitler's desk in his New Reich Chancellery office, where he
continued to work in the final months of the war.
Note books on both sides of his desk.

immediately hanged anyone caught behind the lines without permission. The trees near the front, Goebbels observed with satisfaction, dangled with the corpses of uniformed German soldiers with placards around their necks that declared I AM A DESERTER. I REFUSED TO PROTECT GERMAN WOMEN AND CHILDREN AND HAVE THEREFORE BEEN HANGED. Goebbels liked the compelling simplicity of Schörner's message: At the front, you face the risk of being shot; in the rear, you are sure to be executed.

Hitler agreed. Schörner was a model commander. He would have to promote him at the next opportunity. As often happened with Hitler, a single remark could trigger a series of associations that could occupy him for hours, which was clearly the case on this Sunday night, for he spent the next two hours musing on "examples" of leadership in their own day or, as was becoming increasingly evident in his view, the absence of it. He complained that in recent months his own generals had repeatedly subverted his authority, depleting the eastern front to bolster Berlin for a Soviet assault that he was certain would never come. He had placed Himmler in charge of the eastern armies in the hope of seeing his "loyal Heinrich" instill discipline among the generals, only to watch Himmler turn against him as well; in defiance of Hitler's explicit orders, and at the ultimate peril to the Reich, Himmler, too, was beginning to reinforce Berlin. This would bring catastrophe, Hitler predicted.

Why not discipline Himmler for this insubordination, Goebbels wondered. It was futile, Hitler said. There were too many ways to subvert authority. In the end, he would be proved right, but by then it would not matter. The war would be lost. Instead, Hitler said he was developing an alternate plan for rescuing the Reich: to divide the enemy politically, to ally himself with one of the parties and force an end to the fighting.

He told Goebbels he had detected fissures among the enemy. The British alliance with the Soviets was clearly one of convenience, even desperation. Initially, he had hoped to ally with the British against the Soviets, but the current political constellation in England made this impossible. "Churchill has run amok, and set himself the single and insane goal of exterminating Germany, even if it means the destruction of England as well," Hitler told Goebbels. "Thus, we have no choice but to look around for other opportunities."

Unfortunately, he said, a similar dynamic prevailed in the United States. Roosevelt had driven the Europeans into war in the first place, and was intent on letting them destroy themselves. Thus, Moscow remained the only viable option. "It has to be our goal to drive back the Soviets in the east and extract an exceptionally high toll in blood and equipment. Then the Kremlin might become more flexible with us,"

Hitler said. "A separate peace agreement with them would naturally alter the situation with the war radically." Unlike Churchill or Roosevelt, he said, he did not worry about public opinion. He could alter Soviet policy at will. The solution was clear: Moscow had to be turned. Hitler's strategy was to fan German hatred of the Anglo-Americans for forcing Europe into war, for bombing German cities into ruin, for laying waste to the Continent, then, with equal force, steel German resolve in the east, bleed the Soviet armies, deliver a series of decisive blows that would blunt the Russian advance, then negotiate peace. End the fighting in the east, Hitler said, echoing Schlieffen's wisdom, and the rest will take care of itself.* He instructed Goebbels: "Preach revenge against the east and hatred against the west."

This was the Hitler Goebbels knew: defiant, ruthless, commanding, calculating, visionary. As Goebbels departed Hitler's office late that night, he passed a clutch of generals waiting in the foyer. They appeared exhausted, weary, defeated. "A tired crowd that is really depressing," Goebbels wrote in his diary that night, recording his gift of Carlyle's book. "It is shameful that the Führer was able to find so few respectable colleagues. In this circle, he is the only person of distinction."

WHEN GOEBBELS HANDED Hitler the abridged German translation of Carlyle's biography of Frederick the Great, a sprawling twenty-one-hundred-page epic published between 1858 and 1865, he was not only fueling Hitler's lifelong preoccupation with Frederick the Great but handing him a book by an author whose notions of leadership and history Hitler had long embraced.

---

* In his copy of Hugo Rochs's Schlieffen biography, Hitler has marked in pencil a passage on page 61 that anticipates this fallback measure. "The most difficult campaign plans are those in which one must defend oneself against much stronger and more powerful enemies. Then one must take refuge in politics and seek to divide one's enemies from within or to separate one or the other of them from the rest by offering advantages."

As a pioneer of the great leader theory, Carlyle believed that "the history of what man has accomplished in this world is at bottom the History of the Great Men who have worked here." He despised representational government. "Democracy never yet, that we heard of, was able to accomplish much work, beyond that same canceling of itself," Carlyle once observed. Imperious leaders were to be revered, studied, and emulated, no matter how flawed. "One comfort is, that Great Men, taken up in any way, are profitable company," Carlyle wrote. "We cannot look, however imperfectly, upon a great man without gaining something." Carlyle hated Irishmen and Jews and once authored a racist tract he belligerently titled "An Occasional Discourse on the Nigger Question."

A critic once claimed that Carlyle had spent seven "miserable" years trying to make Frederick "presentable" to a European public. In fact, Carlyle reveled in the enterprise. He expressed nothing but admiration for this eighteenth-century despot who "left the world all bankrupt," in "bottomless abysses of destruction," with his enemies "in quite ruinous circumstances." He was fascinated by the king's "quiet stoicism," his "great consciousness and some conscious pride," and, in particular, his eyes, "potent brilliant eyes," which were at once "vigilant and penetrating," and emanated "a lambent outer radiance springing from some great inner sea of light and fire in the man." Carlyle found Frederick "miraculous," a man who tottered repeatedly on the brink of disaster, even once contemplated suicide in the face of overwhelming odds, and yet had "defended a little Prussia against all Europe, year after year, for seven long years, till Europe had had enough, and gave up the enterprise as one it could not manage." William Butler Yeats once called Carlyle "the chief inspirer of self-educated men."

Carlyle's lyrical blend of brutality and sentimentality spoke to Hitler's own toxic emotional constitution. Carlyle's works occupied shelf space in Hitler's first bookcase in his Thiersch Street apartment, and may have inspired Hitler to fashion himself as the "drummer"—*Trommler*—of the early Nazi movement, a designation that Carlyle similarly assigns to the young regent in chapter six of book one of his Frederick biography, when his "Fred" reveals his nascent martial spirit by taking a drum in hand and banging away much to his father's delight. "The paternal heart ran over with glad fondness, invoking Heaven to confirm the omen," Carlyle writes, noting that the man who began his career as a "drummer" went on to conquer a continent.

"It is wondrous when the English historian Carlyle emphasizes that Frederick the Great, so help him God, lived a life devoted solely to the service of his people," Hitler said in the closing remarks of his 1924 trial. He continued to invoke Carlyle for the rest of his life. "There is much to be said about leaders, and it is certain that a leader is of tremendous importance for a people, but of equal importance is the people itself," Hitler said in May 1927, while addressing a group of Nazi Party leaders. "Carlyle wrote that Frederick the Great was not only a great monarch but also that the Prussian people deserved a great monarch. The people also have to be worthy."

Hitler invoked this same Carlylian notion two decades later, as his Reich began to crumble. "If the German people must acquiesce in this war, then they were too weak," Hitler declared on August 4, 1944, two months after the Allies had splashed ashore at Normandy to breach his Fortress Europe, and "they would not have passed their test before history and would be destined to nothing other than destruction." In March 1945, with the obliteration of his Reich inevitable, Hitler issued his infamous "Nero Order," which called for the destruction of Germany's public infrastructure, invoking the same Carlylian logic. "It is not necessary to worry about what the German people will need for elemental survival," Hitler told Albert Speer. "For the nation has proved itself weaker, and the future belongs solely to the stronger eastern nation."

On that Sunday night in mid-March, when Hitler spoke of "exceptional men" and of comporting oneself for posterity, he was clearly echoing his readings of Carlyle, just as he was when he outlined his intentions for a political solution to the looming military catastrophe. As a lifelong student of Carlyle, Hitler could not have missed the parallels

between his own situation and Carlyle's depiction of the darkest hour of
the Prussian king:

> Since December 9th, Frederick is in Breslau, in some remainder of his
> ruined Palace there; and is represented to us, in Books, as sitting amid
> ruins; no prospect ahead of him but ruin. Withdrawn from Society;
> looking fixedly on the gloomiest future. Sees hardly anybody; speaks,
> except on matters of business, nothing.

Carlyle observes that by late 1861, Frederick's empire is on the verge
of ruin with the great forces of continental Europe—Austria, France,
and Russia—assembled against him with overwhelming odds. German
cities are occupied or in ruins. In a letter dated January 18, 1862, to the
Marquis d'Argens, Frederick contemplates suicide—he speaks of a "little
Glass Tube" that will end it all—and seeks solace in the hope of some
unforeseen turn of events. "If Fortune continues to pursue me, doubt-
less I shall sink," Frederick writes. "It is only she that can extricate me
from the situation I am in. I escape out of it by looking at the Universe
on the great scale, like an observer from some distant Planet; all then
seems to me so infinitely small, and I almost pity my enemies for giving
themselves such trouble about so very little."

Frederick goes on to say that he finds refuge in his books. "I read a
great deal," he writes. "I devour my Books, and that brings useful allevi-
ation. But for my Books, I think hypochondria would have had me in
bedlam before now. In fine, dear Marquis, we live in troublous times and
in desperate situations."

Frederick concludes the letter with a description of himself as a
"Stage Hero; always in danger, always on the point of perishing." He
hopes only that "the conclusion will come; and if the end of the piece be
lucky, we will forget the rest."

Then comes sudden and unexpected news from Petersburg. The day
after Frederick pens this despairing missive, he learns that his sworn
enemy, the tsarina Elizabeth, is dead, victim to an illness as unantici-

pated as it is fatal. "[T]hat the implacable Imperial Woman, INFAME
CATIN DU NORD, is verily dead. Dead; and does not hate me any
more," Frederick jubilates. "Deliverance, Peace and Victory lie in the
word!" Better still, Elizabeth is succeeded by her nephew, Peter, who as
chance should have it, is an unapologetic Germanophile who "has long
been privately a sworn friend and admirer of the king; and hastens, not
too SLOWLY as the king had feared, but far the reverse, to make it
known to all mankind."* Peter III sunders Russia's alliances with Austria
and France, withdraws the Russian armies from the battlefields, and dis-
patches an envoy to Berlin. Prussia is saved. The miracle of the House of
Brandenburg has come to pass. Carlyle observes, "Frederick is difficult
to kill."

Huddled amid the ruins of Berlin—with the Ministry of Propaganda
across the street a gutted shell, the adjacent old Reich Chancellery
damaged by bombs, and the vast walls of the New Reich Chancellery
stripped of tapestries and paintings, its library evacuated of books in
anticipation of destruction—Hitler may well have taken delusional comfort in the pages of Carlyle on that Sunday night, or at least at some
point in the weeks that followed. Hitler's preoccupation with the belea-
guered but ultimately triumphant Prussian king is also evidenced by the
portrait of Frederick that he had hung on the wall of his bunker suite.
His choice of paintings was telling. Among the several Frederick por-

* Hitler's oldest surviving book on Frederick the Great is a nineteenth-century volume,
Histories and Whatever Else There Is to Report About Old Fritz, the Great King and Hero. Written
in verse, it relates the same incident as no less consequential but in slightly quainter terms:

So was the chain that long did dangle
And held Prussia in a murderous strangle
Just as they once together were bound
Fell away in a single round.

*(So wurde die Ringe der grossen Kette
Die Preussen beinahe erdrosselt hätte—
Wie einst an einander gefugt man sie fand—
Jetzt würden abgetrennt nacheinand—)*

traits that he owned—reproduced in a bound volume, *Catalogue of Adolf Hitler's Private Gallery,* among his books at the Library of Congress—he selected a work by Anton Graff, an eighteenth-century artist whom Max Osborn had praised for the "psychological and luminous concentration" he brought to his subjects' eyes. The painting shows Friedrich in his later years, gray-haired and mellow, well "beyond his troublous times and desperate situations," the beneficiary of the sort of unexpected turn of events that Hitler was awaiting; and that seemed to present itself in the second week of April.

On Thursday, April 12, circumstance seemed to collude in this delusional end game. While resting at his private retreat in Warm Springs, Georgia, Franklin Roosevelt suffered a massive brain embolism and died.

WHEN WORD OF ROOSEVELT'S DEATH reached the *Führerbunker,* jubilation swept the subterranean space. There are numerous accounts of how Hitler received the news, but the general consensus seems to follow that given by Albert Speer. "When I arrived in the bunker," he remembered, "Hitler caught sight of me and rushed to me with a degree of animation rare in him in those days. He held a newspaper clipping in his hand. 'Here, read it! Here! Here we have the miracle I always predicted. Who was right? The war isn't lost. Read it! Roosevelt is dead!' " Hitler told Speer that this was proof that Providence was watching over him. Goebbels was beside himself with jubilation. He told Speer that history was repeating itself, that the miracle of Brandenburg had again come to pass. As with Frederick the Great, salvation had come at the last moment.

Hitler seized the moment to rally his battered troops and issued a frontline declaration: "In this hour all of Germany is watching you, my eastern warriors, and only hopes that your resilience, your fanaticism, through your weapons and under your leadership the Bolshevik onslaught will suffocate in a bloodbath. In the moment in which destiny has removed from this earth the greatest war criminal of all time, the turning point in this war has been decided."

It is impossible to know if Hitler believed the words he was offering Germany, or whether they were part of a calculated propagandistic effort to exploit what he saw as a remarkably fortuitous opportunity; whether he was simply harmonizing his rhetoric with that of Goebbels, or whether, in fact, these words emerged from some deeper conviction, a half-pleading, half-hopeful incantation shouted through the mist of self-delusion and into the still denser fog of desperation; or whether, in fact, these words were an expression of Hitler's alleged steadfast conviction that Providence, or chance, had once again seen fit, as with his revered Frederick the Great, to rescue him from ruin.

The circumstances were so unexpected, the timing so uncanny, that even the soberest observers were left pondering Hitler's reaction for years to come. "I don't have a compelling answer even today to the question of what in this declaration was false optimism and what Hitler truly believed," one Hitler adjutant recalled after the war. Another observer of the scene was inclined to believe that Hitler "was literally obsessed with the idea of some miraculous salvation, that he clung to it like a drowning man to a straw."

In the days following Roosevelt's death, Hitler monitored developments to see if he could detect a shift in the political climate. He even considered dispatching Speer to the United States for a meeting with Truman. All the while he scrutinized the military situation for a perceptible shift in battlefield fortunes.

But April 13, the day after Roosevelt's death, saw no abatement in enemy advances. Along the eastern front, the Soviets were bludgeoning the German defenses. In Vienna, they would soon obliterate the last pocket of resistance. A hundred miles to the west, Allied bombers pounded the area in a line from Venice to Linz. Berlin was battered by three successive waves of bombers. Three days later, on April 16, when the Soviet armies unleashed a final massive offensive against the German capital, it became clear there would be no second Brandenburg miracle. On April 20, Hitler's fifty-sixth birthday was "celebrated" in a notably subdued atmosphere, with none of the pomp and celebration that had marked his previous birthday, when, two months before the Allied landings at Normandy, he still commanded the Continent.

One of his gifts in 1944 had been a specially bound facsimile edition of letters from Frederick to his lifelong servant and confidant, Michael Gabriel Fredersdorf, written between 1747 and 1755, in which Frederick muses on mundane affairs such as the expense of owning horses, the quality of operatic performances in Berlin, and dealing with a woman who says she can produce gold from water (he recommends imprisoning her until she can make good on her claim). Bound in white linen, and with an adulatory birthday greeting printed in large gold letters, this oversize album preserves the ostentatiousness and delusional confidence of the occasion, which Hitler attended in a celebratory white uniform.

A year later, stooped and grim, he wore his spattered field jacket. He attended the dinner, shook the necessary hands, then withdrew to his bunker quarters, where later Traudl Junge found him sitting in his armchair with his reading glasses and a book.

After that day, Junge told me, he never again spoke of a divine intervention or of a miraculous turn of events. Hitler spent his last ten days in an atmosphere of increasing gloom as the military situation deteriorated. On April 23, with the Soviet armies on the outskirts of Berlin, Göring sent a telegram from the Obersalzberg requesting decision-making authority in the event that Hitler was unable to exercise his responsibilities from the besieged capital. Sensing betrayal, Hitler had Göring arrested two days later. That same day, April 25, Soviet and American forces met on the bridge at Torgau, on the Elbe, in northwestern Saxony. Instead of exchanging gunfire, they shook hands. That Friday, Hermann Fegelein, Himmler's adjutant and Eva Braun's brother-in-law, was arrested while attempting to flee Berlin with a suitcase full of foreign currency. The next day Hitler learned that Himmler was in

secret peace negotiations with the Allies. For Hitler, this was the bitter-
est disappointment of all. The following day, he had his cyanide capsules
tested on his German shepherd, Blondi, then withdrew to a side room to
dictate his last will and testament.

As if taking a final cue from his mentor Frederick, and in a tradition of
subsequent rulers, Hitler divided this parting document into a personal
and political testament. Unlike Frederick's last will, which was dictated
in his waning years from the elegant though rheumatic circumstances of
Sanssouci and provided his vision for smooth transition and good governance after his demise, Hitler's final words were plaintive, defensive, and
mendacious, dictated shortly after midnight in a bunker room, as he
stood at a table with his head down and his arms outstretched, while
Traudl Junge sat across from him with a pencil and stenographic pad. "It
is untrue that I or anyone else in Germany wanted war in 1939," Hitler
began.

> It was wanted and provoked exclusively by those international states-
> men, who either were of Jewish origins or worked for Jewish interests. I
> have made too many offers for limiting and restricting arms production
> for posterity, with all talk of cowardice aside, to be able to blame me for
> the responsibility for the outbreak of war. Further, I never wanted
> another war with England or even America after the first wretched
> world war.

He went on to detail his eleventh-hour efforts to avert war in the summer of 1939, as dutifully recounted by Sven Hedin, and attributed his failure to the desire on the part of British industry to go to war, and to the
"propaganda of international Jewry." He then detailed the betrayals he
had suffered at the hands of his own associates, and designated the gov-
erning body that was to rule Germany after his death. It seemed a
strange way to write a will, a stranger way still to make provisions for an
empire that had already ceased to exist. Hitler's final act was stranger
yet. "Since I believed during the years of struggle that I could not respon-

sibly contract a marriage, I have now decided before the conclusion of this earthly course to take as my wife that girl who after long years of loyal friendship came to this nearly besieged city to share her fate with mine," Hitler stipulated in his private will. "By her own wish she will go as my wife into death. This will compensate us for what we lost through my work in the service of my people."

While Junge hammered these words in triplicate on a manual typewriter, Hitler walked down the hall to another room that had been set for a small wedding ceremony. With a justice of the peace who had been pulled from the street fighting above, and with Martin Bormann and Goebbels serving as witnesses, Adolf Hitler and Eva Braun were declared man and wife. A round of champagne was poured, glasses were raised, and eventually, shortly after four o'clock in the morning, the last will and testament was signed. Then Hitler and Braun withdrew to their private quarters. The next morning, when Junge encountered the newly minted bride and hesitated, Braun said, "It's all right, you can call me Frau Hitler."

The next two days were spent discussing the respective advantages of suicide by cyanide or pistol shot, the leave-taking of associates, the rumble of approaching gunfire. At one point, a bomb struck overhead, sending a shiver through the bunker complex. On April 30, Hitler and his wife took lunch as usual, in the company of Traudl Junge and another secretary. Hitler ate in silence, his shoulders hunched, his eyes fixed on the table. After lunch, he summoned his entire entourage and bade them farewell, shaking hands and murmuring parting words that were barely audible. Braun bequeathed her silver fox stole to Junge. Hitler promised the Graff portrait to Hans Bauer, and gave his gold party pin to Goebbels's wife, Magda. Shortly before three o'clock that afternoon, Hitler and Braun withdrew to their quarters. At some point between three-thirty and four, a single pistol shot was fired.

When Hitler's adjutants opened the door, they were met with the acrid smell of cyanide and the sight of Braun stretched on the sofa, her

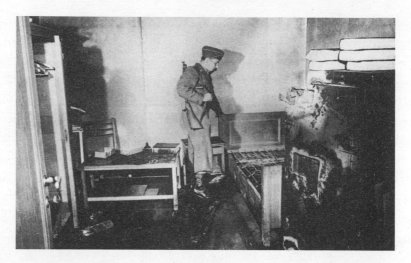

An American soldier inspecting Hitler's bedroom in the Berlin bunker. The room has been stripped of everything personal except Hitler's remaining books.

shoes neatly to the side. Hitler was slumped beside her with a single bullet in his head and a plate-size pool of blood on the floor. They were wrapped in blankets and carried up the narrow stairs to the chancellery garden, where they were placed in a shallow grave, doused with twenty-five gallons of petrol, and set ablaze. One witness remembers watching Braun's blue silk dress eviscerate, revealing for a brief instant her smooth, white skin, gradually charred to black amid the flames. Hitler's bunker rooms were also drenched with petrol and set ablaze, but the flames quickly choked and died in the tight, airless space.

A photograph of Hitler's bedroom at the time shows a spartan and plundered space. The bed has been stripped of its mattress, revealing a simple wooden bed frame and a loose weave of steel springs. Barren clothing hangers dangle in the open closet. A chest-high strongbox dominates the foreground. The thick door has been cut open with a welder's torch. In the far left corner, a simple wooden chair stands against the wall along with a low square table that almost abuts the bed. Nothing personal remains, with the exception of scattered books: five volumes stacked in two piles on top of the breached strongbox, clearly part of a series, possibly one of the Meyer or Brockhaus encyclopedias that Hitler invariably kept in his proximity. A single volume lies on the floor near the closet, and two more near the far wall. One book rests on the table, perched on the corner nearest Hitler's bed. It is the only volume whose spine faces the camera, and appears to be a handsomely bound tome of several hundred pages, as hefty as the abridged edition of Carlyle's *Frederick the Great;* its identity might have been decipherable from the spine were it not for the glare of the flash that blinds us to both author and title.

WE WILL NEVER KNOW the titles of the books Hitler had at his bedside the day he killed himself, but we do know eighty books that were in the bunker complex at the time, some rather recent acquisitions, such as a 1943 book titled *A Prehistory of Roosevelt's War,* by Hans Heinrich Dieckhoff. But there were also books he had acquired as a young man and at some point brought with him to Berlin: a 1913 treatise on Wagner's *Parsifal,* a tract on racial values published in 1917, a 1921 history of the swastika, and a dozen or so books on mystical and occult subjects all from the early 1920s, including a 120-page paperback called *The Prophecies of Nostradamus,* by Carl Loog, published in 1921.

In this cheap paperback, printed on paper that today is rapidly deteriorating, Loog predicts the emergence of a "prophet" "with a raging head"—*mit rasendem Kopf*—who will "liberate" the German people and make himself "heard around the world." In explicating one of Nostradamus's more cryptic passages, this 1921 publication predicts the outbreak of a "second world war" in 1939, with Germany going to war against Poland, France, and England. The author is so certain of the timing and circumstance of this future war—two decades into the future—that he cites the relevant Nostradamus stanza (century 3, quatrain 57) in its entirety and provides a detailed explication. "If you assume in the previous stanzas that Mars stands for war, then it is not difficult today to translate this riddle as 'world war,' " Loog writes. "The remaining Mars stanzas almost certainly then suggest a second or third world war." Loog sees Nostradamus's quatrain 57 as a road map to war:

> Seven times you will see the British nation change
> Steeped in blood in 290 years
> Free not at all from its support Germanic.
> Aries doubt his Bastarnian Pole.

The English nation will "change seven times" and be "steeped in blood" in 290 years' time; war will consume the "Bastarnian Pole." (Loog explains that "Bastarnians" were a Germanic tribe who once occupied an area acceded to Poland after 1918.) Loog sets England's 290-year countdown to bloodshed ticking in 1649, the year Charles I is executed and Oliver Cromwell comes to power, then catalogues the subsequent "changes" as corresponding to the reigns of Charles II, James II, William III, Queen Anne, and finally George I.

"From that point on, the politics of England run pretty much in one direction," Loog writes, noting that the remaining balance of 150 years proceeds with relative calm, bringing him to the fateful year of 1939. "Nostradamus evidently wants to explain that 1939 will go hand in hand with the last and greatest English crisis and a crisis for the reconstituted country of Poland," Loog writes.

When I ordered this particular volume in the rare book reading room at Brown University, it was brought to me in an acid-free gray paper sleeve, marked with the catalogue number 38. As I leafed through the pages, I found no marginalia, no penciled intrusions, either comments or underscorings, no question marks or exclamation points, nor any other revealing artifacts that might give some bearing on Hitler's engagement with this remarkable text. The only evidence that the book had been read was the jagged edge where some pages had been cut with a dull-edged object, perhaps a letter opener, leaving a frayed seam along the top of each page that had grown brittle with time. In studying the volume, I quickly discovered that Hitler, or whoever cut these pages, had sliced only as far as page 42, twenty-six pages before Loog's prediction of the "prophet" with the raging head and a "second world war."

Whether Hitler was aware of Nostradamus's predictions we will never know, but with this particular volume, the Hitler library both fulfills the Benjamin conceit and extends its dimensions: Not only is the collector preserved within his books, but his life is scripted in their pages.

The Fates of Books

WHEN WALTER BENJAMIN WROTE that books "preserve" the collector, he saw the private library not only as the summation of a life in which the collector became "comprehensible" once his last volume was acquired and shelved, but also as the end point to the trajectory of the books themselves, which passed from hand to hand, often through remarkably circuitous routes, until coming to final rest on the shelf of the collector. Like Alois Hudal, Benjamin found wisdom in Latin: *habent sua fata libelli*.

"These words have been intended as a general statement about books," Benjamin observed. "So books like *The Divine Comedy,* Spinoza's *Ethics,* and *The Origin of Species* have their fates. A collector, however, interprets this Latin saying differently. For him, not only books but also copies of books have their fates."

For Benjamin, each volume of a library represented an individual "destiny," each with its own story, its own fated purpose in the life of the collector, whether it be to entertain, to distract, to inform, or to decorate, but ultimately and collectively to bear witness after the collector was "exterminated," like an assembled chorus from a Greek tragedy.

There is, of course, a detectable myopia, even presumption, to this particular Benjamin conceit, for it assumes that a particular book is "fated" for a particular library, that its ultimate raison d'être is to "preserve" its collector, to play the role of posthumous witness, to be pressed into lasting servitude to the memory of the "exterminated" collector. This is certainly a comforting thought to the collector with an eye to posterity, but a blinkered view to the true fate of books, to the fact that few libraries ever survive their collector intact, as Benjamin himself painfully discovered in March 1933. Within weeks of Hitler's seizure of power, Benjamin fled Germany, entrusting his book collection to a neighbor, who eventually forwarded a portion of the collection—"the most precious half"—to Denmark, where Benjamin was staying with the playwright Bertolt Brecht. Benjamin eventually moved to Paris, taking his books with him.

When money grew tight, Benjamin sold individual volumes to make ends meet. His melancholy deepened when he attempted to secure the other half of his library in Berlin, only to learn that his remaining books and papers had been destroyed.

Following the German invasion in 1940, Benjamin was briefly detained by French authorities, then released through the intervention of a French acquaintance. He abandoned the surviving "precious" portion of his library, and fled south to Lourdes, then to Marseille, where he hoped to immigrate to the United States, where fellow German intellectuals were in exile. In a letter to a former student, Hannah Arendt, Benjamin spoke of the "fear-filled life"—*angsterfülltes Leben*—he now faced, not knowing what the next hour, let alone the next day, might bring. At any moment, he could be handed over to the Gestapo. In early autumn, he decided to cross the French-Spanish border at Portbou, an isolated coastal town unpatrolled by French authorities. On the morning of September 27, 1940, Benjamin set off with a small group of refugees on a brief but rigorous walk along a mountain path to Portbou, only to be detained by the Spanish guards who had temporarily closed the border. Exhausted and fearful of being handed over to the French authorities, Benjamin scrawled a brief note that evening—"I am in a hopeless situation and have no other possibility but to end it"—and took his life with an overdose of morphine.

While desperation and terror were certainly the most immediate causes for Benjamin's suicide, Hannah Arendt later surmised a deeper existential crisis: the loss of his books. Standing at that desolate border crossing on the littoral edge of the Continent, he was peering into a future both bleak and threatening, knowing that his remaining books—his refuge, his "dwelling," his livelihood—had passed into the hands of the Paris Gestapo. In reflecting on his final desperate act, Arendt was pained but not surprised. "How was he to live without a library?" she asked. What Arendt did not know, and Benjamin could never have assumed, is that his library in fact survived him. Confiscated by the Gestapo, it was dispatched to Berlin, where it was in turn claimed by the Soviets and taken to Moscow, only to be returned to Germany, first to the Theodor Adorno Archive in Frankfurt and eventually to its own archive in Berlin, where its journey began six decades earlier.

Hitler's own library was rapidly disassembled in the chaos of his collapsing empire. By the time he shot himself, American soldiers were already picking apart his collections in Munich. In Hitler's office at the Nazi Party headquarters in the Brown House, a young lieutenant found the copy of Henry Ford's *My Life and Work* that Hanfstaengl had inscribed back in 1924; the lieutenant eventually took the two-volume set, which "showed evidence of thumbing," back to New York and put it up for sale at Scribner's Bookstore.

At Hitler's Prince Regent Square residence, war correspondent Lee Miller found Hitler's books partially intact. "To the left of the public rooms was a library full of richly bound books and many presentation volumes of signatures from well-wishers," she noted. "The library was uninteresting in that everything of personal value had been evacuated: empty shelves were bleak spoors of flight." A photograph shows Miller seated at Hitler's desk. A dozen or so random books litter the adjacent shelves—paperbacks, hardcovers, a large, scuffed picture book of Nuremberg, three early editions of *Mein Kampf* in their original dust jackets.

Four days later, advance troops of the 101st Airborne Division arrived on the Obersalzberg to find Hitler's Berghof a smoldering ruin. In the second-floor study, the hand-tooled bookcases had been reduced to ash, leaving only charred concrete walls and a soot-blackened strongbox, in which the soldiers found several first editions of *Mein Kampf*. The rest of Hitler's books were discovered in a converted bunker room. "At the far end were arranged lounge chairs and reading lamps," an intelligence officer assigned to the 101st reported. "Most of the books were concerned with art, architecture, photography and histories of campaigns

War correspondent Lee Miller in Hitler's Prince Regent Square residence. Most personal books had been removed by Hitler's staff. Note copies of Mein Kampf *with the original dust jackets.*

and wars. A hasty inspection of the scattered books showed that it [*sic*] was notably lacking in literature and almost entirely devoid of drama and poetry." The classified report identifies only three works by name: *Genesis of the World War,* by the American revisionist historian Harry Elmer Barnes, Niccolò Machiavelli's *The Prince,* and the critiques by the eighteenth-century philosopher Immanuel Kant.

The handsomely bound tomes with their distinctive bookplates became the totem of choice for the victorious soldiers. Newsreel footage records American soldiers picking through Hitler's book collection. One sequence shows a soldier opening a large volume to reveal the Hitler ex libris as the camera zooms in for a close-up; in another, several men emerge from the bunker with stacks of books under their arms. In the weeks that followed, the Berghof collection was picked apart book by book. By May 25, when a delegation of U.S. senators arrived on the Obersalzberg, they had to content themselves with albums from Hitler's record collection. Not a single book remained.

In those same weeks, Hitler's book collection in Berlin was also disassembled. At nine o'clock on the morning of May 2, thirty-six hours after Hitler's suicide, a Soviet medical team entered the nearly abandoned *Führerbunker.* They reemerged an hour later waving black lace brassieres from Eva Braun's wardrobe and carrying satchels filled with diverse souvenirs, including several first editions of *Mein Kampf.* Successive waves of plundering followed. When Albert Aronson arrived in Berlin as part of the American delegation sent to negotiate the joint occupation of the city, his Soviet hosts took him on a tour of Hitler's private quarters and as a courtesy let him take an unclaimed pile of eighty books. In those same weeks, the entire Reich Chancellery library—an estimated ten thousand volumes—was secured by a Soviet "trophy brigade" and shipped to Moscow and never seen again.* The only significant portions

* In the early 1990s, a Moscow newspaper reported on the presence of these books in an abandoned church in the Moscow suburb of Uzkoe. Shortly after the article appeared, the collection was removed and has not been seen since.

of Hitler library's to survive intact were the three thousand books discovered in the Berchtesgaden salt mine, twelve hundred of which made
it into the Library of Congress. The rest appear to have been "duped
out" in the process of cataloguing the collection.

Thousands more lie in the attics and bookshelves of homes of veterans across the United States. Occasionally, random volumes find their
way to the public. Several years ago, a copy of Peter Maag's *Realm of God
and the Contemporary World,* published in 1915, with "A. Hitler" scrawled
on the inside cover, was discovered in the fifty-cent bin of a local library
sale in upstate New York. Following Aronson's death, his nephew
donated the eighty books from the *Führerbunker* to Brown University. In
the early 1990s, Daniel Traister, head of the rare book collection at the
University of Pennsylvania, was given a biography of Frederick the
Great along with several Berghof trophies. An accompanying note read
"Dan, you wouldn't believe how much money people want to offer me
for these things. So far, I haven't met one whom I want to have them.
Here: destroy them or keep them as you wish."

A few years ago, I received a similar note after writing an article on
Hitler's library for *The Atlantic Monthly.* A Minnesota book dealer had
inherited a Hitler book her mother had purchased at auction in the
1970s. Initially fascinated by the acquisition, the mother suffered a double bite of conscience: she was uncomfortable with profiting from a
Hitler artifact and was equally uneasy about the motivations of a potential purchaser. After the mother's death, her daughter inherited both the
book and the dilemma. Having read my article, and sensing that my
interests were purely academic, she offered me the book at cost. A week
later, Hitler's copy of *Body, Spirit and Living Reason,* by Carneades,
arrived in a cardboard box.

The treatise was in remarkably good condition, a hefty tome bound
in textured linen with leather triangles on each corner and a matching
leather spine with title and author embossed in gold. The linen was partially frayed and the leather was scuffed in places, but otherwise the vol-

ume was flawless. Opposite the Hitler ex libris, a typewritten note had
been tipped into the binding recording the volume's provenance:

> This volume was taken from Adolph [*sic*] Hitler's personal library
> located in the underground air-raid shelter in his home at Berchtes-
> gaden. It was picked up by Major A. J. Choos as a souvenir for Mr. E. B.
> Horwath on May 5, 1945.

For several years, *Body, Spirit and Living Reason* haunted the bookshelves of my Salzburg apartment until I, too, grew uncomfortable with

*The Hitler Library in the rare book
and manuscript division at the
Library of Congress, as
photographed in the 1970s.*

its presence. Like the Pennsylvania veteran and the Minnesota book dealer, I had no interest in profiting from the volume and had serious concerns about its further disposition. I ultimately resolved the dilemma by donating the volume to the Archive of the Contemporary History of the Obersalzberg in Berchtesgaden, a private repository established by a resident archivist to preserve the history of the town, including this dark chapter.

After spending nearly a decade behind a glass case in Hitler's second-floor Berghof study—a silent witness to his daytime meetings and late-night reading—the Carneades volume had found its way back to Berchtesgaden, where its journey had begun nearly seven decades earlier. Indeed, *habent sua fata libelli*.

ACKNOWLEDGMENTS

ADOLF HITLER WAS AN unsystematic book collector. He never engaged a professional librarian to organize or catalogue his books, delegating these responsibilities to housekeepers and adjutants. It has been left to a handful of postwar librarians and scholars to impose their own sense of order and significance on the surviving portions of his private library.

The earliest effort to organize Hitler's remnant books was undertaken by Hans Beilhack, a German librarian who tended to Hitler's books in a Munich storage depot following their confiscation by the Americans in the spring of 1945. In the 1950s, Arnold Jacobius sorted the volumes for the Library of Congress while training as a library intern in the rare books and manuscript division. The eminent scholar Gerhard Weinberg included Hitler's books in his landmark catalogue of captured German war documents, which he compiled as a newly minted graduate student.

Robert Waite drew on the collection for his controversial Freudian analysis, *Hitler: The Psychopathic God*, published by Basic Books in 1977. In 2003, the Hungarian scholar Ambrus Miskolczy published *Hitler's Library* with the Central European University Press, a personal memoir of a summer he spent studying the Hitler volumes. Reginald Phelps and Jehuda Wallach have also written insightfully on the collection.*

The most ambitious and successful effort to date is *The Hitler Library* by Philipp Gassert and Daniel Mattern. This dense, 550-page volume,

* Reginald H. Phelps, "Die Hitler Bibliothek," *Deutsche Rundschau* 80 (September 1954): 923–31; Jehuda Wallach, "Adolf Hitlers Privatbibliothek," *Zeitgeschichte* (1992): 29–50.

published by Greenwood Press in 2001, provides the first annotated catalogue of the 1,244 known Hitler books in the United States, which comprise at most 10 percent of Hitler's original collection. I am particularly grateful to these two scholars for their comprehensive work. Their book provides a veritable road map through Hitler's surviving books.

Before thanking those individuals who generously provided guidance and assistance with this book, I would like to acknowledge a number of former Hitler associates who shared with me details of Hitler's reading and book-collecting habits.

Herbert Döring, the Berghof manager from 1936 to 1941, detailed the disposition of books at Hitler's alpine retreat, and his sorting and shelving habits. Margarete Mittlstrasser, also at the Berghof, from 1936 until 1945, detailed Hitler's nocturnal reading habits: one book per night, either at his desk or in his armchair, always with a cup of tea. Traudl Junge, the private secretary whose memories of Hitler's final days inspired the film *Downfall,* spent half a day with me studying copies of pages with Hitler marginalia. Hitler's telephone operator Rochus Misch provided details of Hitler's book-littered quarters in the Berlin bunker.

As with any project involving archives, there are numerous individuals and institutions to be thanked. Let me first express my appreciation to the staff of the rare book collection at the Library of Congress, stewards to the largest remnant collection of Hitler's books. In the last six years, they have assisted me with the highest degree of courtesy, professionalism, and, most of all, patience. In this regard, I owe special thanks to Mark Dimunation, chief of the Rare Book and Special Collections Division, and Clark Evans, reference specialist in the Rare Book Reading Room.

Similar thanks are also due to Samuel Streit and his staff at the John Hay Library at Brown University; Daniel Traister, curator of research services for the rare book collection at the University of Pennsylvania; Leslie Morris, curator at the Houghton Library at Harvard University; Carol Leadenham, reference archivist, Ronald Bulatoff, archival specialist, at the Hoover Institution Library at Stanford University, Jenny Fichmann, an independent researcher for the Hoover Institution; Dr. Håkan Wahlquist, keeper of the Sven Hedin Foundation; Dr. Reinhard Horn, head of map collection and image archive at the Bavarian State Library; and the superb research and support staff at the Institute of Contemporary History in Munich. Appreciation also to the library research staff of the University of Michigan.

A number of individuals assisted me in my attempt to locate the still-elusive collection of plundered Hitler books in Moscow, in particular Astrid Eckert, Patricia Grimstead, and Konstantin Akinsha, as well as Oliver Halmburg and his research team at LoopFilm, in Munich. Particular thanks to Franz Fleischmann, researcher extraordinaire. Most significantly, I would like to express appreciation to Florian Beierl for his generosity in providing access to the Archive for the Contemporary History of the Obersalzberg in Berchtesgaden, the most extensive collection of primary source material on the Berghof and its residents. I would also like to thank him for sharing with me the original manuscript pages to *Mein Kampf*, and permitting me to use his extensive photographic record of Hitler's surviving books.

As always, I owe an enduring debt of gratitude to Richard M. Hunt and his team of former Harvard University teaching fellows from Literature and Arts C-45, Weimar and Nazi Culture, to my many former colleagues at the Salzburg Global Seminar, and in particular to the Salzburg photographer Herman Seidel. Thanks also to Sebastian Cody and Jonathan Petropoulos for their careful reading of early drafts of the manuscript, to Russell Riley for his help and support, and to Steven Bach who helped frame the idea of a "book about books." I owe particular gratitude to Jonathan Segal at Alfred A. Knopf for his vision, rigorous editing, and patience. The book also owes a great deal to the attentions of the entire team at Knopf, especially Kyle McCarthy and Joey McGarvey. As always, fond appreciation to my agent Gail Hochman, and to Marianne Merola.

And finally, thanks to my wife, Marie-Louise, who, as always, is my single greatest source of support and inspiration, and, of course, to my children Katrina, Brendan, and Audrey, who each helped in their own way.

In closing, I would like to remember Jerry Wager, the former head of the Rare Book Room at the Library of Congress, who passed away recently, unexpectedly, and at much too young an age. When I first began my research, in the spring of 2001, Jerry served as my guide to this collection, revealing hundreds of pages of marginalia that had been overlooked by generations of researchers and scholars. For several years, he continued to update me on his own investigations into the collection. There is hardly a chapter in this book that does not owe some insight or discovery to Jerry, whose spirit of intellectual inquiry and curatorial acuity is preserved in these pages.

APPENDIXES

BY THE END OF HIS LIFE, Hitler maintained private libraries at his residences in Berlin, Munich, and on the Obersalzberg, as well as a book depository at the "Führer Archive" in the basement of the Nazi Party headquarters at the Brown House in Munich. Except for a partial inventory of the Reich Chancellery library in Berlin, which is preserved at the Hoover Institute at Stanford University, there is no surviving catalogue of Hitler's book collection.

However, we do have several firsthand accounts that help us understand the texture of this vanished library. Most significant among these is Frederick Oechsner's description based on interviews with various Hitler associates, which was ultimately published in a 1942 book-length profile of Hitler titled *This Is the Enemy*. Though journalistic by nature and propagandistic in intent, Oechsner's account nevertheless provides, aside from its more sensational and salacious claims, the best portrait we have of Hitler's book collection. In comparison, the other three firsthand accounts are mere snapshot glimpses. The first of these comes from a classified report by the U.S. Army's Twenty-first Counterintelligence Corps, dating from May 1945, detailing the bunker complex beneath the Berghof. It includes a brief description of the vaulted room that served as an air raid shelter for Hitler's Berghof books but mentions only three of them by name. This is especially unfortunate, because in the weeks to follow the room was picked clean by pilfering neighbors, soldiers, and others.

A second postwar account, published by Hans Beilhack in a Munich daily newspaper in November 1946, describes the cache of Hitler's books discovered in a salt mine near Berchtesgaden. Though he mistakenly assumed the three thousand books under his care represented Hitler's entire library, he proved to be remarkably perceptive in gauging the "dilettantish" nature of Hitler's bibliophilic interests.

Finally, we have a Library of Congress memorandum dated January 9, 1952, which details the "Hitler Library" after it arrived in the United States but before it was accessioned into the rare book collection. The in-house report was written by Arnold Jacobius, a trained librarian hired on a temporary basis to provide an expert opinion on the final disposition of the books. Ultimately, Jacobius reduced the number of books to twelve hundred by recommending that the Library of Congress retain only those books with inscriptions, marginalia, or the Hitler ex libris. In the process, Jacobius "duped out" hundreds of Hitler's books that were anonymously absorbed into the main collection or sent to a distribution department, where they were disseminated to public libraries across the United States. It was an understandable and maybe necessary decision, given space constraints, but a good number of Hitler's personal acquisitions almost certainly vanished in the process, including a book that Beilhack notes in his account, a "how-to" book titled *The Art of Becoming a Speaker in a Few Hours.*

These four firsthand descriptions of the Hitler Library are intended to supplement my own account and provide the reader with additional perspectives on the man and his books.

APPENDIX A

From This Is the Enemy, *by Frederick Oechsner, 1942*

I FOUND THAT [HITLER'S] PERSONAL LIBRARY, which is divided between his residence in the Chancellery in Berlin and his country home on the Obersalzberg at Berchtesgaden, contains roughly 16,300 books. They may be divided generally into three groups:

First, the military section containing some 7,000 volumes, including the campaigns of Napoleon, the Prussian kings; the lives of all German and Prussian potentates who ever played a military role; and books on virtually all of the well-known military campaigns in recorded history.

There is Theodore Roosevelt's work on the Spanish American War, also a book by General von Steuben, who drilled our troops during the American Revolution. [Werner von] Blomberg, when he was war minister, presented Hitler with 400 books, pamphlets and monographs on the United States armed forces and he has read many of these.

The military books are divided according to countries. Those which were not available in German Hitler has had translated. Many of them, especially on Napoleon's campaigns, are extensively marginated in his own handwriting. There is a book on the Gran Chaco dispute [the 1932–35 war between Paraguay and Bolivia] by the German General [Hans] Kundt, who at one time (like Captain Ernst Röhm) was an instructor of troops in Bolivia. There are exhaustive works on uniforms, weapons, supply, mobilization, the building-up of armies in peacetime, morale and ballistics. In fact, there is probably not a single phase of military knowledge, ancient or modern, which is not dealt with in these 7,000 volumes, and quite obviously Hitler has read many of them from cover to cover.

The second section of some 1,500 books covers artistic subjects [such] as architecture, the theater, painting and sculpture, which, after military subjects, are Hitler's chief interest. The books include works on surrealism and Dada-ism, although Hitler has no use for this type of art.

One of his ironical marginal notes could be roughly translated: "Modern art will revolutionize the world? Rot!" In writing these notes Hitler never uses a fountain pen but an old-fashioned pen or an indelible pencil.

In drawers beneath the bookshelves he has a collection of photographs, drawings [of] famous actors, dancers, singers, both male and female. One book on the Spanish theater has pornographic drawings and photographs, but there is no section on pornography, as such, in Hitler's library.

The third section includes works on astrology and spiritualism procured from all parts of the world and translated where necessary. There are also spiritualistic photographs, and, securely locked away, the 200 photographs of the stellar constellations on important days in his life. These he has annotated in his own handwriting and each has its own separate envelope.

In this third section there is a considerable part devoted to nutrition and diet. In fact, there are probably a thousand books on this subject, many of them heavily marginated, those marginal comments including the vegetarian observation: "Cows were meant to give milk; oxen to draw loads." There are dozens of books on animal breeding with the photographs of stallions and mares of famous name. One interesting psychological angle here is that where stallions and mares are shown on opposite pages, many of the mares have been crossed out in red pencil as merely inferior females and unimportant compared with the stallion males.

There are some 400 books on the Church—almost entirely on the Catholic Church. There is also a good deal of pornography here, portraying alleged license in the priesthood: offenses such as made up the charges in the immorality trials which the Nazis conducted against priests at the height of the attack upon the Catholic Church. Many of Hitler's marginal notes on this pornographic section are gross and uncouth. Some pictures show Popes and Cardinals reviewing troops at moments in history. The marginations here are: "Never again" and "This is impossible now," showing that Hitler proposes that the princes of the Church shall never again be allowed to gain political positions in which they can command armies and otherwise exercise temporal powers. Hitler is himself a Catholic, though not a practicing one.

Some 800 to 1,000 books are simple, popular fiction, many of them pure trash in anybody's language. There are a large number of detective stories. He has all of Edgar Wallace; adventure books of the G. A. Henty class; love romances by the score, including those by the leading romantic sob sister of Germany, Hedwig Courts-Mahler, in which wealth and poverty, and strength and weakness are sharply contrasted and in which honor and chastity triumph and the sweet secretary marries her millionaire boss. All of these flaming volumes are in neutral covers so as not to reveal their titles. Hitler may read them, but he doesn't want people to know that he does.

Among Hitler's favorites is a complete set of American Indian stories written by the German, Karl May, who had never been to America. These books are known to every German youngster, and Hitler's fondness for them as bedside reading suggests that he, like many a German thirteen-year-old, has gone to sleep with the exploits of "Old Shatterhand" reeling through his brain. Hitler's set, which was presented to him by Marshal Goering, is expensively bound in vellum and kept in a special case. They are much thumbed and read and usually one or two may be found in the small bedside bookcase with its green curtain in Hitler's bedroom.

Sociological works are strongly represented in the library, including a unique book by Robert Ley, written in 1935, on world sociological problems and solutions. This book never was circulated. Six thousand copies were printed, 5,999 were destroyed; the single remaining copy is Hitler's.

The reason: all books and pamphlets on National Socialism have to be submitted to a special Party commission before being released for publication, and books by prominent Nazi individuals have to be shown to Hitler himself. The book, by Ley, a notorious idolater, so idealized Hitler that even he couldn't stomach its being published.

Another suppressed book in Hitler's library is Alfred Rosenberg's work on the proposed Nazi Reich-Church, of which today there are only twelve copies in proof, although typewritten carbon copies of some sections are known to exist and in mysterious ways to have circulated as far as the United States.

In earlier days, when he had time, Hitler used to bind his own damaged books. Hitler's own best-seller, *Mein Kampf*, has yielded him a fancy fortune, estimated by German Banking circles to be about 50,000,000 Reich mark ($20,000,000 at official rates). With part of this sum, Hitler has amassed a collection of precious stones valued at some 20,000,000 Reich marks, which he keeps in a special safe built into the wall of his house at Berchtesgaden.

The stones were bought for him in various parts of the world by his friend Max Amann, head of the Nazi publishing firm the Eher Verlag, in which Hitler has an interest. It was Hitler who put Max Amann in charge of the Eher Verlag, and it has turned out to be a lucrative job; Amann's own fortune today is estimated by bankers at around 40,000,000 Reich marks. With absolute autocratic control over all publishing enterprises in Germany, it is no wonder that the Nazi Eher Verlag snowballed into a phenomenally profitable enterprise for everybody connected with it, including Adolf Hitler. The Reich Chancellor has never found it necessary to use his official salary, a large part of which he turns over to charity.

Among the books in Hitler's library is one volume covering a field in which he has always shown particular interest: namely, the study of hands, including those of as many famous people throughout the ages as could be procured. Hitler, in fact, bases a good deal of his judgment of people on their hands. In his first conversation with some personality, whether political or military, German or foreign, he usually most carefully observes his hands—their form, whether they are well cared for, whether they are long and narrow or stumpy and broad, the shape of the nails, the knuckle and joint formation and so on. Various generals and diplomats have wondered why Hitler sometimes, after starting a conversation in a cordial and friendly way, became cool as he went along, and often closed the discourse curtly or abruptly without much progress having been made. They learned only later that Hitler had not been pleased by the shape of their hands.

APPENDIX B

*From a classified report by the U.S. Army Twenty-first
Counterintelligence Corps, May 1945*

IN ADDITION HITLER HAD a private library of a large but undetermined number of books. At the far end were arranged lounge chairs and reading lamps. Most of the books were concerned with art, architecture, photography and histories of campaigns and wars. A hasty inspection of the scattered books showed that it was noticeably lacking in literature and almost totally devoid of drama and poetry.

There were many books illustrating types of architecture throughout the world, one tracing the early domestic architecture of Pennsylvania and another of American public buildings.

Immanuel Kant's *Critiques* were there as well as Machiavelli's *The Prince.* One of the few American authors represented was Harry Elmer Barnes's *The Genesis of the World War.*

A big folio size book printed in heavy Gothic type outlined Hitler's genealogy and a note penned on the fly-leaf showed that it was worked out and presented by an admirer.

Many of the books bore Hitler's bookplate, "Ex Libris Adolf Hitler." This consisted of a black engraved eagle with outstretched wings carrying the swastika in his claws.

None of the books examined gave the appearance of extensive use. They had no marginal notes or underlinings.

"The Library of a Dilettante: A Glimpse into the Private Library of Herr Hitler," by Hans Beilhack, Süddeutsche Zeitung, *November 9, 1946*

FOUR FREIGHT CARS FILLED with National Socialist literature of every kind will be heading on a journey from Munich to the U.S.A. in the coming days. The extensive collection, which includes Hitler's private library, is being sent to the American Library of Congress and will be used as a reference work for students and other interested individuals who want to trace the development of Nazism. For the first time the *Süddeutsche Zeitung* is reporting on Hitler's library.

Among the many "Nazi Holy Relics" that have fallen into the hands of the Americans is the private library of Herr Hitler. They had been kept in the elaborate bookcases in the Berlin Reich Chancellery until recently. A few weeks before Berlin was taken into the grip of the Allied pincers, they came to Munich. Just how quickly that happened was shown by the way they were packed. They were stowed in old schnapps crates addressed to the Reich Chancellery. Evidently, they were dispatched in great haste.

The library itself, seen as a whole, is only interesting because it is the library of a "great" statesman and yet so uninteresting. It is the typical library of a dilettante. You can see Hitler's hatred of the "educated," who "in truth alienate themselves more and more from the world until they end up either in a sanatorium or as a politician" (*Mein Kampf,* Chapter 2). For anyone familiar with his "Kampf," the quality of his library will not come as a surprise. A man who could say, "In a few years I created [through impassioned reading in my youth] the foundation of knowledge on which [!] I still draw today" didn't really need a methodically selected library in the more mature years of his life. Even if he did eventually decide to become a politician.

A large portion of his library consists of French works on art and architecture, including magnificent bibliophilic publications in old, richly ornamented Moroccan volumes, numerous monographs about individual artists as well as special collections of old and new works on theater architecture. The volumes that are not bound are all uncut and show no trace of use. The entire French literature was obviously never even perused by Hitler. In addition, the architecture is represented by a large number of English works, which also show no signs of having been used. There are very few German books on art and architecture, with the exception of the few and very rather incomplete series of old newspapers.

When it comes to political literature, the library contains almost exclusively party writings; high-level politics is not represented, there are not even the works of Bismarck or other German statesmen, nor is there the extensive memoir literature about the First World War and the politics after 1918. The famous works of Wilson, Churchill, Poincaré, the great special collection of the Carnegie Foundation are also missing as are the works of the great statesmen of the past (Cromwell, Napoleon, Talleyrand, etc.). For Frederick the Great there are only four volumes from a large collective edition still packaged in their wrapping from the publisher.

Also completely missing from Hitler's official Berlin library are the significant works on religion, philosophy, world history, the history of warfare, geography. There are no works on national economy and the history of economics (with the exception of [Gustav] Ruhland), nor are there any standard works from the national sciences and technology. There is not a single work in the library that reminds us that there was ever a German poet of world stature, for you cannot consider the novels that we do have, all from the Eher Verlag, as belonging to German literature. As said, while good German literature before 1933 is missing almost entirely, there are individual works by living authors who are represented with books dedicated to Hitler. [Edwin Erich] Dwinger, Hans Johst, Agnes Miegel, Hans Hienz Ewers ("Horst Wessel"), among others, attempt to outdo one another in superlatives and groveling.

The library contains a valuable series of the *Leipziger Illustrierte Zeitung* that is nearly complete. Of particular note is an annual report from 1940 for the Daimler Benz Company that consists of fifty-four (!) large parchment volumes with countless photographs from the factory. Based on this report, it is clear that the company's entire economic life was infused by the Nazi Party and was misused for the party's political purposes. Even the workers' free time was stolen down to the last minute by party activities. In contrast, there is extensive pseudo-scientific literature represented that deals with the big questions of religion and philosophy in a dilettantish and unintentionally humorous manner. Among these are the so-called "How to Succeed" books by Schelbach, among others, or the quaintly presumptuous booklet "The Art of Becoming a Speaker in a Few Hours."

A large number of photo albums, almost all of them tastelessly bound in leather or parchment, show the formation of various local organizations, [and] party festivities recall the opening celebrations of youth homes and similar things. A large number of architectural plans deal with the various party buildings on the Obersalzberg, in Berlin, Munich, Nuremberg, etc. There is not a single sketch or design or instructions to an architect in Hitler's own hand! None of the books in the library contain numbers or any sort of catalogue number; only a few are decorated with the Hitler ex libris, a state symbol surrounded by an oak wreath. This library in no way reflects the state of German spiritual life or the sophisticated German book culture. There is not a single area of knowledge that is systematically represented, not even his hobby horses like architecture and art; even though he was "firmly convinced to eventually make a name for himself as an architect." Hitler's library is that of a man who never systematically sought to gain comprehensive knowledge and learning in any one area. That this library is completely lacking in those things which would be absolutely necessary to making the proper decisions in moments of important matters of state (world history, the history of warfare, economic geography, state politics, etc.) is characteristic of the basis of knowledge on which Hitler made his decisions.

APPENDIX D

"Report on the Adolph [sic] Hitler Collection and Recommendations Regarding Its Arrangement," by Arnold J. Jacobius, Intern, to Frederick R. Goff, Chief, Rare Books Division, Library of Congress, January 9, 1952

THE MAJORITY OF THE BOOKS in the Adolph [*sic*] Hitler Collection deal with, or are related to National Socialism, its leaders, history and ideological background. German classic and fictional writers, generally associated with German private libraries, are almost entirely lacking. There are a number of books on history and art dating back to periods preceding the Nazi era, but most of these, too, bear some relationship to Nazi ideologies.

Among the materials in the collection we can discern the following groups:

1. Books especially printed and/or bound for Hitler (100)
2. Books available to the public at the time they were incorporated into Hitler's collection—many of them deluxe editions and dedication copies (1,400)
3. Scrolls, honor diplomas—on parchment or mounted and bound—dedicated to Hitler (100)
4. Photo albums, some of them containing short typewritten captions, descriptions and/or ornamented dedication pages (100)
5. Portfolios containing reproductions of works of art, photographs, etc. (50)
6. Miscellaneous items such as letters, clippings, mounted photographs, posters, memoirs, etc. (2 shelves)
7. Bound periodicals (150)

Spot checks revealed little in the way of marginal notes, autographs or other similar features of interest; indeed, it seems that most of the books have never been perused by their owner. In the majority of cases the books can be identified as having belonged to Hitler by his personal bookplate or by inscribed dedications. However, in a considerable number of items ownership cannot be established on the basis of direct evidence. Unfortunately it appears that in the process of transportation of Hitler's books to their present location some extraneous materials have been intermixed with them, so that it is difficult to determine with certainty whether or not some books belonged to the Hitler library.

NOTES

PREFACE: The Man Who Burned Books

xi HE RANKED *DON QUIXOTE*: Adolf Hitler, *Monologe im Führerhauptquartier*, steno-graphed by Heinrich Heim, ed. Werner Jochmann (Hamburg: Albrecht Knaus Verlag, 1999), p. 281.

xi "THE DEVELOPMENT OF": Ralf George Reuth, ed., *Joseph Goebbels Tagebücher, band 3, 1935–1939* (Munich: Piper Verlag, 1999), February 1, 1939, p. 1195.

xi HE CONSIDERED SHAKESPEARE: Ibid.

xii HE APPEARS TO HAVE: For references to Shakespeare quotes, see index to *Adolf Hitler: Reden, Schriften, Anordnungen: Februar 1925 bis Januar 1933*, ed. Institut für Zeitgeschichte, 5 vols. in 12 parts (Munich: Institut für Zeitgeschichte, 1992–1998).

xiii "THE FIRST KARL MAY": Hitler, *Monologe*, p. 281.

xiv "DATES, PLACE NAMES": Walter Benjamin, "Unpacking My Library: A Talk about Book Collecting," *Illuminations*, ed. Hannah Arendt, trans. Harry Zohn (London: Fontana Press, 1992), p. 65.

xiv QUOTING HEGEL, BENJAMIN: Ibid., p. 68.

xv "NOT THAT THEY": Ibid., p. 69.

xvii "THIS WATER PESTILENCE": Paul Lagarde, *Deutsche Schriften* (Munich: J. F. Lehmanns Verlag, 1934), p. 276.

xvii "THE COMBINATION OF HITLER'S": Ian Kershaw, *Hitler, 1889–1936: Hubris* (New York: W. W. Norton, 1999), p. xiv.

BOOK ONE: Frontline Reading, 1915

4 "FALSE ALARM": All citations related to conditions at the front in November 1915 are taken from the RIR 16 Regimental Daily Log at the Bayerisches Kriegsarchiv, Munich.

5 "I WAS REPEATEDLY": Anton Joachimsthaler, *Korrektur einer Biographie: Adolf Hitler, 1908–1920* (Munich: Herbig Verlags, 1989), p. 143.

5 DURING THE FIRST DAY: Photostat copy of letters written to Assessor Ernst Hepp in Munich, in folio in the Third Reich Collection, Library of Congress. For the exact quote, see the transcription of Hepp's letters in Eberhard Jäckel and Axel Kuhn, eds., *Hitler: Sämtliche Aufzeichnungen, 1905–1924* (Stuttgart: Deutsche Verlag-Anstalt, 1980), p. 68.

6 "THE BATTLE FOR": Daily Log of the RIR 16, Bayerisches Kriegsarchiv, Munich, October 25, 1915.

7 "TWO OF OUR COMPANY": Fridolin Solleder, *Vier Jahre Westfront: Geschichte des Regiments List, RIR 16* (Munich: Verlag Max Schick, 1932), p. 193.

10 OSBORN ARRIVED ON: References to Osborn's time at the front can be found in Max Osborn, *Drei Strassen des Krieges* (Berlin: Verlag Ullstein, 1916).

12 "THE BOSCHES ARE": Ibid., p. 183.

12 "BY THE WINTER": Adolf Hitler, *Mein Kampf*, trans. Ralph Manheim (New York: Houghton Mifflin, 1998), p. 165.

12 "I THINK SO OFTEN ABOUT": Jäckel and Kuhn, eds., *Hitler: Sämtliche Aufzeichnungen*, p. 69.

13 "EVEN IF I CAME IN": Joachimsthaler, *Korrektur*, p. 127.

14 "MESSENGER, REGIMENTAL HEADQUARTERS": Adolf Meyer, *Mit Adolf Hitler im Bayerischen Reserve-Infantrie-Regiment 16 List* (Neustadt an der Aisch [Mittelfranken]: Georg Aupperle, 1934), p. 33.

16 "ONE COULD NOT ATTEND": Hitler, *Mein Kampf*, p. 20.

16 THERE WAS WILHELM KUH: Descriptions of the various artists can be found in Solleder, *Vier Jahre Westfront*, pp. 187–99.

18 "IN WYTSCHAETE ALONE": Hitler's letter to Hepp reprinted in Jäckel and Kuhn, eds., *Hitler: Sämtliche Aufzeichnungen*, p. 68.

18 ONE RECENT OBSERVER: Joachimsthaler, *Korrektur*, p. 136.

19 "ORGIES OF AN UNSPEAKABLE": Max Osborn, *Berlin* (Leipzig: Seeman Verlag, 1909), p. 3.

20 "THE ULTIMATE": Ibid., p. 198.

20 "ITS COLUMNS HAVE": Ibid., p. 198.

20 "THE KING, ENTIRELY A CHILD": Ibid., p. 171.

21 "THE BERLINERS WERE": Ibid., p. 181.

21 "I ALWAYS LIKED": For Hitler's quotations on his early impressions of Berlin, see Adolf Hitler, *Monologe im Führerhauptquartier*, stenographed by Heinrich Heim, ed. Werner Jochmann (Hamburg: Albrecht Knaus Verlag), pp. 100–102.

22 "THIS TRIP IS": Jäckel and Kuhn, eds., *Hitler: Sämtliche Aufzeichnungen*, p. 75.

23 "THE MESSAGE RUNNERS": Joachimsthaler, *Korrektur*, p. 165.

23 "WHAT A CHANGE": Hitler, *Mein Kampf*, p. 191.

25 "RAUCH UNDERSTOOD": Osborn, *Berlin*, p. 236.

25 "THE CITY IS TREMENDOUS": Werner Maser, *Hitlers Briefe und Notizen: Sein Weltbild in handschriftlichen Dokumenten* (Düsseldorf: Econ Verlag, 1973), p. 106.

25 "THE ENTIRE FLOOR": Osborn, *Berlin,* p. 293.

25 IN HIS SKETCH: For a description of the sketch, see Frederic Spotts, *Hitler and the Power of Aesthetics* (Woodstock, N.Y.: Overlook Press, 2002), p. 188.

26 "ON A HILL SOUTH": Hitler, *Mein Kampf,* p. 202.

BOOK TWO: The Mentor's Trade

28 FIRST TRENCH COAT: Adolf Hitler, *Monologe im Führerhauptquartier, 1941–1944,* stenographed by Heinrich Heim, ed. Werner Jochmann (Hamburg: Albrecht Knaus Verlag, 1980), p. 208.

29 "THIS MAN IS": Margarete Plewnia, *Auf dem Weg zu Hitler: Der "volkische" Publizist Dietrich Eckart* (Bremen: Schünemann Verlag, 1970), p. 67.

30 "ECKART WAS THE MAN": Otto Dietrich, *Zwölf Jahre mit Hitler* (Cologne: Atlas Verlag, 1955), p. 178.

30 "FOLLOW HITLER": Plewnia.

30 HITLER HAILED ECKART: Hitler, *Monologe,* p. 208.

31 "MY IMPRESSION WAS": Adolf Hitler, *Mein Kampf,* trans. Ralph Manheim (New York: Houghton Mifflin, 1998), p. 218.

32 "AS A RESULT": For quotations from Drexler, see Anton Drexler, *Mein politisches Erwachen* (Munich: Deutscher Volks-Verlag, 1919), p. 31.

33 "ONCE I HAD": Hitler, *Mein Kampf,* p. 220.

33 "NOW WE HAVE AN AUSTRIAN": Anton Joachimsthaler, *Korrektur einer Biographie: Adolf Hitler, 1908–1920* (Munich: Herbig Verlag, 1989), p. 252.

34 "WILL YOU FINALLY": Eberhard Jäckel and Axel Kuhn, eds., *Hitler: Sämtliche Aufzeichnungen, 1905–1924* (Stuttgart: Deutsche Verlags-Anstalt, 1980), p. 342.

34 "A POWERFUL FOREHEAD": Ibid., p. 342.

35 "WE NEED SOMEONE": Konrad Heiden, *Adolf Hitler. Ein Biographie.* Vol. I (Zurich: Europa-Verlag, 1936), p. 76.

36 "I HAD BEEN ADMIRING": Plewnia, *Auf dem Weg zu Hitler,* p. 63.

36 WHEN THE TWO MEN: Hitler's visit to Berlin with Dietrich Eckart, as well as the use of an aircraft and the reference to Kapp's press spokesman as a "Jew," can be found in Jäckel and Kuhn, eds., *Hitler: Sämtliche Aufzeichnungen,* p. 117.

36 "LET'S GO, ADOLF": Dietrich, *Zwölf Jahre mit Hitler,* p. 179.

37 "I FELT MYSELF DRAWN": Plewnia, *Auf dem Weg zu Hitler,* p. 66.

38 "BUT WHAT DID HITLER": Karl Dietrich Bracher, *Adolf Hitler: Archiv der Weltgeschichte* (Munich: Scherz Verlag, 1964), p. 38.

38 "HORRIFIED": Hitler, *Mein Kampf,* p. 52.

38   "NOT UNTIL MY": Ibid., p. 51.

38   "AS ALWAYS IN SUCH": Ibid., p. 56.

39   "DIETRICH ECKART HIMSELF": Jäckel and Kuhn, eds., *Hitler: Sämtliche Aufzeich-nungen*, p. 341.

39   "BURNING THEIR SYNAGOGUES": Dietrich Eckart, *Der Bolschewismus von Moses bis Lenin: Ein Zweigespräch zwischen Adolf Hitler und mir* (Munich: Hoheneichen Verlag, 1924), p. 46. All further quotations from the conversation can be found on pp. 46–47.

41   "I EXPERIENCED": Dietrich Eckart in a letter to Ibsen's son, dated June 11, 1912. Copy in Archiv zur Zeitgeschichte der Obersalzberg, Berchtesgaden.

41   "LET ANYONE WHO": Ibid.

42   ECKART HAD "PEER GYNT" EMBOSSED: Wilhelm Grün, *Dietrich Eckart, als Pub-lizist* (Munich: Hoheneichen Verlag, 1941), p. 50.

42   IN HIS YOUTH: Hitler, *Monologe*, p. 281.

42   "AS A BOY": Letter from Paula Hitler to Sven Hedin, December 14, 1951. Copy in Archiv zur Zeitgeschichte der Obersalzberg, Berchtesgaden.

42   HITLER RECALLED THAT: Hitler, *Monologe*, p. 284.

43   FOUR SEPARATE RECORDINGS: The recordings are listed in a seven-hundred-page, three-volume catalogue registered in the Library of Congress as ML158.S3 1936, which contains Hitler's complete Berghof record collection. Volumes I and II list the recordings by category—instrumental music, opera, operetta, light music, dance music, songs—with the composers arranged alphabetically. Volume III lists the recordings by title.

44   "WHEN THE CURTAINS": Reviews in Eckart's *Peer Gynt* adaptation.

46   "TO BE FORWARDED": Werner Maser, *Sturm auf die Republik* (Düsseldorf: Econ Verlag, 1994), p. 265.

47   "THE JEWISH QUESTION": Otto Dickel, *Auferstehung des Abendlandes* (Augsburg: Gebrüder Reichl Verlag, 1921), p. 81.

48   "WHEN, AFTER THREE TEDIOUS": Albrecht Tyrell, *Vom "Trommler" zum "Führer"* (Munich: Wilhelm Fink Verlag, 1975), p. 261.

49   FOR A FULL WEEK: Joachimsthaler, *Korrektur*, p. 240.

50   ERNST "PUTZI" HANFSTAENGL: Ernst Hanfstaengl, *Unheard Witness* (New York: J. B. Lippencott, 1957), p. 49.

51   "AT THE TIME, I BECAME": Friedrich Krohn, *Mein Lebenslauf*, Institut für Zeitgeschichte Archiv, Munich, undated, ZS 89, p. 5.

52   "FOR HIS PART, SCHELLING": Dickel, *Auferstehung des Abendlandes*, p. 269.

52   "AS A SIMPLE MAN": Tyrell, *Vom "Trommler" zum "Führer,"* p. 122.

52   "HITLER WAS CERTAINLY": Ibid., p. 117.

54   "AS BUSINESSMEN, THEIR SONS": Dickel, *Auferstehung des Abendlandes*, p. 81.

54   "I ACCUSE THE PARTY": Jäckel and Kuhn, eds., *Hitler: Sämtliche Aufzeichnungen*, p. 437.

54 "THE IMMEDIATE SUMMONING": Maser, *Sturm auf die Republik*, p. 269.

54 "I LIKE AND VALUE HITLER": In a letter from Gottfried Grandel to Dietrich Eckart, August 12, 1921.

55 "NO HUMAN BEING": Maser, *Sturm auf die Republik*, p. 280; *Völkischer Beobachter*, August 4, 1921.

55 "DO WE NEED": Ibid.

55 "MR. OTTO DICKEL FROM": Jäckel and Kuhn, eds., *Hitler: Sämtliche Aufzeichnungen*, p. 480.

58 "EGYPTIAN DREAM": Ibid., p. 532.

58 "PROFESSOR WHOSE DETACHMENT": Ibid.

58 "ANY DICKEL": Ibid., p. 460.

58 "WHERE WAS THE PROMISED": *Adolf Hitler: Reden, Schriften, Anordnungen: Februar 1925 bis Januar 1933*, ed. Institut für Zeitgeschichte, 5 vols. in 12 parts (Munich: Institut für Zeitgeschichte, 1992–98), vol. I, pp. 95–96.

58 DICKEL ALSO HAUNTS: Hitler, *Mein Kampf*, pp. 35–36.

58 DICKEL ALSO SEEMS: Ibid., p. 356.

58 AND WHEN I FINALLY: Ibid., p. 370.

59 "ACH HERR PROFESSOR": Hanfstaengl, *Unheard Witness*, p. 131.

BOOK THREE: **The Hitler Trilogy**

61 THE ECLECTIC NATURE: In the confiscation report at the archives of the rare book collection in the Library of Congress, written by Hans Beilhack, a German librarian employed by the U.S. Army, contains a detailed account of the rather adventurous confiscation process, including details of the Braille copies of *Mein Kampf*.

61 "WRITING THEM": Walter Benjamin, *Illuminations,* ed. Hannah Arendt, trans. Harry Zohn (London: Fontana Press, 1992), p. 65.

62 "WRITERS ARE REALLY": Ibid.

63 "EVEN IF YOU DECLARE": Eberhard Jäckel and Axel Kuhn, eds., *Hitler: Sämtliche Aufzeichnungen, 1905–1924* (Stuttgart: Deutsche Verlags-Anstalt, 1980), p. 1216.

64 "ONLY A SINGLE LIGHT BURNED": In Hans Kallenbach, *Mit Adolf Hitler auf Festung Landsberg* (Munich: Verlag Kress und Hornung, 1939), p. 106. The Library of Congress has Hitler's personal copy of Kallenbach's book, *With Adolf Hitler in the Landsberg Fortress: Newly Revised by Fellow Inmate Retired Lieutenant Hans Kallenbach, former Machinegun Unit Leader of the "Assault Unit Adolf Hitler 1923,"* with an introduction by Hitler and thirty-seven photographs, some of which are previously unpublished. The book is personally inscribed by Kallenbach—"God protect our Führer!"—and dated October 6, 1939. An accompanying letter describes the origins of the book and Hitler's personal endorsement of its contents.

64 "A THOROUGH SETTLING": Jäckel and Kuhn, eds., *Hitler: Sämtliche Aufzeich-nungen,* p. 1233.

65 "MAKE MY HAIR": Ibid., p. 1270.

65 "HE IS EXPECTING": Werner Maser, *Hitlers Mein Kampf* (Munich: Bechtle Ver-lag, 1966), p. 24.

65 ERNST HANFSTAENGL, WHO: Othmar Plöckinger, *Geschichte eines Buches: Adolf Hitlers "Mein Kampf," 1922–1945* (Munich: R. Oldenbourg Verlag, 2006), p. 35.

65 "THAT IF A COLLECTOR'S EDITION": Ibid., p. 37.

66 STAGE-MANAGE THE BANNED: Among the extensive materials on the early his-tory of the Nazi Party in the Third Reich Collection at the Library of Congress is a document with the stamped signature "Rolf Eidhalt."

66 "HERR HITLER HAS ANNOUNCED": Jäckel and Kuhn, eds., *Hitler: Sämtliche Aufzeichnungen,* p. 1241.

66 HITLER REDUCED: See Anna Maria Sigmund, *Des Führers bester Freund* (Munich: Ullstein, Heyne List, 2003), p. 54.

66 HE ABANDONED HIS: Hess letter, June 29, 1924, in Plöckinger, *Geschichte eines Buches,* p. 50.

67 "THE CONNECTION TO": Ibid.

67 "PERSONALLY, I HAVE": Jäckel and Kuhn, eds., *Hitler: Sämtliche Aufzeichnungen,* p. 1232.

68 "THE ADMIRATION OF GANDHI": Ibid., p. 206.

68 "IT IS QUESTIONABLE": Carl Ludwig Schleich, *Die Weisheit der Freude* (Berlin: Rowohlt Verlag, 1924), p. 27.

69 "IN THIS BOOK": Otto Strasser, *Hitler und ich* (Constance, Ger.: Johannes Asmus Verlag, 1948), p. 78.

69 "THE WALL BESIDE": "Berlin Hears Ford Is Backing Hitler," *The New York Times,* December 20, 1922, p. 2.

69 "I READ IT": "Documents from the Nuremberg Trials, 1945–1948," *The Avalon Project: Nuremberg Trial Proceedings,* vol. 14, p. 367.

70 IN ONE SPEECH: *Adolf Hitler: Reden, Schriften, Andornungen: Februar 1925 bis Januar 1933,* ed. Institut für Zeitgeschichte, 5 vols. in 12 parts (Munich: Institut für Zeit-geschichte, 1992–98), October 18, 1928, vol. III, part 1, p. 163.

70 "THEY SAY THAT": Ibid., May 2, 1928, vol. II, part 2, p. 828.

70 "EVERY YEAR SEES THEM": Ibid., February 12, 1926, vol. I, p. 292. This is nearly a verbatim quote from *Mein Kampf.*

70 "GERMANY IS TODAY": "Did the Jews Foresee the World War?," chapter 14 of *The International Jew: The World's Foremost Problem* (Dearborn, Mich.: Dearborn Publishing Co., 1920), vol. 1, pp. 153–54.

71 "IT IS COMPLETELY": Adolf Hitler, *Mein Kampf,* trans. Ralph Manheim (New York: Houghton Mifflin, 1998), p. 308.

71 "I REGARD FORD AS": Bill McGraw, "Forced Labor and Ford: History of Nazi Labor Stares Ford in the Face," *Detroit Free Press*, December 21, 1999, p. B1.

72 TYPED IN PICA: The Hitler manuscript was subjected to forensic analyses by four independent experts. According to Bernard Haas at the State Office of Criminal Investigation for Baden-Württemberg, the pages were typed in Pica Ra 58. The Haas report, dated January 23, 2007, is available at the Archive for Contemporary History of the Obersalzberg in Berchtesgaden.

72 "IT IS NOT BY": From the original typescript of *Mein Kampf.* Photocopy in Archiv zur Zeitgeschichte des Obersalzberg, Berchtesgaden.

74 "I SAW ONE": Adolf Hitler, *Monologe im Führerhauptquartier,* stenographed by Heinrich Heim, ed. Werner Jochmann (Hamburg: Albrecht Knaus Verlag), p. 259.

75 "THE PROBLEM FOR ME": Jäckel and Kuhn, eds., *Hitler: Sämtliche Aufzeichnungen,* p. 1270.

75 AS MANY AS SEVEN: Werner Maser, *Hitler's Mein Kampf,* trans. R. H. Berry (London: Faber & Faber, 1970), p. 23.

75 "YOU CANNOT SAY": Ernst Hanfstaengl, *Unheard Witness* (New York: J. B. Lippencott, 1957), p. 134.

76 "WE STRUGGLED FOR WEEKS": Maser, *Hitler's Mein Kampf,* p. 23.

76 ILSE DESCRIBED HITLER'S WRITING: Ibid., pp. 49–51.

76 WHEN HE DISTILLED: Ibid., p. 24.

76 THE *FRANKFURTER ZEITUNG*: Plöckinger, *Geschichte eines Buches,* p. 227.

77 "PARTIAL DOUBTS ABOUT": Ibid., p. 226.

77 ONE CRITIC: Ibid., p. 226.

77 *"Sein Krampf"*: Ibid., p. 225.

77 "GENERAL LAUGHTER BROKE": See Otto Strasser, *Hitler und ich* (Constance, Ger.: Johannes Asmus Verlag, 1948), p. 80.

78 "FOR OLD TIME'S SAKE": Maser, *Hitler's Mein Kampf,* p. 14.

78 EMIL MAURICE RECEIVED: Sigmund, *Des Führers bester Freund,* p. 73.

78 FOR CHRISTMAS THAT YEAR: Joseph Goebbels, *Joseph Goebbels Tagebücher band 1, 1924–1929,* ed. Ralf Georg Reuth (Munich: Piper Verlag, 1999), December 30, 1925, p. 215.

78 "HERE I WAS REALLY": Hitler, *Monologe,* p. 206.

78 "IF AT THE BEGINNING": Hitler, *Mein Kampf,* p. 679.

79 AS OTTO BRUCKMANN: Plöckinger, *Geschichte eines Buches,* p. 160.

80 "I HAVE READ": Ibid., p. 160.

80 "HE IS ALREADY REFLECTING": Ibid., p. 159.

81 "IN THE SPRING": Ibid., p. 160.

82 "WE RUN FORWARD": Werner Maser, *Hitlers Briefe und Notizen: Sein Weltbild in handschriftlichen Dokumenten* (Düsseldorf: Econ Verlag, 1973), pp. 92–95.

82 "BUT THIS IS": Ernst Jünger, *Feuer und Blut: Ein kleiner Ausschnitt aus einer großen Schlacht* (Magdeburg: Stahlhelm Verlag, 1925), p. 86.

83 "THE THROTTLING CONCUSSION": Ibid., p. 107.

84 "THE BATTLE IS": Ibid., p. 26.

84 "WITH THE ASSISTANCE": Christa Shröder, *Er war mein Chef* (Munich: Georg Müller Verlag, 1985), p. 213.

85 AN ACCOMPANYING MEMORANDUM: Initially, "Target No. 589" was reviewed by American intelligence officers and classified as relatively insignificant—"priority three"—then dispatched to the United States with millions of other Nazi documents. The manuscript was discovered by Gerhard Weinberg, a recently minted doctoral student, who immediately recognized its significance. He published it with his mentor Hans Rothfels and a colleague, Martin Broszat, at the Institut für Zeitgeschichte in Munich in 1961, under the title *Hitler's Second Book*. In a subsequent edition, the title had changed to *Foreign Policy Position After the Reichstag Election, June–July 1928*, to better reflect the content of the manuscript, and to avoid sensationalism and sensitivity on the part of the Germans.

88 "TROSTLOS": Goebbels, *Joseph Goebbels Tagebücher, band 1: 1924–1929*, May 21, 1928, pp. 290–91.

88 "WE WILL CONTINUE": *Adolf Hitler: Reden, Schriften, Anordnungen: Februar 1925 bis Januar 1933*, ed. Institut für Zeitgeschichte, 5 vols. in 12 parts (Munich: Institut für Zeitgeschichte, 1992–98), vol. 2A, p. 847.

88 "ALONE AND ISOLATED": Adolf Hitler, draft manuscript, *Mein Kampf*, can be found at the Archiv zur Zeitgeschichte des Obersalzberg, Berchtesgaden.

92 "ICH BIN KEIN SCHRIFTSTELLER": Maser, *Hitler's Mein Kampf*, p. 43.

93 "IF I HAD HAD ANY IDEA": Ibid., p. 28.

93 "I AM CERTAINLY GLAD": Albert Speer, *Inside the Third Reich* (New York: Macmillan, 1970), p. 86.

BOOK FOUR: The Lost Philosopher

94 "SUFFICE IT TO QUOTE": Walter Benjamin, *Illuminations,* ed. Hannah Arendt, trans. Harry Zohn (London: Fontana Press, 1992), p. 62.

94 "FOR YEARS, FOR AT LEAST": Ibid.

94 "SUDDENLY THE EMPHASIS": Ibid.

95 LARGEST TAX DEDUCTION: Oron James Hale, "Adolf Hitler: Taxpayer," *American Historical Review* 60, no. 4 (July 1955): 836.

95 IN MORE RECENT TIMES, TWO SCHOLARS: Philipp Gassert and Daniel S. Mattern, *The Hitler Library: A Bibliography* (Westport, Conn.: Greenwood Press, 2001).

98 DURING THE WAR: This incident is recounted in Henriette von Schirach,

Der Dreis der Herrlichkeit: Erlebte Zeitgeschichite (Munich: Herbig Verlag, 1975), p. 289.

99 THE VOLUME IS DEDICATED: The Library of Congress collection also contains several other books on the 1936 Olympics, including a volume devoted to the Winter Olympics; a book in Hungarian, *A Berlini Olimpia;* and one for young people, titled *The Meaning of the Olympic Games.*

99 "FRÄULEIN RIEFENSTAHL CAME": Joseph Goebbels, *Joseph Goebbels Tagebücher, band 3: 1935–1939,* ed. Ralf Georg Reuth (Munich: Piper Verlag, 1999), November 6, 1936, p. 1002.

102 "THESE TRAITORS": Leni Riefenstahl, *Memoiren, 1902–1945* (Frankfurt: Ullstein Verlag, 1990), p. 186.

102 "FRÄULEIN RIEFENSTAHL, I KNOW": Ibid., p. 197.

103 "I CAN'T, I CAN'T": Ibid., p. 198.

103 "I AM SORRY": Ibid.

103 "HOW ABOUT IF": Ibid.

103 STEPHEN BACH, AUTHOR OF: See Steven Bach, *Leni: The Life and Work of Leni Riefenstahl* (New York: Alfred A. Knopf, 2007).

106 THE INVENTORY OF THE REICH CHANCELLERY LIBRARY: This reference is included in a partially preserved inventory list of approximately fifteen hundred books from the Reich Chancellery library. The list was discovered in the ruins of the Reich Chancellery by an American soldier in the spring of 1945. The originals are now in the Hoover Institution at Stanford University. Books given to Hitler as gifts are identified with an *x* in the records.

106 "PHILOSOPHICAL GOD": Ernst Hanfstaengl, *Unheard Witness* (New York: J. B. Lippencott, 1957), p. 217.

106 "FROM THAT DAY AT POTSDAM": Ibid., pp. 217–18.

106 RIEFENSTAHL PROVIDES: Riefenstahl, *Memoiren,* p. 249.

106 "WHEN A PERSON 'GIVES' ": Ibid.

107 "NO, I CAN'T REALLY": Ibid.

107 "OVERTHROW OF THE": *Adolf Hitler: Reden, Schriften, Andornungen: Februar 1925 bis Januar 1933,* ed. Institut für Zeitgeschichte, 5 vols. in 12 parts, (Munich: Institut für Zeitgeschichte, 1992–98), vol. III, p. 156.

107 "SPEECHES TO THE GERMAN NATION": Ibid.

108 "THE TITLE *FÜHRER*": Adolf Hitler, *Monologe im Führerhauptquartier,* stenographed by Heinrich Heim, ed. Werner Jochman (Hamburg: Albrecht Knaus Verlag), p. 174.

108 "TO CUT OFF": Johann Gottlieb Fichte, *Sämmtiche Werke,* ed. I. H. Fichte (Berlin: Veit, 1846), vol. I, part 2, p. 293.

110 "RACIAL GÜNTHER": Gerwin Strobl, "The Bard of Eugenics: Shakespeare and Racial Activism in the Third Reich," *Journal of Contemporary History* 34, no. 3 (July 1999): 328.

112   J. F. LEHMANN VERLAG: Gary D. Stark, "Publishers and Cultural Patronage in Germany, 1890–1933," *German Studies Review*, 1, no. 1 (February 1978): 66.

113   THE HUNGARIAN SCHOLAR: Ambrus Miskolczy, *Hitler's Library* (Budapest: Central European University Press, 2003), p. 20.

114   "DISTINCTIVE FINE PENCIL": Ibid., p. 22.

114   "IT WOULD BE MORE TYPICAL": Ibid., p. 21.

114   HITLER'S OWN THEORY OF READING: Adolf Hitler, *Mein Kampf*, trans. Ralph Manheim (New York: Houghton Mifflin, 1998), p. 36.

115   "THE MAN IS A GENIUS": Goebbels, *Tagebücher, band 3*, February 1, 1938, p. 1195.

115   "BOOKS, ALWAYS MORE": Alfred Kubizek, *Adolf Hitler, Mein Jugendfreund* (Graz: Leopold Stocker Verlag, 1953), p. 244.

115   ANOTHER EARLY HITLER ASSOCIATE: Brigitte Hamann, *Hitlers Wien: Lehrjahre eines Diktators* (Munich: Piper Verlag, 1996), p. 576.

115   "DEADLY SERIOUS BUSINESS": Kubizek, *Adolf Hitler*, p. 244.

116   "A TOPIC THAT HE HAD READ": Christa Schröder, *Er war mein Chef* (Munich: Herbig Verlag, 2002), p. 177.

116   "HITLER, EXCESSIVELY EXACTING": Ibid.

117   THIS PROCESS IS: For all quoted passages in Lagarde, see Paul Lagarde, *Deutsche Schriften* (Munich: J. F. Lehmanns Verlag, 1934).

BOOK FIVE: Book Wars

122   "THE HORRIFIC CRUCIFIXES": Alfred Rosenberg, *Der Mythus des 20. Jahrhundert: Eine Wertung der seelisch-geistigen Gestaltenkämpfe unserer Zeit* (Munich: Hohenichen Verlag, 1935), p. 701.

122   "RECOMMENDED" TITLES: Dominik Burkard, *Häresie und Mythus des 20. Jahrhunderts: Rosenbergs nationalsozialistische Weltanschauung vor dem Tribunal der Römischen Inquisition* (Paderborn: Ferdinand Schöningh Verlag, 2005), p. 43.

122   "RECENTLY, I HEARD THAT THE TWO": Ludwig Volk, ed., *Akten Kardinal Michael von Faulhabers* (Mainz: Mathias-Grünewald Verlag), vol. 1, p. 842.

122   "I DON'T WANT THAT BOOK": Conversation between Hitler and Schulte recorded in Bernhard Stasiewski, ed., *Akten deutscher Bischöfe über die Lage der Kirche 1933–1945, band I* (Mainz: Mathias-Grünewald Verlag), pp. 539–40. Schulte's full report on the meeting can be found in Konrad Repgen and Reihe A. Quellen, eds., *Veröffentlichungen der Kommission für Zeitgeschichte, band 5* (Mainz: Mathias-Grünewald Verlag), pp. 539–40.

124   ON THE NIGHT OF JUNE 30: The Hitler library contains three books that preserve traces of the infamous "Night of the Long Knives." The commemorative volume of the Beer Hall Putsch is dedicated to Hitler "in loyal obedience" by Gregor Strasser, who was shot dead through his prison cell window that

night; another volume, about Silesian storm troopers, is inscribed to Hitler by Edmund Heines, the SA man who was found in bed with a young man in a hotel room and shot on the spot. The third book, a seventy-five-page treatise on "Indo-Aryan metaphysics" based on the Bhagavad Gita, was given to Hitler in the aftermath of the bloody purge "as a sign of loyalty in these most difficult times" from its author, Wilhelm Hauer, founder of the pro-Nazi German Faith Movement.

125 "THE BOOK SCORNS": Burkard, *Häresie und Mythus*, p. 75.

127 "THAT WHICH I MAINTAIN": See epilogue to *Studien zum Mythus des 20. Jahrhunderts, Kirchlicher Anzeiger für Erzdiözese Köln* (Cologne: Badhemdruck, 1935).

127 BY 1935, THE BOOK: Rosenberg, *Der Mythus*, pp. 67–70.

128 "IN *L'OSSERVATORE*": Burkard, *Häresie und Mythus*, p. 179.

129 "THUS AND IN THIS SENSE": Ibid.

130 "THERE YOU HAVE MADE": Alois C. Hudal, *Römische Tagebücher* (Stuttgart: Leopold Stocker Verlag, 1976), p. 119.

130 "THE SWASTIKA HERE": At least two alleged press interviews with Grüner appeared in the summer of 1933, one in France and one in Germany, both of questionable authenticity. Grüner was eighty-two years old and, according to monastery records, growing senile. Nevertheless, there was a popular impression that the swastika at the Lambach monastery, carved in the mid-nineteenth century and inspired by an abbot's visit to India, was the source of Hitler's inspiration for the use of the swastika. Lambach became known as the Monastery of the Swastika. Hitler himself never referenced Lambach as an inspiration for the swastika, instead crediting other sources.

131 "AND THE POWER": Hitler speech, February 10, 1933.

131 "THAT A PRELATE": Franz von Papen, *Der Weisheit eine Gasse* (Innsbruck: Paul List Verlag, 1952), p. 431.

131 "BOOK OF BISHOP HUDAL": Joseph Goebbels, *Joseph Goebbels Tagebücher, band 3: 1935–1939*, ed. Ralf Georg Reuth (Munich: Piper Verlag, 1999), June 19, 1936, p. 962.

132 "IN ORDER TO KEEP": Burkard, *Häresie und Mythus*, p. 210.

132 HE "ENDORSED" THE BOOK: Hudal, *Römische Tagebücher*, p. 132.

132 "IF I HAD NOT": Burkard, *Häresie und Mythus*, p. 211.

132 "HIS SPEECH IS A": Goebbels, *Tagebücher, band 3*, September 25, 1935, p. 892.

133 "TRIALS AGAINST THE CATHOLIC CHURCH": Ibid., October 21, 1936, p. 993.

133 " 'A JEW REMAINS' ": Volk, ed., *Akten Kardinal Michael von Faulhabers*, October 23, 1936, pp. 179–80.

134 FAULHABER NOTED: Burkard, *Häresie und Mythus*, p. 45.

134 THE OBERSALZBERG WAS: See the report on Faulhaber's meeting with Hitler, November 4, 1936, 11:00 a.m. to 2:00 p.m., recorded in Volk, ed., *Akten Kardinal Michael von Faulhabers*, pp. 184–94.

137 "HAD REALLY LET": Goebbels, *Tagebucher, band 3*, November 10, 1936, p. 1006.

138 "IN THE END, I SUCCEEDED": Papen, *Der Weisheit eine Gasse*, p. 432.
139 "AS THE AUTHOR HIMSELF": Hudal, *Römische Tagebücher*, p. 129.

BOOK SIX: **Divine Inspiration**

141 IN THE EARLY 1930S: Walter Langer Report, Memorandum from Edward Deuss to Professor Crane Brinton, "Recollections of Adolf Hitler Gained from Personal Contact, Interviews and on Airplane Campaign Tours with Hitler from September 1931–May 1933," Box 1, undated, p. 1, National Archives, College Park, Maryland.

141 HITLER'S "ASPIRATIONS": "Zur Entstehung und Bedeutung der Entwürfe zu Hitlers Buch 'Mein Kampf,'" lecture, Seventh International Congress of the Gesellschaft der Forensic Schriftuntersuchung, Dr. Othmar Plöckinger, Salzburg, Austria, 2007.

141 HELENE HANFSTAENGL: John Toland, *Adolf Hitler* (New York: Doubleday, 1976), p. 12.

142 "I BELIEVE THE GOOD LORD": Paula Hitler, postwar debriefing interview, copy in the Archiv zur Zeitgeschichte des Obersalzberg, Berchtesgaden.

142 "I CONFRONTED THE PROFESSOR": Adolf Hitler, *Monologe im Führerhauptquartier*, stenographed by Heinrich Heim, ed. Werner Jochmann (Hamburg: Albrecht Knaus Verlag), p. 103.

142 "THE WORST BLOW": Ibid., p. 41.
142 "THERE EXISTS IN EVERY": Ibid., p. 40.

143 "A HUNDRED AND SIXTY-NINE OF THEM": Hitlers *Tischgespräche im Führerhauptquartier*, stenographed by Henry Picker (Berlin: Ullstien Verlag, 1999), p. 101.

146 "WHOEVER GOES FAR": Bertold Otto, *Der Zukunftsstaat als sozialistische Monarchie* (Berlin: Putkammer und Mühlbrecht, 1910), p. 391.

146 "THAT WHICH DISTINGUISHES": Hitler, *Monologe*, p. 302.

146 "WHAT I PHYSICALLY": Carl Ludwig Schleich, *Die Weisheit der Freude* (Berlin: Rowohlt Verlag, 1924), p. 93.

146 "OUR BODY": See Ernst Schertel, *Magie: Geschichte, Theorie, Praxis* (Prien: Anthropos Verlag, 1923), p. 56.

147 "EVEN IF YOU TAKE": Hitler, *Monologe*, p. 149.

149 "I HOPE YOU HAD": Carl J. Burckhardt, *Meine Danziger Mission, 1937–1939* (Munich: Verlag Georg D. W. Callwey, 1960). Burckardt includes in his memoir the verbatim exchange with Hitler that he prepared as a report to the League of Nations following the meeting with Hitler, pp. 264–70.

152 "A VIEW OF THE UNTERSBERG": Hitler, *Monologe*, p. 204.
152 "YES, I AM CLOSELY": Ibid., p. 207.

153 "ALL MY GREAT": Ibid., p. 207.

155 "AT FIRST WE": Nicolaus von Below, *Als Hitlers Adjutant, 1937–1945* (Mainz: Hase und Koehler Verlag, 1980), p. 183.

158 "WE WILL AT BEST": Hitler, *Monologe*, p. 40.

159 "GENIUS AND TALENT": Schleich, *Die Weisheit der Freude*, p. 26.

160 "GENIUS BELONGS TO": Ibid., p. 27.

160 "EVERYTHING OF THE MIND": Schertel, *Magie*, p. 69.

160 "TRULY EKTROPIC": Ibid., p. 63.

161 "EUROPEAN HUMAN TYPE": Ibid., pp. 34–35.

162 "ON THE OTHER SIDE": Max Domarus, *Reden und Proklamationen, 1932–1945*, vol. 2 (Munich: Süddeutscher Verlag, 1965), p. 1234.

162 "OUR ENEMIES HAVE": Ibid.

162 "ESSENTIALLY, IT DEPENDS": Ibid.

163 "GOAL: EXTERMINATION OF": Franz Halder, *Kriegstagebuch, band I vom Polenfeldzug bis zum Ende der Westoffensive* (Stuttgart: W. Kohlhammer Verlag, 1962), pp. 22–25.

BOOK SEVEN: **Frontline Reading, 1940**

169 "KANNENBERG WAS NOT": Christa Schröder, *Er war mein Chef* (Munich: Georg Müller Verlag, 1985), pp. 53–54.

169 "EVENING WITH THE FÜHRER": Joseph Goebbels, *Joseph Goebbels Tagebücher, band 3: 1935–1939*, ed. Ralf Georg Reuth (Munich: Piper Verlag, 1999), August 22, 1938, p. 1257.

169 "SOME 7,000 VOLUMES": See Appendix A, p. 235.

170 "RUMMAGING THROUGH": Adolf Hitler, *Mein Kampf*, trans. Ralph Manheim (New York: Houghton Mifflin, 1998), p. 6.

170 "IN THESE YEARS": Interview with Hermann Esser, 1.4.1964. Vol. 1; copy in Archiv zur Zeitgeschichte des Obersalzberg, Berchtesgaden.

171 "HE SORT OF": Ibid.

172 HITLER'S OLDEST EXTANT: Ernst Moritz Arndt, *Katechismus für den deutschen Krieg- und Wehrmann, worin gelehret wird, wie ein christlicher Wehrmann seyn und mit Gott in den Streit gehen soll* (Cologne: H. Rommerskirchen, 1815).

174 WALLS WERE SO THIN: See Wilhem Keitel, *Mein Leben: Pflichterfüllung bis zum Untergang: Hitlers Feldmarschall und chef des Oberkommandos der Wehrmacht in Selbstzeugnissen* (Berlin: Edition, 1998) p. 265.

174 "AFTER THE ELIMINATION": Percy E. Schramm, ed., *Die Berichte des Oberkommandos der Wehrmacht 1939–1945, band I* (Munich: Verlag für Wehrwissenschaften, 2004), p. 141.

176 "WHAT DOES HE": Keitel, *Mein Leben*, p. 228.

176 "I RECALL ONLY": Ibid., p. 253.

177 "AN UNIMAGINATIVE KNOCK-OFF": Franz Halder, *Hitler als Feldherr* (Linz: Johann Schönleitner Verlag, 1949), p. 27.

177 "MY OPERATION IS": Ibid., p. 193.

178 "REICHENAU HAS THE ORDER": Ibid., p. 301.

178 "HE RAGES AND YELLS": Ibid., p. 302.

178 "HE LACKED THE": Erich von Manstein, *Verlorene Siege* (Bonn: Bernhard und Graefe Verlag, 2004), p. 123.

178 "THE SELF-ASSUREDNESS": Ibid., p. 39.

179 "IT IS BETTER IF": Eberhard Jäckel and Axel Kuhn, eds., *Hitler: Sämtliche Aufzeichnungen, 1905–1924* (Stuttgart: Deutsche Verlags-Anstalt, 1980), p. 1202.

179 "HE HAD AN EXCEPTIONAL": Otto Dietrich, *Zwölf Jahre mit Hitler* (Cologne: Atlas Verlag, 1955), p. 93.

179 "A REFERENCE TO": Halder, *Hitler als Feldherr*, p. 21.

180 "ETERNAL DOUBTS": Erich von Manstein, *Verlorene Siege* (Bonn: Bernard und Graefe Verlag, 2004), p. 75.

180 "HITLER WAS WONT": Albert Speer, *Spandau: The Secret Diaries* (New York: Macmillian, 1976), p. 347.

180 "BUT THEN AGAIN": Rochs, *Heinrich von Schlieffen*, p. 51.

182 "WHEN THE NEWS": Adolf Hitler, *Monologe im Führerhauptquartier*, stenographed by Heinrich Heim, ed. Werner Jochmann (Hamburg: Albrecht Knaus Verlag), p. 92.

BOOK EIGHT: **Hitler's History of the Second World War**

188 MEMORY NO LONGER: Werner Maser, *Hitlers Briefe und Notizen: Sein Weltbild in handshriftlichen Dokumenten* (Düsseldorf: Econ Verlag, 1973), p. 201.

189 "THE RUSSIAN": For Halder's recounting of the incident, Franz Halder, *Hitler als Feldherr* (Linz: Johann Schönleitner Verlag, 1949), p. 52.

190 "YOU WILL BUILD": Hermann Giesler, *Ein anderer Hitler* (Leoni am Starnsverger: Druffel Verlag, 1977), p. 390.

190 "I LIVE AND WORK": Ibid., p. 402.

190 "IT JUST DOESN'T WORK": Ibid., p. 404.

190 "MY NERVES ARE SHOT": Max Domarus, *Reden und Proklamationen, 1932–1945*, vol. 2 (Munich: Süddeutscher Verlag, 1965), p. 1911.

190 "THE BITTER FIGHTING": *Die Berichte des Oberkommandos der Wehrmacht 1939–1945, band 3, 1 Januar 1942 bis 31 Dezember 1942* (Munich: Verlag für Wehrwissenschaft, 2004), p. 292.

192 "KEEP IN MIND": See Sven Hedin, *Ohne Auftrag in Berlin* (Tübingen: Internationaler Universitätsverlag, 1950), pp. 85–86.

192 "AFTERNOON WITH THE FÜHRER": Joseph Goebbels, *Joseph Goebbels Tagebücher, band 3: 1935–1939*, ed. Ralf Georg Reuth (Munich: Piper Verlag, 1999), October 24, 1942, p. 1337.

193 "IT IS THIS SATANICALLY": Sven Hedin, *Amerika im Kampf der Kontinente* (Leipzig: Brockhaus Verlag, 1942), p. III.

194 "THE VICTOR WILL": Ian Kershaw, *Hitler, 1936–1945: Nemesis* (New York: W. W. Norton, 2000), p. 209.

194 "NO QUESTION IS": Hedin, *Amerika*, p. 42.

195 "A HEALTHY SOCIAL POLICY": Ibid., p. 46.

195 "ALL OF ADOLF": Ibid., p. 48.

195 "IT IS RARE": Ibid., p. 64.

196 "MOST HONORABLE HERR": Reprinted in Hedin, *Ohne Auftrag in Berlin*, pp. 277–78.

198 "WE ARE FIGHTING": For Hitler's speech, November 9, 1942, see Domarus, *Reden und Proklamationen*, p. 1933–1940.

200 MOST "MISERABLE" SPEECH: Domarus, *Reden und Proklamationen*, p. 1932.

200 "EVERYONE KNOWS THAT": Joseph Goebbels, *Joseph Goebbels Tagebücher, band 4: 1940–1942*, ed. Ralf Georg Reuth (Munich: Piper Verlag, 1999), November 9, 1942, p. 1830.

200 "NOW THIS IS": For a detailed account of the developments leading up to this turning point in the war, see Tim Clayton and Phil Craig, *The End of the Beginning* (London: Coronet Books, 2002).

BOOK NINE: A Miracle Deferred

201 BIOGRAPHY OF FREDERICK THE GREAT: Thomas Carlyle, *History of Friedrich II. of Prussia, called Frederick the Great in Four Volumes* (London: Chapman and Hall, 1858), vol. 4, book 20, p. 438. See this edition for all subsequent Carlyle quotes relating to Frederick the Great.

202 "THERE HAS NEVER BEEN": Max Domarus, *Reden und Proklamationen, 1932–1945*, vol. 2 (Munich: Süddeutscher Verlag, 1965), p. 2212.

203 "PROVIDE RESISTANCE": Ibid.

203 BEFORE GOEBBELS COULD GIVE: Joseph Goebbels, *Joseph Goebbels Tagebücher, band 5: 1943–1945*, ed. Ralf Georg Reuth (Munich: Piper Verlag, 1999), p. 2127.

203 "IT MUST ALSO BE": Ibid., March 12, 1945, p. 2149.

204 I AM A DESERTER: For a description of the last days of the war see Joseph Goebbels, *Joseph Goebbels Tagebücher 1945: Die letzten Aurzeichnungen* (Hamburg: Hoffman und Campe, 1977), February 25, 1945, pp. 196–207.

206 "A TIRED CROWD": Ibid., p. 206.

207 AS A PIONEER OF: Thomas Carlyle, *On Heroes, Hero-Worship, and the Heroic in History* (London: Chapman and Hall, 1894), pp. 1–2.

207 CARLYLE HATED: Thomas Carlyle, *Selected Writings*, edited and introduction by Alan Shelston (New York: Penguin Books, 1971), p. 31.

207 A CRITIC ONCE CLAIMED: Ibid., p. 21.

207 "THE CHIEF INSPIRER": Carlyle, *Selected Writings*, p. 8.

208 "IT IS WONDROUS": Lothar Gruchmann and Reinhard Weber, eds., *Adolf Hitler: Reden, Schriften, Anordnungen der Hitler Prozess 1924*, Teil 4: 19–25, Verhandlungstag (Munich: K. G. Saur, 1999), p. 1578.

208 "THERE IS MUCH": *Adolf Hitler: Reden, Schriften und Anordnungen, band 2, Teil I,* p. 425.

208 "IF THE GERMAN PEOPLE": Domarus, *Reden und Proklamationen*, August 4, 1944, p. 2139.

208 "IT IS NOT NECESSARY": Albert Speer, *Inside the Third Reich: Memoirs*, trans. Richard and Cara Winston (New York: Macmillan, 1970), p. 440.

211 "PSYCHOLOGICAL AND LUMINOUS": Max Osborn, *Berlin* (Leipzig: Seemann Verlag, 1909), p. 192.

211 "WHEN I ARRIVED": Speer, *Inside the Third Reich*, p. 463.

211 "IN THIS HOUR": Domarus, *Reden und Proklamationen*, p. 2224.

212 "I DON'T HAVE": Nicolaus von Below, *Als Hitlers Adjutant, 1937–1945* (Selent: Pour le Mérite, 1999), p. 409.

212 "WAS LITERALLY OBSESSED": Ian Kershaw, *Hitler, 1936–1945: Nemesis* (New York: W. W. Norton, 2001), p. 792.

214 "IT IS UNTRUE": Werner Maser, *Hitlers Briefe und Notizen: Sein Weltbild in handschriftlichen Dokumenten* (Düsseldorf: Econ Verlag, 1973), pp. 356–59.

215 "IT'S ALL RIGHT, YOU": Interview with Traudl Junge, July 2001. See also Traudl Junge, *Bis zur letzten Stunde. Hitlers Sekretärin erzählt ihr Leben* (Berlin: Ullstein Verlag, 2003).

217 THE PROPHECIES: Carl Loog, *Die Weissagungen des Nostradamus: Erstmalige Auffindung des Chiffreschlüssels und Enthüllung der Prophezeihungen über Europas Zukunft und Frankreichs Glück und Niedergang, 1555–2200*, 4–5 ed. (Pfullingen in Württemberg: Johannes Baum Verlag, 1921). Quotations from Loog on pp. 68–70.

AFTERWORD: The Fates of Books

220 "THESE WORDS HAVE BEEN": Walter Benjamin, *Illuminations*, ed. Hannah Arendt, trans. Harry Zohn (London: Fontana Press, 1992), pp. 62–63.

222 "SHOWED EVIDENCE: Neil Baldwin, *Henry Ford and the Jews: The Mass Production of Hate* (New York: Public Affairs, 2002), p. 182.

222 "TO THE LEFT": Antony Penrose, ed., *Lee Miller's War* (London: Thames and
     Hudson, 2005), p. 191.
223 "AT THE FAR END": Confidential intelligence report by the U.S. Army Twenty-
     first Counterintelligence Corps, dated May 1945, detailing the bunker complex
     beneath the Berghof; copy in Archiv zur Zeitgeschichte des Obersalzberg,
     Berchtesgaden.
224 BY MAY 25: Florian Beierl, *Hitlers Berg* (Berchtesgaden: Beierl Verlag, 2005),
     p. 164.

INDEX

Page numbers in *italic* refer to illustrations.

Hanfstaengl, Ernst "Putzi," 50, 51, 59, 62,
65, 67, 93, 103n–4n, 106, 109–10, 125,
222
Mein Kampf edited by, 75–6
Hans Westmar (film), 103n
Harrer, Karl, 31, 35, 46, 58
Harvard University Rare Book Library, 78
Hauer, William, 257
Häusler, Rudolf, 115
Hearst, William Randolph, 38
Hedin, Sven, 42, 50, 186, *187*, 188, 191–8,
197, 199
Hegel, Georg Wilhelm Friedrich, xiv, xv
Heine, Thomas Theodor, 38
Heines, Edmund, 257
Henty, G. A., 237
Hepp, Ernst, 12–13, 18, 81
Hess, Ilse, 76
Hess, Rudolf, 67, 72, 76, 132, 134
Hiegl's Handbook of Tanks, *171*, 172
Himmler, Heinrich, 97, 167, 205, 213–14
Hindenberg, Paul von, 124
*Histories and Whatever Else There Is to
Report About Old Fritz, the Great King
and Hero*, 210n
*History of Friedrich II of Prussia, Called
Frederick the Great* (Carlyle), 201, 203,
206–11, 217
Hitler, Adolf, *53*, 197
Abrechnung of, 63
anti-Semitism of, 30, 38, 40, 50, 55, 67,
77, 78–9, 92, 142, 199
biographers of, 79
bookcases of, 26, 50, 51, 52, 95, 207
on books, vii
Burckhardt's negotiations with, 149–51
casualty report of, 24
Catholicism and, 120, 122–3, 128–9, 133,
134–7, 141–3, 236–7
compartmentalized mind of, 116

on "education at state expense," 68, 71
emotional transformation of, 12–13
ex libris bookplate of, xvi, 186, 226,
240, 243
failed Bavarian coup of, 40, 62–3, 65,
66, 78, 88, 97, 102, 198, 256
fiftieth birthday of, xviii, *xviii*
on Ford, 70
Foundations of National Socialism and,
132
on Gandhi, 68
in hospital, 23–5, 26
Iron Crosses of, 14, 18
Lehmann read by, 109–14
marginalia of, xvii, 68, 108, 112, 113, 114,
117–19, 145–6, 173, 181, 182, 183–4, *183*,
185, 218
marriage of, 215
memory of, 115
Mercedes desired by, 74–5
military books of, 169–73, 235, 240
as military tactician, 175–80
on *The Myth of the Twentieth Century*,
122–3, 126, 127, 132
Nazi leadership given up by, 66
Nazi resignation of, 54–5
Nazi salute by, 99
New Yorker profile of, 95
occult reading of, 143–8, 155–62, 236
personal papers of, 84
philosophy and, 67, 104–9, 161
and plan for Nazi merger, 47
political classes taken by, 31, 49, 52
poor spelling of, 52, 72, 104
in prison, 60, 63–9, *64*, 71, 72, *73*, 74–5,
86, 170
promotion to chancellor, 93, 102,
118–19, 124, 134
recommended reading list of, 56–7,
57, 69

PAGES frontispiece, xviii, 53, 64, 105, 154, 174, 204   Bayerische Staatsbibliothek Photoarchiv Hoffmann, Munich

PAGES xii, 9, 15, 24, 43, 45, 111, 113, 121, 144, 147, 165, 171, 202   Courtesy of the Rare Books and Special Collections Division, Library of Congress, Washington, D.C.

PAGES xiii, 57, 73   Private Archive

PAGES 5, 6   Reprinted from Adolf Meyer, *Mit Adolf Hitler in Bayr. Reserve Inf. Reg. 16 List.* Courtesy of the Rare Books and Special Collections Division, Library of Congress, Washington, D.C.

PAGES 8, 17   Reprinted from Max Osborn, *Berlin.* Courtesy of the Rare Books and Special Collections Division, Library of Congress, Washington, D.C.

PAGE 19   Reprinted from *Hitler's Aquarellen,* Heinrich Hoffmann, Berlin, 1935. Courtesy of the Rare Books and Special Collections Division, Library of Congress, Washington, D.C.

PAGE 29   Reprinted from *Peer Gynt.* Courtesy of the Rare Books and Special Collections Division, Library of Congress, Washington, D.C.

PAGE 33   Courtesy of Franz Fleischmann, Munich

PAGE 83   Reprinted from Ernst Jünger, *Feuer und Blut.* Courtesy of the Rare Books and Special Collections Division, Library of Congress, Washington, D.C.

PAGE 87   Reprinted from the archives of Institut für Zeitgeschichte, Munich-Berlin, F19/9; with the permission of the Bayerisches Staatsministerium der Finanzen, Munich. The image is reproduced as part of a critical study. The author and publisher expressly distance themselves from the contents of this excerpt.

PAGE 96   Courtesy of the Bundesarchiv, Berlin

PAGE 100   Inscription reprinted from *Fichte: Sämtliche Werke.* Vol. 1. Courtesy of the Rare Books and Special Collections Division, Library of Congress, Washington, D.C.

PAGE 126   Courtesy of the John Hay Library, Brown University, Providence, Rhode Island

PAGE 153   *Die Kunst im Deutschen Reich,* October 1939

PAGE 158   Drawing reprinted from Max Riedel, *Gesetz der Welt.* Courtesy of the Rare Books and Special Collections Division, Library of Congress, Washington, D.C.

PAGES 166, 183   Hugo Rochs, *Schlieffen.* Courtesy of the Rare Books and Special Collections Division, Library of Congress, Washington, D.C.

PAGES 187, 197   Hedin Letter republished with permission from the Sven Hedin Foundation and the Swedish National Archives, Stockholm

PAGE 216   Courtesy of the National Archives and Records Administration, Washington D.C.

PAGE 223   David E. Scherman, © Lee Miller Archives, England, 2008. All Rights Reserved.

PAGE 226   *Die Welt,* June 18, 1977

A NOTE ABOUT THE AUTHOR

Timothy W. Ryback is author of *The Last Survivor: Legacies of Dachau*. He has written on historical memory for *The Atlantic Monthly*, *The New Yorker*, and *The New York Times*, and has appeared in television documentaries in Europe and America. He cofounded the Institute for Historical Justice and Reconciliation in The Hague, and currently works at the Académie Diplomatique Internationale in Paris. He is married and has three children.

A NOTE ON THE TYPE

This book was set in Monotype Dante, a typeface designed by Giovanni Mardersteig (1892–1977). Conceived as a private type for the Officina Bodoni in Verona, Italy, Dante was originally cut only for hand composition by Charles Malin, the famous Parisian punch cutter, between 1946 and 1952. Its first use was in an edition of Boccaccio's *Trattatello in laude di Dante* that appeared in 1954. The Monotype Corporation's version of Dante followed in 1957.

Composed by North Market Street Graphics,
Lancaster, Pennsylvania

Printed and bound by R. R. Donnelley,
Harrisonburg, Virginia

Designed by M. Kristen Bearse